Oil, Power and Politics

Oil, Power and Politics

Conflict in Arabia, the Red Sea and the Gulf

Mordechai Abir

FRANK CASS : LONDON

First published 1974 in Great Britain by
FRANK CASS AND COMPANY LIMITED
67 Great Russell Street, London WC13BT, England

and in the United States of America by
FRANK CASS AND COMPANY LIMITED
c/o International Scholarly Book Services Inc.
P.O. Box 4347, Portland, Oregon 97208

ISBN 0 7146 2990 1

Library of Congress Catalog Card No. 72–92951

Printed in Great Britain by William Clowes & Sons, Limited,
London, Beccles and Colchester

To Ruta
who helped produce this book, and to our neglected children
Ronit and Anat who impatiently awaited its completion.

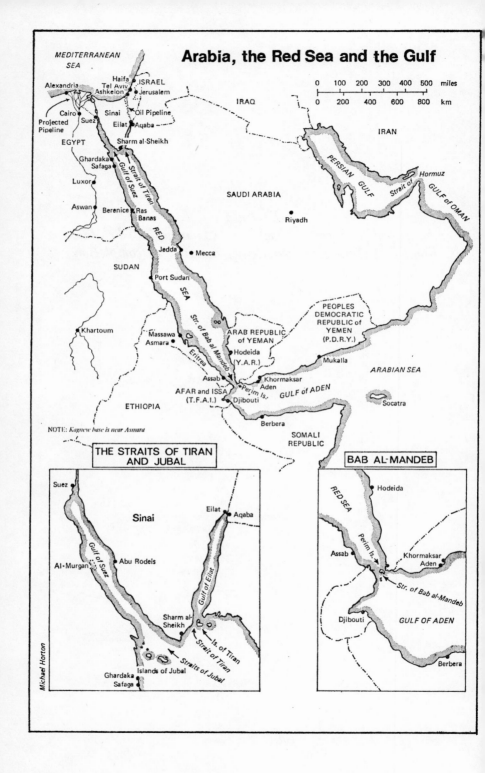

Arabia, the Red Sea and the Gulf

Contents

vii

Maps

Abbreviations

AFP	Agence France Presse
ARB	Africa Research Bulletin
ARP	Africa Report
ANA	Aden News Agency
ARR	Arab Report and Record
BBC	British Broadcasting Corporation
CDL	Commerce de Levant (Beirut)
CSM	Christian Science Monitor
DT	Daily Telegraph
EG	Egyptian Gazette
EH	Ethiopian Herald
EM	Egyptian Mail
FAZ	Frankfurter Allegemeine Zeitung
FBIS	Foreign Broadcasting Information Service
FT	Financial Times
FYSR	Free Yemeni South Radio
G	The Guardian
IHT	International Herald Tribune
INA	Iraq News Agency
JP	Jerusalem Post (Israel)
M	Le Monde
MD	Le Monde Diplomatique
MENA	Middle East News Agency (Cairo)
NCNA	New China News Agency
ND	Neues Deutschland
NME	New Middle East
NYT	New York Times
Observer, FNS	Observer, Foreign News Service
RWA	Review of World Affairs
T	The Times (London)

Acknowledgements

In 1970 I was invited to join the Middle East Study Group (Van Leer Institute, Jerusalem) as an 'expert' on the Horn of Africa and the southern peripheries of the Arab countries. In addition to offering my thanks for opening a new field to me, I must now confess to my friend, Professor Saul Friedlander (who organised this group), that, although a student of the modern history of the region, my knowledge of its contemporary politics was at the time quite limited. Not wishing to show my ignorance to my colleagues, I read extensively on the affairs of the area and quickly became fascinated by the impact of power politics on conflicts in the Red Sea and the Arabian/ Persian Gulf.

A year's fellowship (1971–1972) at the Centre for International Studies of the London School of Economics was probably the most important catalyst for producing this book. It made possible the continuation of my previous research in depth, gave me access to source material otherwise out of reach and enabled me to meet a large number of experts in my new field of interest and to exchange ideas with them. I am, therefore, greatly obliged to the Centre's steering committee and especially to Professors Goodwin, Joll and Shapiro for the fellowship and for their limitless kindness and help. Professor Shapiro introduced me as well to Mr. Brian Crozier, Director of the Institute for the Study of Conflict, whose interest in my work led to my publishing a short monograph called 'The Contentious Horn of Africa' in the 'Conflict Series' of his institute. Part of a far more extensive study of the tensions in the Horn of Africa, this monograph served as the foundation for chapter 4 in this book. I am grateful to Mr. Crozier not only for initiating this essay but also for putting at my disposal the facilities of his institute.

Professor John Kelly's most stimulating seminar on the Arabian Peninsula and the Gulf (Area Studies Centre, School of Oriental and African Studies, University of London, 1971–1972), in which I participated, led to my producing two essays which appear in this book. Originally invited to read in the seminar a paper on 'Red Sea Politics', I was later requested, because of a change in the seminar's programme, to prepare instead a paper on the 'People's Democratic Republic of Yemen' (PDRY). This short paper led to my writing in Jerusalem a year later the essay in this book called 'Crisis in Southern Arabia'. Mr. François Duchene, Director of the International Institute for Strategic Studies, who heard of my research into 'Red Sea Politics' discussed the subject with me and persuaded me to write a short article for the Adelphi Series of the IISS. Mr. Duchene not only edited my article but also convinced me that I was utterly ignorant of the use of military terminology and I am grateful to him for pointing this out. Although obviously more interested in the strategic aspects of my research, he is indirectly 'guilty' for my producing the more extensive essay on 'Red Sea Politics' included in this book.

Unable to complete my book before leaving England, the rapid and important developments in 1972–1973 in the region covered by the different papers necessitated additional research and rewriting of part of certain essays, as well as preparing 'Crisis in Southern Arabia', which I began to write only after my return to The Hebrew University at the end of 1972. I wish to acknowledge my indebtedness to the Leonard Davis Institute for International Affairs of The Hebrew University, whose generous help made this stage of my book possible.

Credit should be given to my local research assistant, Miss Rachel Simon, for her help and patience and to my friend and visiting colleague, Dr. Victor Low, who tried to edit the atrocious English of some of the material written in Jerusalem. I am also grateful to the Shiloah Institute of Tel-Aviv University for enabling me to use their facilities, to Miss Kempbell and her staff in the press cutting library of the Royal Institute for International Affairs (Chatham House) for their kind help, and to the librarian of the Institute for the Study of Conflict and Mr. Lynn Price, senior research officer of the above institute, for their friendliness, keen interest and the many cups of coffee which they prepared for my wife and myself. Last, but not least, I am indebted to my friends, Elie and Sylvia Kedourie, for their encouragement and for some very wonderful meals and stimulating evenings.

Preface

Until recent years the logic of grouping together in one book studies on the politics and conflicts of an area including both the Horn of Africa and the Arabian/Persian Gulf would have been questioned by many. Among the poorest and climatically most difficult parts of the world, the Red Sea and the Gulf have served from the earliest times as a bridge between the Far East, the Mediterranean and Europe. But while notable as a bone of contention between the Great Powers, the region gained little in the past from its relative importance and the luxurious transit trade which went through it and which enriched and helped develop other lands. The endless conflicts between the largely poor and backward peoples of the Red Sea and Gulf littoral, mainly over the meagre resources of the region, were, in most cases, local in character and of little wider significance. The decline of British power and western interests in the Red Sea, followed by the persistent expansion of Russia's presence and influence in the region and the dramatic growth in importance of the Gulf's oil resources, have completely transformed the situation. These changes polarised existing conflicts, created new ones, and made it quite evident that not only did these conflicts have many common denominators but so interrelated were they that no single one could be isolated from another and studied by itself.

The essays in this book, are the outcome of research which I began in 1970. These papers were written during 1972 and 1973 under different circumstances and for various purposes. The book was the idea of the publishers, who suggested that I publish my work concerning the politics of the Horn of Africa and Arabia in this form. I was at first hesitant to put together these studies, at the time in various stages of completion, and in some cases slightly overlapping. But, although its analytical side may suffer from a lack of historical perspective, such a book,

I am convinced, will prove useful to the student of the contemporary history of the Red Sea and the Gulf as well as to the many who, perplexed by the staggering impact of Middle East oil politics on the Western world, would like to know the background to events in this now vital area. From past experience I know how difficult it is to obtain up-to-date, factual, analytical studies of recent developments in this region. Hence this book.

* * *

The transcription of Arabic words is always a problem. We have adopted here the line of least resistance, omitting for the most part diacritical marks on the grounds that Arabists will know the correct Arabic, while others will not know the difference. 'Ains and hamzas are indicated by ' and ' respectively, as is conventional, and where names etc. are widely known in Anglicized form, this is generally used.

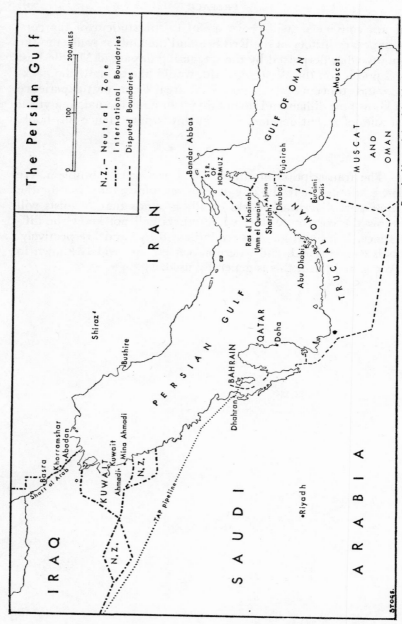

The Persian Gulf

N.Z. – Neutral Zone
– · – · – International Boundaries
– · · – Disputed Boundaries

0   100   200 MILES

IRAQ

IRAN

Basra
Shatt al Arab
Khorramshar
Abadan
Kuwait
KUWAIT
Ahmadi Mina Ahmadi
N.Z.
N.Z.
Shiraz
Bushire
Tap pipeline

SAUDI

ARABIA

Riyadh

PERSIAN GULF

BAHRAIN
Dhahran
QATAR
Doha

Bandar Abbas
STR. OF HORMUZ

Ras el Khaimah
Umm el Quwain
Sharjah Ajman
Dhubai
Abu Dhabi
TRUCIAL OMAN

Fujairah
Buraimi Oasis

GULF OF OMAN

Muscat

MUSCAT AND OMAN

STGS.

I

Saudi Arabia and The Gulf

Gulf Oil and the Great Powers

Ever since Britain reversed its 'East of Suez' policy in 1968, the Persian Gulf has been a focus of world attention. Increasingly more essential to the international economy, the vast oil reserves of the area bestow upon the countries of the Gulf an importance far out of proportion to their population, power and development. In a generation for which pollution has become a major problem and consumption of energy continuously grows, oil (especially Gulf oil) is, despite a constant rise in price, one of the cheapest and cleanest sources of energy. Although unreliable, recent statistics indicate that 60% of the world's proven oil reserves are to be found in the Persian Gulf area, compared to 7% in the United States and an estimated 14% in the Soviet Union. Described[1] as mere puddles relative to new oil strikes in the Persian Gulf countries, North Sea, Alaskan and Siberian oil and gas strikes may halt slightly the world's growing dependence on Gulf fuel but will not bring a meaningful change in the chart of proven oil reserves.[2] At present Gulf countries are already supplying about one-third of the world's fuel consumption, but as the oil and natural gas sources of the western hemisphere are being gradually exhausted whereas global energy consumption rises annually by about 10%, the constantly increasing proportion of fuel imported from the Gulf will probably rise even more sharply in the near future. This fact, of which consumers and producers alike became aware in recent years, is already influencing the local and world economy, politics and strategy.[3]

Notwithstanding intensive efforts to diversify its sources of energy after the 1956 Suez crisis, Europe still imports (on the average) about 60% of its fuel from the Persian Gulf even while intensifying the search for oil and gas in the North Sea.[4] It is doubtful if in the coming decade Europe will be able substantially to reduce the proportion of fuel imports from the Gulf. With 90% of its total oil importation coming from the Gulf countries, Japan, the third largest industrial country in the world, is at present utterly dependent on this source. Even if it were to reach an understanding with the Soviet Union regarding the exploitation of Siberia's fuel resources,[5] Japan will still have to obtain most of its fuel from Persian Gulf sources. For political–strategic reasons the United States has been reluctant to import oil from the Middle East and only 3% of its fuel requirements have come from the Gulf. However, with its own oil sources rapidly dwindling and its annual growth of energy consumption (about 12%) not compensated for by the discovery of oil sources in the western hemisphere or the development of atomic energy plants, the United States government is already forced to permit the increase of oil imports from the Middle East and especially from the Gulf. But determined not to become too heavily dependent on Gulf oil in the coming decade,[6] the United States is trying to accelerate the exploitation of Alaskan and new off-shore fields and at the same time to diversify its sources of supply.[7]

The Soviet Union is still considered a net exporter of oil, although an inconsequential one. Undeterred by cost, especially if in roubles, Russia has proceeded in its plans to exploit the (according to Soviet sources) substantial oil and natural gas fields in Siberia. In fact oil from the Tyumen field east of the Urals is gradually replacing Russia's partially exhausted traditional sources of fuel in the Caucasus and elsewhere. Moreover, a pipe-line from the Tyumen field was linked in April 1973 with the 'friendship' pipe-line network carrying fuel from Russia to several European countries.[8] Western experts are sceptical about glowing Soviet reports concerning the magnitude of the oil and gas resources in Siberia. They point out as well that the technical complications and prohibitive cost of developing the Siberian resources have already forced Russia to seek the co-operation of the United States and Japan. It is claimed therefore that at the present growth-rate of energy consumption in the Soviet Union and despite the development of its Siberian fields, Russia will soon become a net importer of oil. This, *inter alia*, explains Russia's increasing interest in recent years in cheap Middle Eastern oil in general and the Persian Gulf resources in particular. Growing Soviet involvement in the extraction and marketing of this oil has in fact already proven profitable financially and politically.[9]

Emerging from the Cultural Revolution, the People's Republic of China is trying to overcome the adverse economic and other effects of this period. At present China's oil production is sufficient to answer all its needs. Some experts claim that in view of China's limited oil reserves and the country's annual rate of economic growth it will soon have to import oil from the Middle East; others, claim that China possesses vast untapped oil reserves. Be that as it may, China has already manifest in recent years its interest in the Gulf countries. Possibly an outcome of its rivalry with the Soviet Union and its efforts to gain support among Third World countries, China's interest in the area may also be a result of the Gulf's economic and strategic importance based on its oil reserves.[10]

It is now generally accepted that the phasing out of the role of Western companies as producers of oil in the Middle Eastern countries will be accelerated in the near future. The loss of several billion dollars annually to Western economies through such a process is however insignificant compared to other financial and political repercussions arising from the growing dependency of most of the world and especially of the West on Gulf fuel. The 'seller's market' and OPEC's muscle-flexing have already led, since 1971, to an unprecedented rise in the cost of fuel to consumers. This process is further accelerated by the 'participation agreements', the partial or full nationalisation of the assets of Western oil companies and the United States' 'energy crisis'. As the population and rate of economic growth of the most important producing countries is (with the exclusion of Iran) absurdly small and their market relatively inconsequential, developments in the oil industry are beginning to create for the industrial countries a balance of payments problem which will become far more serious in the near future. The new developments in the oil market are already bringing to the Gulf countries a fantastic flow of capital. Constantly growing, the revenues of these countries in the early 1980's are estimated at tens of billions of dollars annually[11] compared to several billions in 1972 and only several hundred millions a decade ago. Unable to absorb funds of such magnitude in their own economies (again with the exception of Iran), the previously poor and unimportant Gulf countries and sheikhdoms may acquire considerable influence over international finance, economy[12] and politics.

Aware of the serious effects of these developments in the oil industry on their economies, the United States and Europe are accelerating oil prospecting in the North Sea and North America as well as research into technologies concerned with the production of 'clean' energy from fuels other than oil.[13] This however is a complicated, costly and somewhat lengthy matter. To maintain fuel supplies flowing to Europe and America at reasonable prices in the interim period the West is determined to preserve the *status quo* in the Gulf. While gradually giving in to the financial and other demands of the producing countries the west is strengthening 'friendly' conservative régimes in the region. The Soviet Union, on the other hand, would for economic, strategic and ideological reasons obviously gain from a collapse of the present *status quo* in the Gulf.

Far from being a mere product of economic or ideological considerations, the Soviet Union's foreign trade and aid policy is also shaped by her political and strategic interests. The Russians successfully operate a gas pipe-line from Persia to Europe and are planning a similar oil pipe-line. Their participation in exploiting Iraq's Rumeila field,[14] expanded by the Iraqi–Soviet agreement of April 1972, has not only proved most rewarding economically, but prompted Baghdad to nationalise IPC's Kirkuk field. Clearly Russia is unable to absorb or find a market for the vast quantities of oil produced in the Gulf and other Arab countries, Nor can it pay the producing countries with 'hard currencies' or high quality commodities and machinery, as does the West. But it is determined to play a more active role in the international oil market and particularly in the Gulf. In addition to the gain to its economy and power Soviet interest in the oil industry and the Gulf provides the producing countries with an alternative outlet for their fuel, neutralises to some extent Western ability to resort to gun-boat diplomacy and encourages oil-rich countries to gain partial or full control of their resources to the potential detriment of the West.

It is difficult to determine whether Russia's activities in the Red Sea before 1968 were connected with its aspirations in the Gulf.[15] There is little doubt however that the British government's decision in 1968 to evacuate its forces from the Gulf influenced Soviet policy and strategic planning. The small Soviet flotilla which appeared in the western part of the Indian Ocean in 1968 has helped to establish Soviet influence in the countries of the region and indirectly Soviet interest in the Gulf. It was also meant to impress upon the West the fact that it no longer has a monopoly of power in the region and should take Soviet interests into account. Russian warships occasionally began to visit the Iraqi port of Umm-Qasir,[16] but, prudently biding their time, the Russians awaited more opportune circumstances to establish a presence in the Gulf. Such conditions gradually began to emerge as a result of Iraq's relative isolation in the Arab world and its conflict with Iran and the West.[17] Yet the Russians patiently continued to await the independence of Britain's clients in eastern Arabia and the withdrawal of its forces from the region.

In contrast with their previous policy of non-interference the Russians became in 1971 indirectly involved in subversion in the Gulf, both through Iraq and the PDRY (People's Democratic Republic of Yemen) and by helping PFLOAG (Popular Front for the Liberation of the Occupied Arab Gulf).[18] Possibly an outcome of rivalry with China, the Soviet policy was more likely an attempt to undermine Western influence and interests in the region. The Soviet Union was among the first to accord recognition to Bahrain, Qatar and the Union of Arab Emirates (UAE) once they became independent. Russian officials and delegations of different sorts began to tour the Gulf in an effort to foster diplomatic, trade and cultural relations with the newly independent governments.[19] Unrelated to the size and population of the new 'states', the scope of Soviet activities indicated Russia's determination to establish its presence in the region. Flattered by Soviet attentions and hoping that Russian recognition would counter the subversive activities of local radicals and the pressures of their aggressive neighbours, some Gulf rulers at first welcomed this new policy.

Facing grave external and internal problems and frustrated by Western-initiated 'arrangements' in the Gulf,[20] Iraq was exceedingly keen to ally herself with the Soviet Union. The latter, however, reassessing her policy in the Third World and the Arab countries (in particular after its debacle in Sudan), insisted on a binding and meaningful treaty which would ensure its investments and foothold in the future. Hence a treaty of co-operation and friendship was signed between the two governments in April 1972 which made Iraq far more dependent on Russia than any Arab country had been in the past.[21] On the surface quite harmless, this treaty introduced into Gulf politics a new and most serious element: in addition to facilitating further Soviet participation in the extraction and marketing of Iraq's oil, the Soviet Union gained a firm bridgehead in the upper part of the Gulf and became a factor in its politics. Among other things, the agreement (it is claimed) enabled the Soviet Union to develop and use Iraqi naval and other military facilities;[22] significantly, a Soviet flotilla sailed into the Iraqi port of Umm-Qasir shortly after it was signed.

Anxious not to harm the extremely delicate relations developed over the years with Iran and with most Arab countries, the Soviet Union tried to play down the importance of the agreement with Iraq and maintained, for a time, a low profile in the Gulf. The Shah of Iran has clearly indicated on several occasions in the past his strong objection to the Great Powers, especially the Soviet Union (but also the United States), establishing bases within the Gulf. Once the Soviet–Iraqi treaty was signed his attitude towards a Western presence in the region and participation in its defence began to change.[23] Moreover, unlike the Mediterranean, the Gulf is not a region of confrontation between the Arabs and Israel and its wealth is considered essential for the success of Arab economic and political aspirations. Russian interest in this area is, therefore, regarded by most Arab countries with suspicion if not hostility. Aware of this delicate situation the Soviet Union is extremely cautious in the execution of its policy there. Visits of the Soviet navy to Umm-Qasir are not publicised and are relatively short. Claims that they intend to establish a permanent presence in the Gulf are strongly denied by the Russians, as well as by their Iraqi allies.[24] Nevertheless, Russia was accused of being partly responsible for renewed tension between Iraq and

Kuwait in March–April 1973, an episode closely connected with expansion of the naval base of Umm-Qasir.[25]

Having become the focus of Russian interest in the Middle East after the erosion of Soviet relations with Egypt in 1972, Iraq is receiving substantial military and economic aid from Moscow. Despite the recognition Russia granted to the new Gulf states and her declared friendship with them, in co-operation with the PDRY, Iraq supports attempts to undermine their régimes. Openly inimical to Iran, she encourages and abets every attempt to subvert and overthrow her present government.[26]

Until 1971 Britain and the United States believed that if British troops were withdrawn from the Gulf the Soviet Union would not have the incentive and would refrain from entering the area. The West pinned its hopes on the ability of local moderate powers such as Iran and Saudi Arabia (and to a certain extent Kuwait) to overcome pressures from local radicals and maintain stability in the Gulf. As the West was mainly concerned with uninterrupted flow of oil at reasonable terms to its markets, this seemed in the circumstances the best possible solution. Events in the Gulf since the end of 1971 and especially following the Soviet–Iraqi agreement of April 1972 have, however, completely shaken Western confidence in the viability of these arrangements patiently negotiated since 1968 for maintaining the *status quo*. Evidently the Soviet Union does not intend to play the game according to Western rules and is determined gradually to establish its influence in the Gulf. Even more clearly than in the past it is now realised that the immensely rich, weak, underpopulated and disunited states of eastern Arabia possess all the ingredients of instability. Their conservative autocratic régimes, unable to present a common front and already suspicious of each other and of the local super-power (Iran), would be unable to withstand by themselves the mounting pressures within and around them. In far more difficult circumstances the West, now determined to preserve its fuel supply in the coming crucial period has, it seems, decided to adopt a far more active policy concerning the Gulf and nearby regions.

The Arab Principalities of the Gulf on the Eve of Independence

After the independence of Southern Yemen in 1967 the Arabian Peninsula was divided into fourteen political entities, twelve of which shared its eastern coast. With the creation of the UAE late in 1971, the number of 'states' in eastern Arabia was, at least nominally, reduced to six. Except for Saudi Arabia and possibly Oman, anomalies such as the Gulf states, with ludicrously small populations and vast oil resources, owe their existence to the growth of British interests in the Gulf since the nineteenth century; had it not been for these interests, the political map of the region would most probably have looked very different today.

During the nineteenth and twentieth centuries Britain signed a great number of treaties of 'friendship and protection' with the rulers of Kuwait, Bahrain, Qatar, Oman and sheikhs of the trucial coast of Oman. These treaties fossilised nineteenth century political fragmentation in eastern Arabia and interfered with the social mobility typical of the region's tribal society. They enhanced the power of contemporary rulers, producing on the trucial coast permanent ruling dynasties.[27] Geographically and ethnically the trucial Oman principalities are part of greater Oman, but British interests and the discovery of oil in the Gulf created and preserved boundaries in areas where they had never existed in the past. Political dynamism was arrested and the probable unification of most, if not all, of eastern Arabia by Abdul Aziz Ibn Sa'ud in the first decades of the twentieth century was prevented by the treaties of local rulers with England.

The decision of the British government in 1968 to reverse its 'East of Suez' policy terminated nearly a century and a half of British hegemony in the Gulf. Although determined to annul all their commitments in the area by the end of 1971, the British realised the dangers to the stability of the Gulf and to Western interest in it arising from their decision. They also felt a moral obligation towards their 'clients' who, having co-operated with them despite the pressure of Arab nationalism, were previously led to believe that they could rely on the British umbrella in the 1970s. Aware of the weakness of the tiny trucial principalities, Qatar and Bahrain and the growing internal and external threat to their existence, the British were keen to federate the nine political units before their departure. Such a federation, it was thought, would be more viable from an economic point of view and better able to defend itself against internal subversion and external aggression.

Most Gulf rulers, realising that their very existence depended on British protection, at first tried frantically to reverse the British decision.[28] Involved as they had been for generations in hostilities, rivalries and petty jealousies, the idea of a federation looked unrealistic and had no appeal for them. A similar federation which the British created in southern Arabia had proved to be a complete failure and the main cause of the overthrow of the traditional rulers in that area in 1967. However, once convinced that the British decision was irrevocable, with Iraq's attempt to annex Kuwait (1961) still fresh in their minds and Saudi Arabia and Iran's claims to parts of eastern Arabia still pending, the sheikhs and amirs concerned became more amenable to the idea of a federation. Consequently, negotiations between them began in 1968.

The difficulties involved in creating a Gulf federation looked at first insurmountable. In addition to territorial claims by different parties which threatened the negotiations, the rulers concerned were unable to overcome their endless differences. Another major difficulty was the disparity of population and revenue between the various units involved in the planned federation. The smaller principalities feared domination by Bahrain, which despite its meagre resources had the most developed economy and whose population, the most advanced in the region, was larger than that of all the trucial states put together.[29] Qatar, with its relatively large population, increasing oil revenues and puritanical Wahhabi government, was the natural antidote to Bahrain. Involved in territorial dispute with Bahrain and Abu Dhabi, Qatar maintained a lukewarm attitude to the idea of a federation and opposed any concession which could strengthen the position of its rivals. A crucial factor to the success of the negotiations was, of course, the attitude of the Arab countries.

Although all the Arab countries, each for its own reason, welcomed Britain's decision to evacuate its forces from the Gulf, the same did not apply to the British-planned federation.

TABLE I

Country	Area (in thousand square miles)	Population[1]	Revenue[2] from oil in 1971 (in millions of dollars)	Estimated number of foreigners (percentage of total)	Pupils[3] in elementary schools	Pupils in secondary schools	Students in higher education institutions
Saudi Arabia	850-920	5,000,000-7,000,000	1,500[4]	5%-10%	421,000	1,500	5,000-10,000
YAR	74	4,000,000-6,000,000			70,000	2,600	1,000[5]
PDRY	112	1,000,000-1,500,000	133	10%	45,000		
Oman	130[6]	500,000-750,000					
Fujairah	0·4	3,500-10,000					
Ras al-Khaima	0·6	12,000-25,000					
Umm al-Qaiwain	0·3	4,500					
Ajman	0·1	4,200					
Sharja	0·1	15,000-38,000					
Dubai	1·5	60,000-70,000	50[7]	up to 50%	12,421		
Abu Dhabi	32	25,000-70,000	500	about 45%	10,704		600 (abroad)
Qatar	4	85,000-150,000	240	about 25%	48,000		
Bahrain	0·25	216,000[8]	40	about 20%	87,000	5,000[9]	840
Kuwait	5·8	750,000	1,300	about 53%			2,000[10]

With the exception of Kuwait and Bahrain, where censuses were held, the figures for all the other political entities are based on estimates. The substantial differences in these estimates are the outcome of a constant inflow of immigrant labour into the oil producing countries and the movement of nomadic population. This table was compiled in January 1973, and it is expected that in 1973–4 oil revenues have more than trebled in most of the Gulf's oil-producing countries.

1. Saudi—'The modernisation of Saudi Arabia', talk by H. E. Muhammad J. Nadir, Minister Plenipotentiary, Embassy of Saud Arabia, Washington, at Morgan State College, 2.3.71. Fujairah—*Time Magazine*, 7.2.72. Ras al-Khaima—*T*, 14.8.71. Umm al-Qaiwain—*Time Magazine*, 7.2.72. Ajman—*CDL*, 28.8.71. Sharja—*Time Magazine*. Dubai—*Time Magazine*, 7.2.72. Abu Dhabi—*T*, 21.12.71, special supplement. Qatar—*Time Magazine*, 7.2.72, *T*, 23.2.72; *JP*, 23.2.72. Kuwait—*Ha'aretz* (Israel), 1.10.71.

2. Oman—*FT*, 7.7.71. Abu Dhabi—*T*, 21.12.71, special supplement. Qatar—*Observer*, 19.8.71; *Time Magazine*, 7.2.72. Bahrain—*World Survey*, p. 4. Kuwait—*JP*, 25.4.72.

3. Saudi Arabia—Muhammad J. Nadir, *op. cit.* Qatar—*FT*, 24.4.72. Bahrain—*T*, 16.12.71.

4. It is estimated that as a result of recent agreements this will rise to $2,500 million in budgetary year 1971–72 (starting September).

5. More than 1,000 students in the USSR—A. Yodfat, *New Outlook*, March 1971, p. 47.

6. Including Dhofar.

7. In addition to rapid growth in oil revenue, Dubai earned in 1971 about $300 million from trading activities, mainly from smuggling gold—*DT*, 19.7.71.

8. *Al-Hayat* (Lebanon), 25.7.71, according to census taken in 1971.

9. Each year. *T*, 16.12.71.

10. 1,000 from local university and 1,000 from abroad—*Ha'aretz*, 1.10.71.

Iraq, prevented by British intervention from annexing Kuwait during Qasim's régime, had never given up its territorial aspirations in the Gulf.[30] The British decision presented Iraq's extremist Ba'th régime with a golden opportunity to undermine the conservative, Western-oriented governments of the area, diffuse its ideology and expand its influence. The Iraqis realised at the same time that the planned federation was meant to conserve the *status quo* in the region and to protect, to some extent, Western interests in it. In the name of Arab nationalism, Iraq opposed the federation and secretly used every possible method to sabotage the negotiations leading to its creation.

On the other side of the Arabian Peninsula, the poverty-stricken Marxist régime of Southern Yemen (later PDRY), having overcome a British attempt to establish a puppet federation in Southern Yemen, denounced the newly sponsored Gulf federation as an 'imperialist farce'. It openly pledged its support to revolutionary movements which would overthrow the 'reactionary' régimes in the Gulf. Significantly, the 'Dhofar Liberation Front', supported by the PDRY (and China), changed its name in 1968 (at a congress at Hirmin) to 'The Popular Front for the Liberation of the Occupied Arab Gulf' (PFLOAG). The new movement adopted a Marxist programme and declared that its goal was to liberate the Gulf from 'the imperialists and their lackeys—the feudal rulers'[31] Despite similar bombastic declarations in the following years, PFLOAG's activities remained limited mainly to the area of Dhofar.

Several 'incidents' which occurred in the middle of 1970 in the mountains of Oman proper (Jebel Akhdar), Ras Masandum and Ras al-Khaima, heralded the birth of 'The National Democratic Front for the Liberation of Oman and the Arab Gulf' (NDFLOAG). This organisation, as it later came out, had cells in Oman's towns and in most of the principalities and sheikhdoms of the Gulf. Although originally supported by the Syrian Ba'th, NDFLOAG became later a tool in the hands of the Iraqi Ba'th and is discreetly supported by it. It draws its members mainly from among Arab immigrant communities (Palestian and others) in the Gulf and from the local intelligentsia. Although probably far smaller in numbers than PFLOAG and not as well equipped, it presented a far more serious threat to the régimes of the Gulf and to stability in the area. In fact, had it not been for several tactical errors of its leaders and the prompt action taken by British-commanded security forces in 1970–71, this organisation could have become an extremely serious factor in the Gulf and a threat to its oil industry.[32] The reverse suffered by the NDFLOAG, following its initial success in 1970, was probably a reason for the closer co-operation, at least in the field of propaganda, which developed between it and PFLOAG in 1971. Encouraged by the PDRY and Iraq, and possibly on the USSR's initiative, this co-operation became even more essential as the time of the British evacuation of the Gulf approached. Coerced by their respective patrons and hard pressed by British forces and British-commanded local security forces, the two organizations merged at the beginning of 1972. It seems, however, that while co-ordinating some of their activities they maintained their separate operational framework, ideology and allegiances.[33] Moreover, whereas PFLOAG is a Marxist-led rural guerrilla movement of backward Dhofari tribesmen, NDFLOAG is mainly an urban, Ba'th-inspired, intelligentsia-based subversive movement with cells in most of the towns of eastern Arabia.

In contrast to the hostility of Iraq and the PDRY to the proposed Gulf federation, and possibly partly because of it, the UAR welcomed the British plan. By 1968 Egypt had abandoned her ideology of 'unity of ranks' and her role of champion of revolutions in Arab countries whose régimes she considered detrimental to Arab unity and progress. Supported financially and politically after 1967 by the conservative oil-rich Gulf countries led by Saudi Arabia, she has a vested interest in maintaining the *status quo* and stability in the Peninsula. In view of her tense relations with Iraq and her continuous confrontation with Israel, she even began to cultivate better relations with Iran, Saudi Arabia's partner in the Gulf.[34] Instability in the Gulf, an area crucially important to the world's economy, would certainly divert international and possibly Arab attention from her conflict with Israel and might deprive Egypt of the substantial subsidies she was receiving from there.[35] Thus the PDRY's and Iraq's intention to turn the Gulf into a region of conflict clashed with the UAR's interests. The UAR hoped that a larger and stronger Arab political unit in the Gulf could better withstand the pressures of extremist Arab régimes and would continue its support of Egypt. Hence Egypt not only supported the planned Gulf federation but was involved behind the scenes in negotiations concerning its formation.[36]

Until World War II Saudi Arabia was forced to reconcile herself to the *status quo* in eastern Arabia, upheld by the British presence there. This did not mean that the Saudis gave up their aspirations to annex the eastern coast of the Peninsula or at least part of it.[37] In fact, the discovery of oil in Arabia only hardened Saudi Arabia's attitude concerning her claims to parts of Qatar, the trucial states and Oman. But in this period the emerging kingdom was in no position to challenge the might of Britain and while repeatedly reiterating its territorial claims, Riyadh bided its time.

Relations between Saudi Arabia and Britain gradually deteriorated after World War II when American oil companies stepped up their activities in the kingdom and as the oil potentialities of eastern Arabia were fully realised. By then the Saudi claims revolved mainly around the coastal strip adjacent to Khaur al-Udaid (between Qatar and Abu Dhabi), large parts of the interior of Abu Dhabi and northern Oman. Although the British had since the late 1940s appeared willing to discuss the Saudi territorial demands, they exploited the period of negotiations gradually to establish and consolidate the borders of their different client-principalities. Outmanoeuvred by the British and feeling that time was working against them, the Saudis, possibly encouraged by ARAMCO, occupied in 1952 part of the Buraimi region. Being patrons of Abu Dhabi, Qatar and Oman and having their own oil interests at heart, the British strongly denounced this unilateral action. But they reopened negotiations on the demarcation of the region's borders. Finding the Saudis unwilling to relinquish the territories they had occupied or to modify what they considered their minimal claims, the British resorted to force and in 1955 evicted the small Saudi garrison from Buraimi.[38] Still unable to challenge the superior military power of Britain, the Saudis left matters as they were, although they constantly repeated that this did not mean an acceptance of the situation.

In the coming years Riyadh is said to have tried to meddle

with the affairs of principalities protected by the British in order to undermine the latter's position in eastern Arabia. Most outstanding was Saudi support of the Ibadhi imam of Oman, Ghalib, who 'rebelled' against the Sultan of Muscat in 1957. Oil interests were once again involved. The sultan, a British protégé, was only nominally the master of Jebel Akhdar in the hinterland of Oman's coast. Encouraged by reports about the prospects of finding oil in the area, he began in the early 1950s to extend his authority into the interior. The tribes of the area, most of whom supported the imam, resisted this change in the *status quo*, but could do little against the superior forces of the sultan commanded by British officers. In 1957, however, after receiving funds and arms from the Saudis and led by the imam's brother, they intensified their resistance to the sultan. Despite the traditional character of the movement and its leadership, it was fighting 'British imperialism' and therefore also received the full support of Egypt's propaganda machine.[39] The rebellion was finally broken in 1960 only through a massive British intervention. Imam Ghalib and his closest supporters found refuge in Saudi Arabia, which remained until the end of 1971 the main champion of his cause.

As a result of the revolution in Yemen in 1962 and the UAR's intervention there, Saudi Arabia found herself on the same side of the fence as the British. Nevertheless she remained opposed to the British presence in the Peninsula. Since the mid-1960s she has supported to some extent the rebellion in Dhofar, but even more the attempts of several rulers in Southern Yemen and the 'South Arabian League' (SAL) to liberate their country from British rule. Ironically, the Marxist 'National Liberation Front' (NLF), which emerged in 1967 victorious in Southern Yemen, declared a 'crusade' against all the conservative régimes in the Peninsula and became the patron of the Dhofari rebellion. Although they had stopped supporting the Dhofari rebellion even earlier, the Saudis refused to co-operate with the Omani sultan (in fact with the British) to suppress PFLOAG as long as their territorial claims were not recognised.

Saudi Arabia welcomed Britain's announcement in 1968 concerning the termination of her commitments in the Gulf. She hoped that following the withdrawal of British forces from the area she would be able to assert her authority over areas which she had unsuccessfully claimed in the past. Since it could complicate her plans, the British-envisaged Gulf federation was at first received coolly, if not with hostility, by Saudi Arabia. Moreover, the obvious weakness of such an entity and its proposed government could present progressive and radical elements with an ideal opportunity to establish themselves in the federation and penetrate its government, perhaps overthrow it. As it soon emerged, Iraq and the PDRY were determined to foster subversion and revolution in the Gulf. Clearly, if they were to succeed it would become exceedingly difficult to curb the wave of 'radicalism' from making further inroads into Saudi Arabia proper. Thus the annexation of eastern Arabia as soon as the British left looked even more desirable to the Saudi government.

A combination of factors brought Saudi Arabia to change her attitude to the federation. Nevertheless the change was relatively hesitant and slow. Egypt, for instance, advised Faisal to welcome any arrangements which would ensure the withdrawal of British forces from the region. The United States, taken aback at first by the British decision, had no intention of assuming Britain's role in the Gulf, and tried to convince her local allies that it was up to them to fill the vacuum created by the British withdrawal. The creation of a federation of traditional principalities, she pointed out to the Saudis, would prevent anarchy and conflicts which otherwise might follow.[40] On their part, the British did their best to mollify Riyadh, hinting that territorial adjustments could be far more easily arranged between the Arab rulers than enforced by the West.[41] It was, however, the intention of the Conservatives, who came to power in England in 1970, to re-examine the Labour government's Gulf policy which finally changed Riyadh's attitude to the proposed Gulf federation, although not its opposition to its suggested borders. Thereafter Saudi Arabia joined Kuwait and Iran in their efforts to bring together the rulers concerned in the planned federation.[42]

The Shah of Iran, among the first to welcome the British decision of 1968, has also been instrumental in overcoming Faisal's opposition to the federation and in persuading him to undertake jointly the role of preserving stability in the Gulf.[43]

Iran's policy underwent fundamental changes during the 1960s. The détente with the Soviet Union left her free to focus her attention on the Gulf, the life-line of her economy. Iran's oil exports gradually increased from the fall of Musadeq's government in 1953 until by 1969 she had become the largest oil producer in the Middle East and by 1971 the largest in the world.[44] The socio-economic reforms, the so-called 'white revolution', pursued by the Shah and his multi-year development plans, depended on a steady inflow of oil receipts and the expansion of the oil industry. As the Gulf is still Iran's only outlet to the high seas, she is exceptionally sensitive to the problem of stability in this area and wishes, for this and other reasons, to establish her predominance in it.

In the 1950s and 1960s Shi'i Iran's cool relations with the Sunni-Arab countries of the Middle East further deteriorated as an outcome of the aggressive policy of Arab nationalism led by President Nasser. Egypt was strongly opposed to Western-oriented regional alliances which Iran supported and inimical to the moderate-traditional character of Iran's régime. More-over, panarab ideology embraced all the territories inhabited by Arabs from the Gulf to the Atlantic, including Persia's province of Khuzistan with its largely Arab population. Rela-tions between Iran and most Arab countries greatly improved, however, after 1967 when Egypt moderated its policy con-cerning 'traditional' régimes in the Peninsula and the Gulf. The new mood in Egypt was most welcome to Iran whose policy, by this time, was to foster better relations with her Arab neighbours. But this new policy, did not include Iraq, with her extremist Ba'th régime whose interests clashed with those of Iran and which tried to subvert the government of the Shah. Although Iraq took up Egypt's erstwhile role as cham-pion of 'preserving' the Arab character of the Gulf, she did not enjoy Egypt's prestige and influence nor was Iraq, with a population of 8 million, grave internal problems and tense relations with most Arab countries, a match for Iran.

With more than 25 million inhabitants Iran is more populous than all the Arab Gulf countries put together. Two decades of stability, reforms and development under the Shah's govern-ment, enhanced by increasing oil revenues, have made Iran militarily, economically and politically the strongest and the most stable country in the region. Massive purchasing of modern weapons from the West (mainly the United States) and from the Soviet Union and the reorganisation of Iran's armed forces, created the most powerful military in the Gulf littoral countries.[45] Iran is in the enviable position of having all the pre-requisites for developing a strong diversified economy. She has capital, water, sufficient arable land, a variety of minerals, cheap energy, skilled labour, an educated class and a sufficiently large home market. Although it still has a long way to go, the Shah's government is gradually succeeding in developing Iran's communications infra-structure and agriculture and industrialising the country. Hence the standard of living of the masses in general has been rising, a relatively large middle class has emerged and technocrats replace the traditional administrators and aristocracy. All this has been achieved, and a measure of democracy established, without the country having to undergo a major political upheaval. Thus despite foreign-encouraged subversion[46] Iran has become one of the most politically stable countries in the Middle East.[47]

After 1968 Iran was determined to foster further her traditional relations with the Gulf principalities. A remnant of her expansionist policy in past centuries, her traditional claim to the Bahrain archipelago and smaller Gulf islands, was a stumbling block to her new policy. Convinced that the claim to Bahrain with its largely Arab population and relative unimportance was detrimental to Iran's interests, the Shah sought a formula which would enable him to withdraw it without losing face. Solving the Bahrain problem became even more urgent in view of a possible reversal of the British policy and because Iran's claim complicated the negotiations for a wider Gulf federation. Hence, having consulted Faisal and other Arab rulers, the Shah agreed in the beginning of 1970 to a United Nations supervised referendum in Bahrain on the future of the islands.[48] When, as expected, most Bahrainis voted against unification with Iran the Shah renounced his country's claim to these islands.

Wahhabi Saudi Arabia and Shi'i Iran began to develop closer relations from the late 1950s, as an outcome of the UAR's policy and propaganda directed against their traditional régimes. Once the British announced their intention to evacuate the Gulf the Shah became determined to reach an understanding with Saudi Arabia, the largest conservative Arab country in the Peninsula, concerning the future of the Gulf. Such co-operation became especially desirable in view of the common interests of the two countries and the PDRY's and Iraq's intention to support revolution and sedition in the region. Hence following the Shah's visit to Riyadh in 1968 and several meetings between the Irani and Saudi rulers and their representatives which followed this visit, an 'understanding' and possibly a secret agreement of co-operation concerning the future of the Gulf was reached.[49] When Sir William Luce, the Conservative government's special representative, met the two rulers in 1970 he found them united in their determination to take over the British role in the Gulf and to resist a change in Britain's previous policy.[50]

Although Iran had improved her relations with most Arab countries after giving up her claim to Bahrain, she still maintained the claim to the islands of Abu Musa, greater and lesser Tumb, belonging to Ras al-Khaima and Sharja respectively.[51] As they controlled the straits of Hormuz (about 20 miles across at its narrowest point) and used daily by hundreds of tankers and other vessels,[52] these islands were considered vital by Iran. Still licking her wounds after Iran unilaterally asserted what she claimed were her rights of navigation in the Shatt al-Arab,[53] Iraq was strongly opposed to her neighbour's claims to the three islands. Apprehensive of the building-up of Iran's military power by the West[54] and her 'arrangements' with Saudi Arabia (apparently with the West's blessing) concerning the future of the Gulf, Iraq, whose only outlet to the open seas was through Hormuz, tried to mobilise Arab public opinion against Iran, claiming that she was threatening the 'Arab character' of the Gulf.[55] As expected, Iraq was soon joined by the PDRY which called upon the Arab countries to beware of imperialist plots concerning the Gulf and its islands. Later these radical countries were joined by Libya who, for her own reasons, opposed the surrender of 'holy Arab land' and tried to coerce the trucial rulers concerned not to give in to Iran's pressure.[56]

The propaganda of the radical Arab countries concerning Abu Musa and the Tumbs and the attack on the Israeli tanker

by Palestinian guerrillas in Bab al-Mandeb in mid-1971 made
Iran even more determined to assert her authority over the
islands which she claimed were historically hers.[57] As the time
for the British evacuation of the Gulf was approaching and the
latter still hedged regarding the problem of the contested
islands, Iran repeatedly reiterated her intention of reasserting
her sovereignty over them, if necessary by force. Thus although at first Iran's claims to these tiny and semi-deserted
islands were either ignored or received little attention, by 1971
they had gradually become a major issue.

Fearing a major rift between herself, Iran and the Arabs,[58]
which would threaten the stability of the Gulf, Britain tried to
convince Iran that Abu Musa and the Tumbs had no strategic
value. Refuting this argument, Iran considered the islands so
vital to her interests that she was ready to risk a major confrontation over their possession. Faced with Iran's determination to occupy the islands the British began to negotiate a
settlement which would give the islands to Iran, but outwardly
preserve their 'Arab character'. Evidently the moderate Arab
countries, including Egypt, were not only informed of the
negotiations but there are many indications that they actually
agreed to the British solution. Although the negotiations seemed
at first successful, the ruler of Ras al-Khaima, influenced by
Iraq and his Palestinian adviser, at the last minute rejected the
British–Irani offer. Despite Libya's hysterical reaction and
Iraq's and the PDRY's threats, the reaction of most Arab
governments was relatively mild when Iran occupied the
islands at the end of 1971. Egypt, for instance, denounced Iran
in the mildest possible tone whereas Saudi Arabia expressed
only surprise that a sister Muslim state resorted to force to
occupy contested territories.[59]

*The Birth of the Gulf Federation and the Independence of Bahrain and
Qatar*

Negotiations concerning the Gulf federation were resumed
and accelerated at the beginning of 1971 after Sir William Luce
had convinced his government that it was dangerous, if not
impossible, to reverse the Labour government's decision of
1968. Entrusted with the complicated and delicate task of
winding up British affairs in the Gulf, Sir William met with

innumerable problems. For one, the unwillingness of Teheran to recognise the federation as long as its claims to Abu Musa and the Tumbs were not granted. As the most powerful country in the Gulf and the mainstay of Western hopes for preserving stability in it, Iran's co-operation was vital. Moreover, in addition to her 'understanding' with Saudi Arabia, Iran had gained throughout the years substantial influence over the Gulf principalities and sheikhdoms, some of which had very large Iranian communities.[60]

The Saudis insisted that the planned Gulf federation should include Bahrain and Qatar (to counterbalance the progressive elements in the former) in addition to the seven trucial states. They repeatedly informed the British that unless their territorial claims were met they would not recognise the federation. Bahrain was unwilling to join a federation if not given a dominant position in it. Such demands infuriated Qatar, always jealous of her neighbour, and prompted her to insist on similar terms for joining the federation.[61] Bahrain's and Qatar's demands only served to confirm the suspicions of the rulers of the trucial states that a wider federation would be dominated by their larger neighbours. In fact, some rulers strongly objected to any association with Bahrain, whose politically active intelligentsia and proletariat[62] were bound to influence the population of the whole federation and undermine their authority. Others were apprehensive that by joining a federation they might lose the absolute power which they exercised in their own principalities. All the rulers participating in the negotiations were influenced by traditional animosities, jealousies, boundary problems and above all by the disparity of population and revenue between their respective 'states'.[63]

As the negotiations for a federation of the nine Gulf sheikhdoms reached a deadlock,[64] the ruler of Bahrain announced as early as 1971 that he would opt for independence. Bahrain would have declared its independence in May had it not been for Faisal's insistence on a wider federation. By the middle of the year, however, Saudi Arabia and Kuwait gave up hope of uniting the nine sheikhdoms in a federation and Faisal grudgingly agreed to the British plan of a smaller federation of the seven trucial coast principalities.[65] Bahrain declared its independence in August and Qatar followed suit in September, both becoming members of the Arab League and the United Nations. From May, therefore, convinced that the plan for a larger federation was doomed to failure, the British and other interested parties began negotiations for the creation of a smaller federation consisting only of the trucial coast principalities.

Abu Dhabi, the richest and largest trucial state, was the staunchest supporter of the British federation plans, especially of the smaller federation, of which undoubtedly it would become the leader. Despite the relatively strong army which he has been building since 1968, Sheikh Zaid Bin Nahyan, Abu Dhabi's ruler, realised that once British protection was withdrawn Abu Dhabi by itself had little chance of resisting Saudi pressures. Although cordially received in Riyadh and assured of Saudi support for the planned federation, Sheikh Zaid was also told by Faisal that this did not mean recognition of the British-imposed borders. Having discussed the future of the Gulf in several Arab capitals, Sheikh Zaid was convinced that the only hope of preserving the territorial integrity of his country and indeed its existence lay in a federation sufficiently large to become a member of the Arab League and the United Nations.[66] By 1971 Sheikh Zaid made his peace with his old rival Sheikh Rashid Ibn Maktum, the ruler of Dubai—the second most important trucial state—and won his support for the smaller federation plan. In fact, from May 1971 Sheikh Zaid played a major role in Sir William Luce's efforts to bring about the creation of a federation of the seven trucial states. The original plans to create a unified and cohesive federation were abandoned during difficult negotiations between the rulers so as to overcome the suspicions and fears of some of them and to reach an agreement of a sort. To make the proposal even more attractive, Abu Dhabi declared her readiness to carry the major burden of the federation's budget and established a substantial fund to help the economic development of her poorer sisters.[67]

Besides the fears of the less important rulers that they might lose their autonomy, the major obstacle in the negotiations was the unreasonable demands of Ras al-Khaima's ruler, Sheikh Saqr Ibn Muhammad al-Qasimi. In the nineteenth century Ras al-Khaima, famous for its piratical activities, enjoyed a predominant position in trucial Oman and even beyond it. Its power and influence gradually declined in the twentieth century as a result of the British presence in the Gulf and especially after the discovery of oil in neighbouring countries. Ras al-Khaima's ruler nevertheless enjoyed a special position among his neighbours, four of whom belong to the Al-Qasimi family. Unlike the other principalities Ras al-Khaima is relatively fertile and is among the more populous of the trucial states. Sheikh Saqr therefore persistently refused throughout the negotiations to accept his exclusion from the leadership of the planned federation, reserved for the previously unimportant rulers of Abu Dhabi and Dubai (neither of them Al-Qasimis). His refusal to join the federation at this stage was also the outcome of the fact that oil explorations were under way in Ras al-Khaima throughout the period of negotiations. If oil were found in his territories, Sheikh Saqr assumed he would be negotiating from a position of strength.[68]

In July 1971 the trucial rulers, with the exception of Sheikh Saqr of Ras al-Khaima, agreed in principle to unite their countries in a federation to be called the 'Union of Arab Emirates'—UAE. The presidency of the Union was conferred upon the ruler of Abu Dhabi, while the ruler of Dubai was to be made his deputy. Besides several ministries in the government of the union each member state was also allotted a number of seats in the union's council, in proportion to its population, resources and strength. However, Abu Dhabi and Dubai, the strongest and richest members of the union, reserved for themselves the right to veto in the council.

Feverish attempts were made in the last months of 1971 by the British and several Arab rulers to persuade Sheikh Saqr to join the federation before its final formation and independence. The latter persistently refused to do so, hoping for discovery of oil in Ras al-Khaima and encouraged by Iraq. Basically opposed to the Western-influenced federation, Iraq has been fostering relations with the tiny but strategically important Ras al-Khaima since 1970. Thus, despite Ras al-Khaima's traditionally friendly relations with Teheran, Iraq succeeded in exploiting Sheikh Saqr's grievances to influence him to refuse the settlement with Iran concerning Abu Musa.[69] When the islands were occupied by Iran's army Iraq lauded Sheikh

Saqr's stand and strongly supported his call for joint Arab action against Iran. Probably on Iraq's advice, Sheikh Saqr made his joining the UAE conditional on its support against Iran. This was completely unacceptable to the federation leaders who had been previously involved in negotiations with the Shah and who were anxious to maintain friendly relations with him in the future. Leaving Ras al-Khaima to herself, the UAE with six members declared its independence at the end of 1971 and became a member of the Arab League and of the United Nations. It was recognised by most countries, including the Soviet Union, the CPR and Iran. Shortly afterwards, when all hope of finding oil in his territories had been abandoned and realising that Ras al-Khaima was left in a most awkward position, Sheikh Saqr joined the UAE and Ras al-Khaima became the seventh member of the federation.[70]

Compared to the Gulf federation originally envisaged by the British and their allies, the UAE is far smaller (total population about 200,000), weaker and more loosely organised. Because its 'constitution' safeguard the autonomy and authority of the different rulers in most fields, it has not solved even the absurd fragmentation of trucial Oman, the traditional differences and rivalries.[71] The benefits of the substantial oil revenues of Abu Dhabi, and to some extent Dubai, are not equally spread among the UAE's population despite the sums channelled to the poorer states through the special development fund and the federal government budget. Although the five poorer members of the union[72] have relatively little hope of economic development they are quickly expanding their educational systems and social welfare services. Unless the different rulers of the federation agree to more meaningful unity or at least to further measures leading to the integration of their respective principalities, this situation may create in the future grave social, economic and political tensions which could threaten the stability, if not the existence, of the UAE.

Despite all the drawbacks, the federation provided at least a convenient framework for some co-operation between its members. Among other things the emergence of the UAE enabled its government to take under its wing the Trucial Oman Scouts (TOS), which has become the nucleus of the UAE's defence force. This British-commanded, well-disciplined and organised mobile force of about 1,800 men, had proved its worth in the past by successfully maintaining the peace in the trucial states.[73] Nevertheless, the different rulers still maintain and have even expanded their own British-commanded private armies. Abu Dhabi, for instance, has built up an army of about 9,000 men equipped with the most modern weapons. Although supposed to co-operate with the union's defence army and gradually to be integrated into it, these private armies are not under the jurisdiction of the UAE government. The union's defence army remains, therefore, the most accepted and logical tool for preserving peace and stability within the federation. Since the UAE's independence it has in fact already dealt successfully with tribal warfare, subversive activities and attempted coups.[74]

The UAE's economic and strategic importance and its fragmentation and weakness make it an ideal target for progressive and radical elements in the area. Greatly intensified since the independence of the Gulf states, the activity of local subversive organisations is assisted by Iraq and the PDRY.[75] Already suffering the consequences of such activities, the UAE's president announced in April 1972 that the union's army would smash any attempt to overthrow a member government as well as protect the union from its enemies.[76] However, pressure is already building up for the arabisation of the command of the union's army as well as of Abu Dhabi's defence force. The expansion of these forces and their acquisition of more sophisticated weapons necessitates a larger number of officers and requires that the N.C.O.'s and soldiers now being recruited, have a higher standard of education than in the past.

Once Arab officers replace British commanders of the union's army and of Abu Dhabi's defence force, the confidence of Sheikh Zaid in his ability to control the situation, may prove to be exaggerated.[77]

The UAE's president, Sheikh Zaid of Abu Dhabi, is presently far more preoccupied with the possibility of external aggression than with subversion and internal dissension. Once independent, the UAE received the blessing of all the Arab countries, with the exception of PDRY. But Saudi Arabia refused it recognition because she insisted on first settling her claims to Abu Dhabi territory.[78] Rightly or wrongly, Sheikh Zaid considers Saudi

Arabia far more dangerous to the union (in fact to Abu Dhabi) than the subversive activity of far-away PDRY, or of Iraq, who declares her friendship to the UAE whenever possible. In addition to building up his military power, Sheikh Zaid hastily began to foster the UAE's relations with the Arab countries, Iran and the Great Powers. In contradiction to the expressed wishes of Saudi Arabia and despite his special relations with Britain and Iran he gave his consent to the establishing of extensive diplomatic and trade relations with the Soviet Union. These steps, clearly part of an attempt to safeguard Abu Dhabi's integrity in the face of Saudi pressure, not only enraged Faisal but to some extent undermined Western-sponsored arrangements in the Gulf and may help the Soviet Union and its allies in the area.

Having failed to establish a larger Gulf federation, Saudi Arabia hoped that the new conservative Gulf state leaders would follow her anti-communist policy and, under her leadership, co-operate against subversive organisations and the countries supporting them. The most vulnerable to Marxist subversion, Sultan Qabus of Oman, visited Riyadh at the end of 1971 and all outstanding territorial problems between the two countries were settled. Saudi Arabia blocked PFLOAG's supply routes along the edges of the Rub' al-Khali and granted Oman financial aid while Oman wholeheartedly supported Saudi Arabia's policy in eastern Arabia.[79] On the other hand, Sheikh Zaid's activities constituted a severe blow to Faisal's and Iran's attempts to prevent the Soviet Union from establishing its presence in the Gulf and to contain the spread of its influence in the area. Saudi Arabia therefore mobilised the support of all her friends in eastern Arabia to isolate Abu Dhabi. She even hinted that if the necessity should arise she would not hesitate to use her armed forces to maintain 'peace and stability' in the area.[80] Despite Saudi pressure a Soviet embassy was established in Abu Dhabi. However, Soviet representation in the union, at least for the present, is far more limited than originally intended.

Declining Stability in the Gulf and its Consequences

The tension between Saudi Arabia and Abu Dhabi is only one example among many of how unrealistic were Western hopes that eastern Arabia's moderate régimes would unite, or at least co-operate, to maintain stability in the area. It also demonstrated how fragile are the arrangements which the British left behind them, although when they withdrew from the Gulf eastern Arabia was divided (at least in theory) into only six political entities instead of twelve as in the past. With the exception of Saudi Arabia and to some extent Oman (still enjoying British protection), the UAE, Qatar, Bahrain and even Kuwait, controlling among them a sizeable part of the world's oil reserves, are absurdly small, weak, unstable and have excessively large immigrant communities.

All the smaller Gulf states are governed by conservative rulers, whose power, theoretically absolute, depends on an aristocracy made up of the ruler's kinsmen,[81] members of important merchant families and tribal sheikhs. Wishing to retain the support of their subjects, the rulers are desperately trying to develop their backward countries and diversify their monolithic economies. They also channel the benefits of oil revenues into the indigenous population, but not to the immigrant communities, through welfare services and free educational facilities. By giving preference to their subjects, they hope that the latter will acquire a vested interest in maintaining the existing system of government and will not unite with the immigrants against the régime. All the rulers pay lip service to Arab nationalism and 'buy' the good-will and support of Egypt and some of her allies through generous subsidies and technical and cultural aid agreements.[82]

Paradoxically, by developing the welfare services and the economies of their countries, the ruling dynasties are undermining the foundations of their authority based as it is on the loyalty of backward[83] tribesmen. The new generation which is emerging from local schools and returning from universities abroad is critical of the meaningless fragmentation of the region and the backwardness of their countries and their régimes. This is especially true of Bahrain and Kuwait, where development and free education began earlier. However, even in Qatar and the UAE the pressure is growing and the rulers have prudently established systems of popular representation or consultation, although without real authority. In addition to rapid urbanisation and the dissatisfaction of the immigrant communities, this situation makes the smaller Gulf states extremely unstable and vulnerable to the activities of subversive organisations and external pressures.

There are many indications that unrest and subversive activities in the Gulf have greatly increased since 1971. Violence has already erupted between members of the UAE or tribes belonging to them.[84] Sharja, unsettled in December 1971 by riots and an attempted assassination of its deputy ruler, was severely shaken in the beginning of 1972 by the murder of its ruler[85] during an abortive coup. Encouraged by Iraqi agents and allegedly by Ras al-Khaima and extremist Palestinian guerrilla organisations, subversion and unrest are spreading to other principalities of the federation.[86]

In February 1972 the ruler of Qatar was deposed by his brother in a bloodless coup while visiting Iran. It is generally accepted that the coup was an outcome of a struggle of power within the ruling family. The dismissal of the British commanders of the security forces, the establishment of a consultative council and other insignificant reforms introduced by the new ruler, indicate however that the situation in conservative Qatar is not as stable as it appeared to be.[87] The government of Kuwait was shaken out of its complacency already in 1969–70, when several bombs exploded in the capital. Despite a mass expulsion of immigrants, Kuwait still has a foreign community which is as large as the indigenous population. The different revolutionary organisations of the Gulf have all established cells in Kuwait and Palestinian guerrillas are actually 'taxing' the population. Notwithstanding the rapid progress of the country and the many privileges granted to the indigenous population and even to Arab immigrants, news of terrorist activities in Kuwait has occasionally appeared between 1971 and 1973 in the Arab press.[88] On the other hand, the spontaneous popular support given by Kuwaiti citizens to their government during the recent crisis with Iraq indicates that the inhabitants of the Gulf sheikhdoms have already developed some sort of national identity and that, given a vested interest in the régime, they are ready to defend it.

Bahrain, rather than Qatar and the UAE, seems the most vulnerable among the new Gulf states. The early discovery of oil and the introduction of welfare services and Western education produced in Bahrain a strong politically conscious intelligentsia and proletariat. She therefore emerged in the last decades before independence as the centre for progressive elements and political fermentation, the outcome of which was an eruption of 'labour unrest' and political demonstrations. In recent years, with a more liberal government and open society than its neighbours, Bahrain has become the headquarters of a wide spectrum of progressive nationalist and Marxist movements.[89] Since its independence in August 1971 it has experienced rioting, strikes, demonstrations and even acts of sabotage. Seemingly the product of labour and inter-communal problems, unrest in the islands was motivated, in most cases, by politics.[90] In March 1972, for instance, Bahrain's urban centres were paralysed by wide-spread strikes and rioting. Exploited by radical Marxists and nationalists, a strike in the new aluminium factory and problems concerning the planned dockyard were turned into a challenge to the régime's policy toward the American naval presence, relations with Iran, and the employment of non-Arab labourers. The situation became so serious that only by calling in the army was the government able to overcome the rioters.[91] Despite constant improvement in its relations with Iran, Bahrain is reluctant to join a defence pact sponsored by her which could solve some of her more pressing problems. Apprehensive of the reaction of her population (Arab) and the Arab countries to such a treaty, Bahrain, as well as her neighbours, is becoming fearful of Iran's formidable military power and aspirations. Hence her ruler is trying to gain the support of the majority of his subjects by developing a system which would enable them to participate more actively in the government of their country.[92]

The deterioration of law and order in the Gulf principalities since their independence is attributed (in addition to long-standing traditional tensions) to a co-ordinated policy of Iraq and the PDRY of exploiting local opposition to the régimes as well as to Arab immigrant communities.[93] Iraqi representatives, delegations and ministers frequently tour the Gulf and are to be found in all the capitals of its sheikhdoms. While official Iraqi representatives appear to foster friendly relations with the governments, Iraqi agents are subverting their authority.[94] Across the Peninsula, the PDRY openly supports PFLOAG and other progressive revolutionary elements in the Gulf. In co-operation with the Palestinian Marxist organisations, Iran's communist underground movement and Iraq, it helped establish in eastern Arabia's urban centres cells of revolutionary organisations,[95] whose declared aim is the overthrow of the 'feudal régimes' and the termination of 'Western oil monopolies' in the region. The weakness of east Arabia's 'states', the jealousy and suspicion with which they regard each other and Saudi Arabia, and their growing apprehension of the power of non-Arab Iran, make these régimes easier prey for their enemies.

Although without illusions about the durability of its arrangements for the preservation of the *status quo* in the Gulf, the West was shocked by the rapid erosion of stability in the area. Moreover, Western leaders assumed until 1971 that, following the withdrawal of British troops Russia, not wishing to antagonise Arab nationalists and Iran, would refrain from establishing a presence in the Gulf. Hence, despite evidence of increased Soviet interest in the area,[96] the West has been taken aback by the crudely disguised intention of the Soviet Union to gain footholds in the Gulf since 1971.

A constantly increasing number of Soviet diplomatic representatives and delegations have appeared in the Gulf states since their independence. Their main goal is to expand Russian influence and presence in the newly independent states through diplomatic, trade and cultural relations. The UAE's initial willingness to permit the opening of a Russian embassy in Abu Dhabi and consulates in all other capitals of the union's principalities was a major success for the new Soviet policy in the region. Although coerced by King Faisal and a coalition of ultra-conservative rulers into curtailing the original agreement, the UAE (more precisely its president, Sheikh Zaid) permitted the Russians to open the embassy in Abu Dhabi. While some attempt was made to improve relations with Iran, the main Russian efforts were directed towards Iraq and culminated in the signing of the Soviet–Iraqi agreement of April 1972. The scope of this agreement and its outcome in the following year indicated the extent of Russia's determination to establish its influence and power in the Gulf.[97]

In 1971, when the crucial importance of Gulf oil was

becoming universally recognised, the West began to realise that, left to themselves, its local allies were unable to cope with the situation developing in the region. Forced by the Dhofar rebellion to spend half of his modest oil revenue on his army rather than on badly needed development, Sultan Qabus, who deposed his ultra-conservative father in 1970,[98] failed to gain the support of Oman's population. The local intelligentsia resented the British officers and administrators who were reorganising Qabus's army and the civil service. Moreover, despite the expenditure on military hardware and the British adviser's efforts, the situation in Dhofar quickly deteriorated and subversion spread to Oman proper. Hence many more British officers were seconded to, or hired by, the Sultan's Armed Forces (SAF). Secretly deployed in Dhofar from the end of 1971, British élite troops and RAF units, together with SAF, launched several operations meant to break the PFLOAG stranglehold over the province. British-commanded security forces helped, at the same time, to preserve Qabus's authority in Oman proper.[99]

Although in 1970 the United States even considered withdrawing its symbolic naval presence from the Gulf, it has completely reversed its policy in the region since 1971 and especially after April 1972. The agreement about bases with Bahrain was renewed on the eve of independence and the obsolete vessels of America's tiny Gulf squadron were replaced with more modern ones. Moreover, determined to contain the spread of Soviet influence and to protect the West's interests in the Gulf, America is taking a far more active and aggressive role in the region's politics.[100] Increased United States economic aid to the YAR led to the resumption of diplomatic relations with her in mid-1972 as well as to the growth of American influence in this country neighbouring on the PDRY. Allegedly instrumental in the improvement of relations and co-operation between Saudi Arabia and Oman, the United States is accused by the PDRY of being responsible for the growing pressure on its border. Spurred by the Soviet–Iraqi treaty of April 1972, the United States strengthened its relations with east Arabia's sheikhdoms, sometimes even at the expense of the British. Above all, the appointment of the CIA's ex-chief Richard Helms, as ambassador to Teheran indicated America's determination to frustrate Soviet and Soviet-inspired activities in the region and led to an even closer co-ordination of the policies of the two countries. Even earlier, substantial quantities of sophisticated arms were sold by the Americans to the Irani army and have helped make it the strongest in the region.[101]

Determined since 1968 to establish dominance in the Gulf region and, in co-operation with Saudi Arabia, to preserve stability in it, Iran was opposed to any Western military presence in the area. This policy was maintained even as late as 1971 when the Shah expressed the wish that his navy should participate with Western navies in the defence of the Indian Ocean. Therefore substantial sums of money were spent by Iran on the construction of new bases in the Persian Gulf and the Gulf of Oman and on the modernisation and expansion of its armed forces. Realising by 1972 her inability to cope by herself with developments in the region, Iran, concerned by Saudi Arabia's apathy, reversed her policy and sought the co-operation of the United States in the Gulf proper. After discussions with several American leaders a final understanding was, it seems, reached during President Nixon's visit to Teheran in mid-1972. The Shah's determination to avoid encirclement of his country and to establish its hegemony in the region was fully supported by the Americans. The latter were more than willing to furnish the vast quantities of sophisticated arms which Iran wished to buy as well as the military experts which the new weapons necessitated.[102] The Iranis soon afterwards began to render military aid to Oman. They constructed military bases on several Gulf islands and in the name of 'pollution supervision' sought to gain some control of the maritime traffic through Hormuz.[103] Iraqi subversion in Baluchistan and Khuzistan and, above all, the renewed Iraqui territorial claims against Kuwait allegedly connected with the expansion of Umm-Qasir by the Russians, further cemented the Irani–American 'understanding' and seemed to justify their joint policy in the region.

Although the building-up of Iran's power served to some extent to counter Russian penetration of the region and as a safeguard against Iraqi aggression, the Gulf's Arab countries, including Saudi Arabia, have become somewhat apprehensive of the formidable power of Iran, a non-Arab, non-Sunni country, which has taken upon itself to 'police' the Gulf.[104] Originally, Western plans for maintaining stability in the Gulf envisaged Irani–Saudi co-operation in the matter. Doubts, however, have risen both in Washington and Teheran about Riyadh's ability to carry out the role entrusted to it. Iran and the United States are concerned about Saudi Arabia's internal situation and Faisal's failure to carry out badly needed reforms in his autocratic, conservative régime. The overthrow of the present government in Saudi Arabia would immediately affect all east Arabia's conservative governments, leaving Iran isolated and facing the dangerous necessity of deciding whether to intervene in the situation.[105]

Saudi Arabia

General Background—The Rise of King Faisal

The kingdom of Saudi Arabia, comprising about four-fifths of the Arabian peninsula, emerged in 1932 after the unification of the Najd, al-Hassa, the Hijaz and Assir by Abdul Aziz Ibn Sa'ud. Mainly a desert of different kinds,[106] with half her population (estimated today between 5 and 7 millions) nomads and semi-nomads and a quarter sedentary farmers, the new kingdom was extremely poor. Saudi Arabia would have remained backward and insignificant if not for the discovery of oil in al-Hassa in 1932. Although three-quarters of its population are still employed in agriculture and animal husbandry,[107] Saudi Arabia has become in the meantime one of the world's most important oil producers and her revenue from oil in the fiscal year 1972–73 (ending September 1973) surpassed three and a half billion dollars.

The recent discovery of vast new oil fields in the Rub' al-Khali has increased Saudi Arabia's share of the non-communist world's known oil reserves to about 30%.[108] Sufficient to maintain her present rate of extraction and her annual growth for several decades, Saudi Arabia's oil reserves will enable her to gain an exceptional position in the world's oil industry and economy.[109] As the major supplier of fuel[110] she will become one of the richest countries in the world and could be in a position to exert tremendous financial and political power.[111]

Shortly after his rise to power Ibn Sa'ud faced the necessity of reconciling Wahhabi puritan principles (a return to the simple way of life of seventh century Arabia) with the needs of a country existing in the twentieth century. Although hesitant at first, he was gradually forced to make use of modern technology in order to integrate and govern the vast areas which he had conquered. Ironically, the limited modernisation which he introduced sparked off in the 1920s an uprising of the *Ikhwan*, a military–agricultural settlement organisation, created by him to protect the Wahhabi state. The power of the *Ikhwan* was totally broken by 1930, but despite his unquestionable authority the ruler-imam was himself anxious to preserve the strict theocratic character of his country. Great consideration was given to the advice, opinion and wishes of Wahhabi *ulama*, notables and sheikhs and unless absolutely necessary the king refrained from introducing measures of modernisation or reforms in the country. For these reasons, in addition to its extreme poverty, Saudi Arabia's economic development and the modernisation of its society and government were extremely slow and hesitant until the middle of the century.

Before his death Abdul Aziz separated the functions of the head of state from those of the prime minister. Hence, in 1953 his eldest son Sa'ud, a traditionalist, became king and his second son, Faisal, a modernist, who previously served as foreign minister, became Crown Prince and prime minister. The new king did not have the prestige and authority of his father nor his ability. Ignoring developments in the Middle East and in Saudi Arabia he clung to tradition and insisted on ruling his country in the same paternalistic fashion as his father. Faisal, a man of the world, believed that the time had come for a change through evolutionary reforms and modernisation. The tension which grew between the two brothers forced Faisal into a voluntary retirement and Sa'ud assumed his brother's executive authority. In 1958, however, owing to developments in the Arab world and a financial crisis in the kingdom, the royal family and religious and tribal leadership coerced Sa'ud to transfer full executive powers to Faisal.

Until 1958 the larger part of Saudi Arabia's revenues was divided among the royal family,[112] or paid as subsidies to tribal groups, notables and religious foundations. Very little indeed was left for administration or development, social services and education. When Faisal assumed full authority in 1958 he rationalised the expenditures of the royal household and the princes, curtailed all subsidies and began to reorganise the administration and government. The austerity measures and reforms introduced by Faisal re-established the country's financial stability and benefited the government's budget and the population, but alienated many of his powerful supporters. Sa'ud managed to regain his authority for a time, but in 1962 Faisal successfully turned the tables on him and in 1964 Sa'ud was deposed. Faisal, who was appointed king, immediately combined once again the authority of the head of state with that of the prime minister. He reorganised his government and pursued his policy of evolutionary modernisation by gradually turning Saudia into a welfare state, developing a modern educational system, diversifying the economy and creating a communications infra-structure. His ability and statesmanship were manifested in the coming years by his success in walking the tightrope between traditionalists and modernists and in withstanding the challenge of revolutionary 'socialist' panarabism, led by President Nasser. Faisal's policy, combining pan-Islamism, anti-communism and moderate panarabism[113] may have seemed an anachronism to the sophisticated intelligentsia of the Arab countries, but it had nevertheless some attraction for the orthodox uneducated Arab masses and especially the majority of backward puritan Saudi tribesmen and farmers.

Saudi Arabia, Egypt and Yemen

Relations between Saudi Arabia and Egypt had begun to deteriorate already in 1957. They reached a low ebb following the establishment of the UAR in 1958. Nasser's pan-arab ideology was based, to some extent, on the assumption that the Arabs would regain their past glory only if they were to unite under one leadership (preferably Egypt's). As a large nation, controlling a good part of the world's proven oil reserves and some of its most strategically important waterways, they were bound to obtain their due place in the family of nations. The elimination of the traditional Western-oriented régime in Saudi Arabia was, therefore, essential to the success of such plans. In 1961 Egypt adopted the ideology of 'unity of purpose' and became dedicated to the overthrow of all Arab régimes whose rulers and systems of government stood in the way of Arab unity and progress. The mainstay of the conservative Arab governments and an ally of the West, Saudi Arabia became one of the primary targets of Egyptian propaganda and subversive activities.

When revolution broke out in Yemen in 1962 Egypt immediately supported the new republican government. Nasser hoped that the success of the Yemeni revolution would spark off a chain reaction and bring the collapse of all the traditional régimes in the Arabian Peninsula. Paradoxically, the Yemeni adventure proved to be the undoing of Nasser, who became more and more committed to an endless and costly war against the royalists. As Saudi Arabia was the main source of support for the imam's forces, the two countries were on several occasions at the brink of war and all of Nasser's influence, backed by UAR propaganda, was directed against Saudi Arabia. Faisal, however, not only survived this crisis but his tactics brought Nasser to Jedda in 1965 seeking an agreement which would provide a solution for his predicament. Although little came of the 'Jedda agreement', Egypt's defeat in Sinai in 1967, followed by the Khartoum conference, led to the evacuation of Egyptian troops from Yemen.

Having lost much of his prestige in the Arab world and dependent on subsidies from the oil-rich countries of the peninsula, Nasser completely revised his hostile policy towards their 'reactionary' régimes. Faisal, on the other hand, with his oil revenues increasing from year to year emerged from the struggle with Egypt as one of the more important leaders in the Arab camp and in the Muslim world. From 1968 on Saudi Arabia's relations with the Arab nationalist camp, led by Nasser, quickly improved. The latter was as interested as Faisal in preserving the stability of the Gulf and preventing the growth of Iraq's and the PDRY's influence in the area. He even used his influence to help Faisal with the proposed arrangements for replacing the British presence by a coalition of local moderate states including Iran.

Relations between Saudi Arabia and Egypt became even friendlier after the death of Nasser in 1970. President Sadat, known for his religious orthodoxy, had been responsible for pan-Islamic affairs in the UAR. With such a background he was not only more tolerant of the anti-communist, pan-Islamic policy of Faisal, but actually far more sympathetic to it than Nasser.[114] President Sadat supported Faisal's policy in Arabia and the Gulf and was instrumental in improving relations between Saudia and Syria and further isolating Iraq. He was rewarded for his co-operation by an increase of the Saudi subsidy to Egypt.[115] As Egypt's difficulties continued to grow in 1971 Sadat frequently consulted Faisal on matters of policy despite, or possibly because of, Saudi Arabia's relations with the United States. The expulsion of the Russian advisers from Egypt in July 1972, following a gradual deterioration of relations between Egypt and the Soviet Union since the abortive communist coup in the Sudan in 1971, was more than welcomed by Faisal. The latter had always told the Egyptian president that close relations with Russia only enhanced the spread of communism, radical ideology and atheism in the Arab countries. Hence Egypt is now considered by Faisal and his allies in the Peninsula as a pillar of moderation and her influence and prestige are frequently exploited to counter the influence of 'progressive' and subversive elements.[116]

Saudi Arabia continued to support the royalist forces even after the Egyptians withdrew their troops from the Yemen Arab Republic (YAR) in the last months of 1967. In a bid to smash the Republic, the imam's supporters at the end of 1967 opened a general attack on the republicans and succeeded in putting San'a under siege. However, having failed to take the town by April 1968, their power began to decline. On the other hand, the moderates (third force) who gained the upper hand in the republican camp seemed, from the middle of 1968, more inclined to come to terms with the Saudis and with the royalists.[117] No longer threatened by Egypt and disillusioned by the inability, dissension and greed of the imam's followers, Saudi Arabia gradually began to phase out its support to the royalists. By this time, the extremely radical government of Southern Yemen rather than the Yemen Republic (YAR) seemed to be a far more serious threat to the *status quo* in the Arabian Peninsula.

Shortly after coming to power the government of Southern Yemen and especially the more radical elements of the ruling National Liberation Front (NLF), together with the Chinese, began to support the rebellion in Dhofar. Marxist-oriented, 'atheist' and dedicated to the overthrow of the 'feudal' régimes in the Peninsula, the NLF and PFLOAG were loathed by Saudi Arabia. As British intentions to end their commitments in the Gulf were revealed in 1968, the Saudis became deeply concerned about the goals of PFLOAG and the NLF's socio-political revolutionary programme adopted at its congress in Zanjibar in 1968.[118] Moreover, President Qahtan as-Sha'abi, the leader of the moderate, pan-arab-oriented faction of the NLF which curbed the extremists, was deposed in the middle of 1969. The extreme Marxist NLF faction, which thereafter ruled Southern Yemen (later the PDRY), was dedicated to the implementation of the Zanjibar resolutions. As expected, Saudi Arabia was greatly alarmed by this development and by the stronger relations developed between Southern Yemen, the Soviet Union and, even worse, communist China.[119]

Clashes between Saudi and South Yemeni forces along the disputed border in southwestern Arabia were inevitable. These clashes quickly developed by the end of 1969 into a mini-war.[120] The Saudi government soon realised, however, the disadvantage of deploying its troops and tribal auxiliaries against South Yemen. Such activities, heralded by the communist countries as an invasion of her neighbour's territory, also helped to drive into the arms of the NLF tribes of South Yemen's eastern provinces, some of whom were traditionally inimical to Saudi Arabia and to Saudi tribes. Riyadh therefore turned its attention to the many South Yemenis who escaped after 1967 into Saudi Arabia. Mainly ex-sultans and sheikhs with their followers, members of the moderate South Arabia League (SAL) and tribes who opposed the NLF, these refugees served as a nucleus of the Army of National Salvation (ANS) which invaded Hadramaut in the last months of 1970. However, despite initial success the attempt proved to be a complete failure as a result of dissension, lack of determination and leadership within the ANS. It was then that Saudi Arabia turned its attention to the YAR.

At the end of 1967 the remnants of the pan-arab 'Front for the Liberation of Southern Yemen' (FLOSY), which was defeated by the Marxist NLF in Southern Yemen, found refuge in the Republic of Yemen.[121] So did several rulers whose 'states' were located near the border of Northern Yemen and who escaped into YAR with their armies or followers. In 1968 and 1969 they were joined by thousands of soldiers and officers trained by the British who were purged from the South Yemeni army before and after the overthrow of Qahtan ash-Sha'abi.[122] Considered unreliable by NLF authorities, members and especially sheikhs of the tribes from which the soldiers came were persecuted and also forced to flee northwards. Using the YAR's southern provinces as a base of operations and a refuge, some refugee groups opened, in the beginning of 1968, a sporadic and uncoordinated guerrilla warfare against the NLF régime. The South Yemenis in the YAR were not only more numerous, determined and better trained than the ones in Saudi Arabia, but the difficult terrain between the two Yemens was far better suited for guerrilla warfare than the borders of the Rub' al-Khali. The activities of anti-NLF elements in the YAR were hampered, however, by disunity, lack of arms and funds. The Saudi government was anxious to help. But although sympathetic to the cause of the refugees, the YAR's government, still not fully reconciled with Saudi Arabia, was unwilling to compromise its relations with its southern neighbour.[123]

Relations between the YAR and Saudi Arabia gradually improved throughout 1969. A full settlement of the outstanding problems between them was reached when Yemen's prime minister, Muhsin al-Ayni, attended the Islamic conference in Jedda in 1970. The occasion was used for extensive negotiations which resulted in the termination of all hostilities between republicans and royalists and the establishment of friendly relations between Saudi Arabia and Yemen. Consequently, the imam's dynasty was abandoned by its Yemeni supporters and by the Saudi authorities; the latter also granted the YAR substantial economic aid. Royalist leaders who returned to their country gained an important role in her government, moderated her policy and were instrumental in the development of closer relations with Saudi Arabia. Some republican leaders, including Muhsin al-Ayni (an ex-Ba'thist) had, nevertheless, reservations about allowing their country to be used against the PDRY. Although they feared the PDRY's reaction, they were even more concerned with the effects of Saudi activities on their efforts to overcome traditional sociocultural differences and to consolidate the authority of the central government over the tribes. However, Saudi Arabia's position by this time was so strong and Yemen's economy was in such a deplorable state that the YAR government could not afford to antagonise Riyadh. It preferred to close its eyes to the Saudi anti-PDRY campaign as long as the Saudis acted prudently and refrained from interfering in Yemen's internal affairs.

By the beginning of 1971 Saudi efforts began to bear fruit. The different anti-NLF forces in the YAR established a unified command, which they named 'The Army of National Unity' (ANU). Although just a superstructure co-ordinating the operations of the different groups fighting the NLF, the ANU succeeded in intensifying guerrilla activities in the second, third and fourth provinces of the PDRY. The Army of National Salvation was in the meantime also reorganised, re-equipped and re-activated. It resumed operations in remote Hadramaut and Mahra (fifth and sixth provinces of the PDRY), announcing that it intended to gain the independence of these provinces. The Saudis meanwhile had established (in Najran) a 'clandestine' radio station, called 'Free Yemeni South Radio', which broadcast communiqués of the commands of the two 'Liberation' armies, describing their war as a *jihad* and attacking the NLF government as anti-Islamic and tyrannical. Roads were built from the Hijaz and Nadj to the PDRY's border and to Yemen to facilitate the movement of troops and supplies. Moreover, the Saudis constructed extensive military installations ('military towns' and an airfield)[124] in the south-western corner of their country and Saudi forces, especially units of the national guard, were moved into the area. Alarmed by all these activities the PDRY called the attention of Arab and socialist countries to the 'imperialist-inspired' plots against its integrity.[125] Incapable of challenging the strength of Saudi Arabia it did, nevertheless, take occasional retaliatory actions against the Yemeni Republic.

Premier Muhsin al-Ayni resigned his position in February 1971 as a result of an internal struggle for power in YAR. The short-lived government of Ahmad Noaʿman and that of General Hassan al-Amri were more Western-oriented and more willing to co-operate with the Saudis. In fact, some of the leaders of the

South Yemeni refugees were even appointed to ministerial positions in al-Amri's government. The Saudis were so delighted with these developments that in April 1971 Prince Fahd, Saudi Arabia's deputy prime minister, declared that 'Saudi Arabia and Yemen were the pillars of Islamic solidarity against the elements of destruction'.[126] When Yemen's president Qadi Iryani visited Riyadh in June he was warmly welcomed and obtained further Saudi aid for the development of his country.[127] Even when Muhsin al-Ayni was re-appointed prime minister in the last months of 1971, he maintained the policy of fostering closer relations with the West and allowing Saudi Arabia, and the ANU supported by it, to use the YAR's territory against the PDRY.[128] With supplies and ample funds regularly arriving from Saudi Arabia, the different elements participating in the ANU became throughout 1971 better equipped, larger in numbers and more daring. By the end of the year their operations were stepped up and 'plots and subversion' were reported even in the first province and in the PDRY's capital.

The intensification of guerrilla warfare along the PDRY's borders and the concentration of part of the Saudi army around Najran in the last months of 1971 were no doubt partly connected with the fact that the British were evacuating their forces from the Gulf during this period. The size of the forces involved and the scale of guerrilla activities, however, so alarmed the PDRY that it warned its communist allies and Arab friends that a full-scale invasion of her territory was being prepared by the Saudis and the 'American imperialists'.[129] Although possibly in connection with their plans concerning the Gulf, the extent of growth of Soviet military and other aid to the PDRY since the last months of 1971, indicates the importance attributed by the Russians to their facilities in Southern Yemen and that the warning of her government was not ignored.[130]

The Saudi-supported NSA and ANU were soundly beaten by the PDRY's armed forces on several occasions at the end of 1971 and the beginning of 1972. Nevertheless, to intimidate the YAR's tribal elements which co-operated with the Saudis, the NLF government treacherously killed several important North Yemeni tribal chiefs in March 1972. This act, deplored by everybody in the YAR, antagonised the two important tribal confederations of Northern Yemen (the Bakil and Hashid), previously relatively neutral concerning PDRY affairs.[131] War was about to break out between the two Yemens, and was prevented only by the intervention of several Arab countries and prominent republican leaders. During this period the Russians, with interests in both countries, were put in an awkward position. However, taking into account the increasingly Western-oriented policy of the YAR and its relations with Saudi Arabia compared with the greater strategic importance of the PDRY and the relative political reliability of its Marxist régime, they sided, although not openly, with the latter. Their attitude during this crisis led to a further decline of their influence in the YAR and was probably a major factor in Yemen's alleged decision to request the withdrawal of Soviet military advisers and experts.[132]

Faisal's policy concerning the two Yemens no doubt achieved some success. The YAR was finally won over to the moderate-conservative camp and the Russians (it was alleged) were ordered out of the country. Saudi Arabia's dominant position in the Peninsula was further strengthened and a *cordon sanitaire* of a sort, stretching from Yemen to Oman, was created around the PDRY. The latter is, moreover, constantly harassed by a guerrilla warfare which apart from its political impact, has grave effects on South Yemen's economy. On the other hand, the campaign against the PDRY produced several negative outcomes for Saudi Arabia. It strengthened the NLF hold over the PDRY's government and enabled the régime gradually to expand its control to all parts of the country. It increased the dependence of the PDRY on the aid and support of the communist countries, enabling the Soviet Union and China further to establish their influence and presence in the country. Several 'progressive' Arab countries, as well as elements among the intelligentsia in Yemen and Oman, are becoming increasingly critical of their government's policy and their support of the 'reactionary alliance' led by Saudi Arabia against the PDRY. Although unconfirmed, it is claimed that PDRY agents are partly responsible for the reawakening and expansion of subversive activities within Saudi Arabia.[133] Finally, the campaigns against the PDRY have indirect effects on the authority of the Saudi government and the struggle for power in the country. The funds and arms channelled to the elements fighting the NLF enabled the governors of the provinces bordering Yemen and the PDRY to expand their private armies and entrench their position at the expense of the central government.[134]

The Régime and the Internal Struggle for Power

It is customary to regard Saudi Arabia as an overcentralised, autocratic, absolute monarchy.[135] As king-imam, prime minister and commander-in-chief of the armed forces, Faisal has become since 1964 for all intents and purposes the source of all authority in Saudi Arabia. Since then, it is claimed, he jealously guards his absolute power, overlooks his promise to draw up a modern constitution and refuses to delegate authority to his subordinates. Although he has reorganised the government and established fourteen ministries with specific areas of responsibility, the final decision on every matter of importance lies with Faisal.[136] Although substantial, the king's power in fact depends to a great extent on his personality and achievement, but is clearly not absolute as the government of Saudi Arabia is a long way from being over-centralised.

In a Wahhabi theocracy such as Saudi Arabia the powers of the king-imam derive from the Shari'a, which defines his duties as head of state and protector of belief and permits his deposition if he fails his duties.[137] Even more important today is the fact that the king's authority depends on the support of the vast royal family[138] which represents different interests, power groups and opinions. With roots in tribal society, where the sheikh was *primus inter pares* and consulted rather than commanded the elders of the tribe, Saudi Arabia is governed by a king who, although far more powerful than the tribal chief, still resorts to consultation rather than command. The leaders of the different sections of the royal family, representatives of the religious oligarchy and the most important notables and tribal chiefs are members of the *Shura*, the advisory council. No important decision concerning external or internal policy is taken by Faisal and his government without first consulting and getting the approval of the majority of the *Shura*. Although the king appoints the Crown Prince, it is nevertheless the *Shura* which decides who will succeed the king on his death or in the event of his deposition.[139] Finally, the king's authority depends on the loyalty of the armed forces and the administration and on his ability to control the powerful regional governors-amirs.

Theoretically, the king controls the administration and security of the whole country through his government and national security forces. In reality, although the integration and unification of the different areas conquered by Ibn Sa'ud in the first decades of the century has gone a long way, the process is far from complete and each region maintains, to some extent, its special identity and particular character, customs and loyalties. For administrative purposes Saudi Arabia has been divided into five provinces, which represent the different parts of the Peninsula united by Ibn Sa'ud, namely Najd (central province), the northern frontier province (north of Jebel Shammar), Al-Hasa (eastern), Hijaz (western) and Assir (southern province). Each in its turn is subdivided into districts and sub-districts. The regional governors, as well as those of the main town (*Hakim-Amir*), are appointed by the king and responsible for the administration of their respective regions to the king through the ministry of the interior.[140] In practice, the amirs, who belong to traditional powerful families in the area or are relatives of the king,[141] retain their position for a long duration, if not for life, preserve a large measure of autonomy and are exceedingly powerful. With the exception of judicial problems they are *de facto* the ultimate authority in all matters in their region. Although appointed by the government (usually on the amir's recommendation) the subordinate governors and officials of the region are accountable to the amir. Responsible for upholding law and order in the region, the amirs maintain private armies, the strength of which depends on their resources, family connections and circumstances. Thus, with the exception of certain districts in the west, the Nejd, the east and the main towns, the authority of the king and his government is far from being centralised and absolute.[142]

To ensure himself the loyalty and support of powerful sheikhs and rulers of different regions, Abdul Aziz Ibn Sa'ud took wives who were their daughters or kinswomen.[143] His numerous sons, the outcome of these matrimonial arrangements, enjoyed the support of the family and tribes to which their mothers belonged. On the other hand, such families, through their connection with the royal house, membership in the *Shura* and the system of government, enjoy a special position in the country and its administration. Such, for instance, is the case of the Jiluwi family,[144] exceedingly strong in eastern Arabia, which produced several governors who control the populous and economically important eastern region of the kingdom. Crown Prince Khalid, the first deputy prime minister of Faisal, is Adbul Aziz's son by his Jiluwi wife. Another example is the Sudairi family, extremely powerful in the southern part of the kingdom and to some extent in central Arabia. This family has not only produced a number of outstanding amirs,[145] but its members hold key positions in the administration of Saudi Arabia as well as in some of the smaller states of eastern Arabia. Abdul Aziz's seven sons by his Sudairi wife, together with the Jiluwis, were Faisal's main supporters during his struggle with Sa'ud. They are the leaders of the moderate progressive faction in the royal family and hold several key positions in the present government. Although Khalid is Crown Prince and first deputy prime minister, Prince Fahd, one of the Sudairi brothers, is the most powerful personality in Saudi Arabia next to Faisal. Second deputy prime minister and a close associate of Faisal, he is credited with much of the progress achieved during Faisal's régime.[146] As minister of the interior, the amirs, at least in theory, are subordinate to him. More important is the fact that he is responsible for maintaining the internal security of the country and controls the police and security forces. Sultan, his full brother, the minister of defence and aviation, controls the Saudi army, airforce and navy. A third brother, Turki, holds an important position in the palace administration and is one of Faisal's closest advisers.

The conservative elements in the royal family are led by two full brothers, born to another wife of Abdul Aziz. Muhammad, one of Ibn Sa'ud's eldest sons, held hopes of becoming Crown Prince in the early 1960s and is still considered a candidate for this position in view of Khalid's poor health. Far more powerful though is his brother Abdullah, the commander of the national guard, the so-called White Army, made up of the élite of the tribal forces. Abdullah was able through his position to cultivate special relations with important tribal coalitions and other conservative elements in the rural areas, whereas Muhammad exercises influence among the *ulama* and the conservative elements in the central administration. Many other factions, however, exist among members of the royal family. One, composed of young princes with no hope of achieving power, has been pressing for revolutionary reforms in the régime.

Coalition of different groups within the royal family and the *Shura* are created and later disintegrate as a result of common interest, specific events or outstanding circumstances. Nevertheless, the Sudairis, allied with the Jiluwis and several other groups, have at present the best chance of retaining power, even after Faisal's death. If this were to happen, Khalid would probably be made king while Fahd would become his prime minister with full executive authority.[147] The power of the conservative elements in the royal family and of the *Shura* is nevertheless substantial, especially as they control the national guard and have the support of the religious oligarchy. In 1969–70, just when Faisal's health was failing, plots to overthrow the government were uncovered. The conservatives exploited the circumstances to try to persuade the *Shura* to establish a consultative council of twelve of the eldest members of the royal family. Had they succeeded, such a council, probably composed of ultra-conservatives, would have undermined the power of the Sudairi brothers in a most critical period. As it happened, Faisal, recovered from his illness,[148] and successfully withstood the pressures put upon him and the whole matter was dropped.[149]

Faisal's ability to maintain the equilibrium between 'progressives' and conservatives has been a major factor in preserving the unity of Saudi Arabia despite constant rivalry within the royal family. But if reports that his age and failing health impair his ability to govern are true, a struggle for power may soon break out in Saudi Arabia. Such a struggle and especially Faisal's death in the present circumstances could prove disastrous to Saudi Arabia and the future stability of the Gulf.[150] Unless quickly settled by the *Shura*, it could lead Saudi Arabia into civil war, cause the disintegration of the kingdom or provide the new élites with an opportunity to assert their power.

Development, Modernisation and the Emergence of New Élites

Abdul Aziz Ibn Sa'ud maintained the traditional theocratical character of his country and its government by virtually closing Saudi Arabia to the world and preventing development and modernisation. This, however, was no longer possible, or desirable, in the second half of the twentieth century. Faisal realised that social and political upheavals in neighbouring countries, the pressures building up within Saudi Arabia and the economic needs of the country necessitated a change of policy. He therefore encouraged evolutionary reforms in most fields, so long as such reforms did not undermine the power of the monarchy and were, as far as possible, compatible with the principles of the Wahhabiya. Thus he reorganised the government on relatively modern lines, to enable it to cope with the new problems and challenges faced by the country. The oil revenue, constantly increasing and no longer reserved for the royal household and divided among the princes, notables and tribes, benefits the whole population through a complex system of welfare services and free education. Even more important, it is used to accelerate, whether directly or indirectly, development in most fields of Saudi Arabia's economy.

Aware of the fact that oil is not replenishable and that another source of energy may take its place in the future the Saudi government has been trying since 1962, and especially in recent years, to diversify the economy of the country. In addition to overcoming the danger of complete dependence on oil revenue, such measures could indirectly help Faisal's new foreign policy, strengthen the authority of the central government and solve the many social and other problems arising from the oil-boom and the greater accessibility of Saudi Arabia. Substantial funds were therefore allocated after 1965 to the development of agriculture, industry and the communications infra-structure. Thus in 1971–72 over 40% of the country's 1·5 billion dollar budget was earmarked for development projects related to these fields.[151] The dramatic rise in the price of oil, new participation agreements with the oil companies and the expansion of the extraction of oil, now enable the Saudi Arabian government to divert even larger funds for development.[152] The problem will be, of course, whether the

Saudi government is able to undertake such massive development, and the economy to absorb such large capital investment.

Limited projects of land reclamation and attempts to settle
nomads were carried out by Abdul Aziz. More extensive and
technologically advanced projects were undertaken after World
War II with the help of ARAMCO and the American government. Besides the psychological resistance of the Bedouins to
sedentary farming, the major obstacle was that 99% of Saudi
Arabia's land was considered unsuitable for agriculture and
very little water was to be found in the country. The development of agriculture was essential to make Saudi Arabia, a
sizeable importer of foodstuffs,[153] more self-sufficient. It could
also improve the standard of living of three-quarters of her
population and help solve the problem of the nomads. The
budget of the Ministry of Agriculture has therefore been
gradually increased in the last decade. As a result of the general
growth of the country's budget, this meant a substantial increase in real terms.[154] Modern technology and ample funds
now make possible the reclamation of up to 15% of Saudi
Arabia's land. The discovery of vast subterranean water reser-
voirs in some parts of the country, the building of dams to store
flood-water and the use of cheap energy for desalinisation
plants make the development of agriculture even more attractive and economic.[155] Although impressive, the progress in
agricultural development and the settlement of nomads is
relatively limited. Moreover, the majority of the Bedouins who
give up their traditional way of life prefer the bright lights of
the town to farming.

The availability of capital for the initial investment, in
addition to economic and social considerations, induced the
Saudi government to give preference to industrial development. Important progress in this field was achieved, especially
after 'The General Petroleum and Mineral Organisation'—
Petromin—was established in 1962. The initiative, and in many
cases the capital, for the construction of the most important
industrial projects in Saudi Arabia in recent years came from
Petromin. Although its greatest successes were in fields connected with the oil industry and oil byproducts, Petromin was
partly responsible for the growth of a network of factories
producing consumer goods, foodstuffs and construction

materials, not to mention its share in the development of heavy industry.[156] Despite the availability of capital, cheap energy and some minerals, the prospects of substantial industrial expansion in the near future are limited. By itself the Saudi market is far too narrow and unsophisticated. Raw materials in most cases must be imported and there is an acute shortage of skilled labour, technicians and managerial personnel. Hence in present conditions Saudi products stand little chance of competing abroad with the products of developed countries. The situation may improve in the future, although not dramatically, as a result of the constant rise in the buying power of the Saudi population and bilateral trade agreements signed with neighbouring countries. Great efforts are also made to train badly needed management personnel and manpower for the new factories and other branches of the economy and government technical services.

The need for trained manpower was realised by Ibn Sa'ud when he took the first steps to modernise Saudi Arabia and reorganise its rudimentary administration. The demand for skilled personnel grew dramatically after the discovery of oil and especially after World War II. The problem was tackled at first mainly by the employment of non-Saudi Arabs and other foreigners. Although carefully supervised and screened, the presence of tens of thousands of foreigners, many educated and used to environments different from Saudi Arabia, was bound to affect the local population. The first signs of such 'unsettling influences' appeared in the 1950s in the centres of the oil industry. It was not long moreover before the Saudi government realised the political and economic danger of being so utterly dependent on a large group of non-Saudis.[157] Determined to 'produce' Saudi experts, administrators and teachers Saudi Arabia embarked on developing the country's education system.

The introduction of a modern secular education would have been unacceptable in the first decades of Abdul Aziz's reign. Some hesitant steps to introduce schools combining religious instruction with modern studies were taken by Ibn Sa'ud after 1930. In fact, a few of the king's numerous offspring were sent abroad to acquire modern education. It was, however, only after World War II that the first foundations of a modern education system were laid by the government. Despite some criticism from the orthodox, a Ministry of Education was established by Faisal in 1954 and the system of education completely reorganised. The emphasis at this time was still on elementary education, vocational training and religious studies. The exceptions were the schools and technical colleges opened by ARAMCO in eastern Arabia in the 1950s. These schools produced the first generation of Saudis whose training combined modern secular general education and technical studies.

Developments in the Arab world after 1958 and the increasing need for educated personnel in the administration and the economy of Saudi Arabia prompted Faisal to modernise and expand the educational system. Young Saudis had begun to realise the material and social benefits which modern education can provide and there was tremendous pressure on existing educational facilities. Elementary and secondary education were quickly expanded and in addition to an institute of higher Islamic studies, the government supported two universities and two technical colleges. By 1971 the number of pupils enrolled in schools of different levels approached half a million (compared to less than 200,000 in 1965). By this time between 7,000 and 10,000 young Saudis were studying in local universities and abroad.[158]

Despite its impressive growth, the Saudi educational system remains inadequate and unsatisfactory. Nearly 90% of the population are still illiterate[159] and the majority of existing educational institutions are not geared to the requirements of the country. Not all the blame lies, however, with the schools. Ample job opportunities cause most young Saudis not to pursue their studies beyond the elementary level. Moreover, the majority of students at the secondary and higher levels of education prefer liberal arts and the social sciences to engineering and science. This is because of the stigma attached to anything remotely connected with manual work, and the prestige of professional and government employment. For the same reason, employers are nearly unable to recruit Saudi unskilled labourers and have to rely on Yemenis, Palestinians and other Arab and non-Arab immigrants. Thus, as Saudi Arabia's economy continues to expand and become more diversified, the number of foreigners employed in the country has grown rather than declined.[160] Ironically, the school system which does not adapt itself to the country's needs has already produced a surplus of graduates in certain fields. As many more schools are opened each year without a parallel growth in the country's economy,[161] the outcome could be the unemployment of half-baked intellectuals in the midst of affluence.[162]

To prevent the emergence of an embittered unemployed intelligentsia, the Saudi government employs in non-specialised branches of the administration all school and university graduates who apply for government posts. Hence, some ministries are already encumbered with unsuitable officials with little to do; consequently, they are becoming less efficient and entangled in red tape to the detriment of the population and the economy. Employment of a sort is easily procured by the thousands of semi-literate and illiterate nomads who are annually enticed to the urban centres. If manual work is unacceptable and left in most cases to foreigners, the new town dwellers are cared for by the welfare services until suitable employment is found for them.

The process of urbanisation and the system of education are creating, or enhancing, problems and tensions which may prove dangerous to the régime. The privileges, wealth and position of power enjoyed by the rulers are far more apparent in the towns. In spite of the accelerated economic development and the welfare services, the conservative theocratic régime is blamed by the educated and semi-educated urban population for the slow progress of their country. These Saudis resent the foreigners who work and live in their towns, some of whom enjoy a very high standard of living, and in some cases hold important positions. The contact with these Arabs serves, however, as a catalyst for the young town dwellers' criticism of the backwardness of Saudi Arabia compared with other Arab countries.

Even more critical of the archaic theocratic character of Saudi Arabia are students and other Saudis who have lived in Arab or Western countries and have returned to their homeland. Although employed in high positions and handsomely paid, they are frustrated by conditions in their country and by the control exercised by the orthodox oligarchy over every aspect of life. Through special committees, established in every district, and a special police force, it enforces what is considered by Wahhabi standards high moral conduct and a strict observance of religious duties. The power of the orthodoxy is resented by the intelligentsia and the technocrats who, despite their position and material success, are deprived of the way of life and small pleasures which are common in all other Arab countries. Not less frustrating is the strict prohibition of any form of organisation, democratic representation and freedom of speech, strictly enforced by the security services. Indeed, these and other methods are used by the traditional ruling class to control the increasing power of the technocrats and new élite groups, who in recent years are breaking into the upper strata of Saudi society and government.

The emergence of Saudi Arabia polarised the social stratification among the population of the areas conquered by Ibn Sa'ud. The king governed the country through an oligarchy made up of his kinsmen, sheikhs of important tribes and tribal groups, traditional regional amirs and the *ulama*. Next on the social ladder were the noble tribes, the mainstay of Abdul Aziz's power, considered the upper crust of Saudi society and who enjoyed many privileges. Besides receiving regular subsidies, their chiefs held important positions in the administration and only members of these tribes were recruited to the élite force —the national guard. Not far behind came the other Bedouin tribes who also enjoyed subsidies and privileges and whose members, if they wished, could join the royal army. With the exception of the *ulama*, simple townsmen and sedentary agriculturalists, although essential to the economy, were at the bottom of the social ladder and power structure of Saudi Arabia.[163] Social mobility was possible, but only within one's own group. The 'lower classes' had, therefore, no way of achieving power or of advancement in the administration, especially as any form of organisation, other than for religious purposes, was, and still is, strictly forbidden.[164]

The traditional social stratification, although not completely disappeared, has been gradually eroded in the last two decades under the pressure of developments in the country and around it. Opportunities for social mobility and advancement have been opened by the need for trained personnel in government service, the acquisition of education and the accumulation of wealth. The cabinet and the higher strata of the administration are still dominated by members of the old 'aristocracy'. But an increasing number of 'commoners' are to be found in positions of power and greater consideration is shown to educated and successful entrepreneurs.[165] The new élites, considering themselves better suited to rule, crave for more power and wish to change the archaic character of their country, its government and society. The dissatisfaction of the intelligentsia, although suppressed by extensive security services, erupts from time to time through organisations plotting the overthrow of the government.

Hence the unrest in Saudi Arabia which was manifested in the oil-industry areas during the 1950s. Attempts to gain better pay and to organise the labour force were supported by the small proportion of intelligentsia and were in fact also a manifestation of the growing influence of Arab nationalism. Not surprisingly, violence erupted in the eastern province, following the deterioration of relations between Saudi Arabia and Egypt in the late 1950s. The discontent gradually spread to the major cities and even to Riyadh, where some young princes demanded in 1960 far-reaching reforms in the administration and government of the country. Frustrated by Faisal's policy and success, these princes and their followers escaped in 1962 to Cairo, where they established 'The Committee for the Liberation of Saudi Arabia'. When clashes occurred between Egyptian and Saudi forces following the revolution in Yemen, a number of Saudi army officers and pilots defected to the Egyptians together with a number of intellectuals who also found refuge in Cairo and San'a. 'The Committee for the Liberation of Saudi Arabia' disintegrated about 1965, but shortly afterwards an underground organisation called 'The Union of the Arab Peninsula' was established within Saudi Arabia and at the end of 1966 and the beginning of 1967 exploded several bombs in oil installations, government ministries and American institutions. Several hundred people, including many young officers, were later arrested by the security forces and thousands of Yemenis who worked in Saudi Arabia were deported.[166]

By far the most serious attempts to overthrow the Saudi government occurred in June and September of 1969. Although

details of these abortive coups were suppressed by Saudi censorship, it was reported that thousands of people, mainly young
army and air force officers and many intellectuals, were involved in the plots. Although its centre was in the eastern
regions, the organisation which prepared the attempted coup
established cells in other provinces and in all the major towns.
The scale and seriousness of these plots[167] and the number of
young officers involved in them truly shook the Saudi authorities. Consequently, the culprits were most ruthlessly punished
and the security forces were strengthened and reorganised.[168]

Saudi revolutionaries in the 1950s and 1960s were mainly
influenced by Nasser's type of socialist panarabism and to a
lesser extent by the Ba'th (Syrian) ideology. In recent years,
however, the majority of those actively involved in subversion
in Saudi Arabia were, and are, followers of more radical socio-
political ideologies, inspired and supported by the NLF of the
PDRY, the Marxist Palestinian guerrilla organisations (the
PFLP and PDFLP) and the Iraqi Ba'th. A Marxist-oriented
underground organisation called 'The Sons of the Arabian
Peninsula' (SAP) was already active in 1970 and was said to
have had in its ranks a number of young officers. Despite widespread arrests among its members at the beginning of 1971 the
SAP allegedly was preparing a coup against the régime when
most of its members were arrested by the security services at
the beginning of 1972. As expected, SAP members were even
more ruthlessly treated by the Saudi authorities than members
of other progressive nationalist organisations known to exist in
the kingdom.[169] Although there are signs that cells of the
movement still exist in several Saudi towns and oil-producing
centres, it seems that SAP is kept alive mainly through the
activities of Saudi refugees in Aden, Baghdad and Beirut.[170]
Indeed, despite the seeming political inactivity of the majority
of the Saudi intelligentsia and young officers it is far more likely
that they would tend to support progressive panarab nationalist movements rather than Marxist ones.

In the past the futile attempts to overthrow the Saudi régime
were bound to fail because conditions in the country were not
yet ripe for such a drastic change. Still enjoying the support of
the majority of the backward population, armed forces and the
ulama, the monarchy is able to maintain its control over the

country through a network of security services. The expansion of education, economic development in Saudi Arabia and propaganda and subversion by neighbouring progressive Arab régimes are, however, already affecting the Saudi intelligentsia and enhancing their desire to modernise the country and change the character of its government. Indeed, with more intensive contacts with neighbouring Arab countries, political dynamism in the Arab world is beginning to have an impact even on Saudi tribal society upon whose loyalty the régime mostly depends. Yet, the affluence resulting from the oil wealth, now channelled to the population through welfare services and employment opportunities open to Saudi citizens, strengthens particularist and bourgeois tendencies. Hence elements potentially inclined to press for change and progress are likely to prefer moderate Arab socialism to revolutionary Marxism and evolution to revolution. Be that as it may, the modernists' and revolutionaries' best chance to overthrow the régime in the near future is if civil war breaks out following the death of Faisal. Even then, the future of the country will depend on whether young officers succeed in getting control of the armed forces and lead the revolution, as was the case in most other Arab countries.

The Saudi Armed Forces

After breaking the power of the *Ikhwan*, the spearhead of his tribal forces, Abdul Aziz began in the 1930s to lay the foundations for the modern Saudi armed forces. The mainstay of Ibn Sa'ud's power, the noble tribes of the Najd, contributed the manpower for the national guard (white army) and for the more exclusive royal bodyguard. Organised about the same time, on European lines, the regular army recruited its soldiers from other tribal groups loyal to the régime. The two forces complemented and counterbalanced each other. The army's main duty was to protect the country against foreign aggression, while the national guard could support the army in an emergency, but its main duty was to preserve internal security (including the suppression of military insurgency). Although incorporated in the army in 1964, the royal bodyguard has since been reorganised and is responsible for the personal security of the monarch and his household.

The Saudi armed forces remained poorly equipped and badly organised throughout the 1930s and 1940s. Having acquired a quantity of relatively modern arms Abdul Aziz invited the British in 1947 to form and train a mechanised brigade similar to Trans-Jordan's Arab Legion. But this arrangement was terminated in 1951 when relations between the two countries began to deteriorate. The United States, wishing to prolong her arrangements for the use of Dhahran air base (leased in 1947), was requested in 1951 to train and equip the Saudi army in exchange for the desired extension. An agreement of military assistance signed between the two countries provided for the sale of arms to the Saudis and the training of their army by American personnel. Notwithstanding the termination of the use of Dhahran by the United States in 1962, the American training mission remained in Saudi Arabia. Thus most Saudi officers and technicians are either graduates of United States military academies or were trained by the Americans in Saudi Arabia. By 1970 the services of the American training mission were no longer essential. Nevertheless, it was retained because its presence was considered by the Saudis to be an assurance of the United States' support should the need arise. Because they wished to maintain a low profile in the Gulf and the Peninsula the Americans did not want to expand their presence in the country even though they were interested in strengthening the Saudi armed forces, but they were willing to sell to Riyadh limited quantities of relatively modern arms.[171] Developments in the Gulf since 1971, the strengthening of the PDRY's army by the Soviet Union and above all the Soviet–Iraqi agreement of April 1972 brought a radical change in American policy concerning Saudi Arabia. No longer inhibited by fear of Soviet and Arab reaction and spurred on by her and the West's oil interests, the United States (and her allies) were ready to sell Saudi Arabia vast quantities of sophisticated weapons accompanied by the (civilian) experts to train the Saudi army in their use.[172] It was hoped that by building up its power the Saudi army would be able to maintain the *status quo* in the Arabian Peninsula and help Iran keep the Soviet Union out of the Gulf.

The revolution in Yemen was no doubt a turning point in the development of Saudi Arabia's army. As tension between Egypt and their country mounted Faisal and his ministers realised the inadequacy of their armed forces. At the time, the latter numbered altogether about 40,000 men, armed with obsolete World War II American weapons, and they were no match for the Egyptian army. The Saudi air force and navy were in an even more deplorable state and were it not for the United States the UAR might have taken far more aggressive actions against the Saudis than the occasional bombing of their villages and towns bordering on Yemen. Hence, in 1965, Faisal authorised the expenditure of more than $600 million, over several years, to modernise and expand his armed forces. As can be seen from the table below[173] the Saudi defence budget has grown in recent years far more rapidly than originally planned.

TABLE II

Budget year (ending September)	Total budget (in million Saudi Riyals[1])	Defence budget	In percentage of total
1960–61	1·720	243	14
1964–65	3·112	587	18·9
1970–71	5·966	1·743	30
1971–72	6·600	2·200 (?)	nearly 40 (?)
1973–74	22·310		about 25

1. 4·5 Saudi Riyal = 1 United States dollar, before recent devaluations.

Made possible by the rapid increase in Saudi Arabia's oil revenues, the decision to accelerate the expansion and modernisation of the Saudi armed forces was influenced by political developments in the region since 1968. Following Faisal's decision in 1970 to establish Saudi predominance in and maintain the stability of the Peninsula, the development of the Saudi armed forces became even more urgent. Hence in a projected five-year budget announced in 1971 about 2·2 billion dollars were allocated to defence, substantially increased since.[174]

Between 1965 and 1971 Saudi Arabia purchased from America, Britain and France arms valued at several hundred million dollars. By 1971 the Saudi defence forces numbered over 70,000 men, of whom 40,000 belonged to the army, air force and navy and 30,000 to the national guard. The Saudi armoured units have 85 World War II American M-47 and M-41 medium and light tanks, 25 French AMX-13 light tanks and 50 modern AMX-30 medium tanks. In addition to 200 AML-60s and AML-90s they also have an assortment of armoured cars. An important addition to the Saudi artillery were batteries of Hawk, surface-to-air missiles and Vigilant anti-tank missiles. More dramatic however is the growth of the Saudi air force which by 1972 had an assortment of 75 combat aircraft and was expecting delivery of 140 F-5 and 30 F-4 fighters. The navy, which was still insignificant, was recently augmented by a large number of small vessels of different types and is about to receive several submarines and other warships.[175] Modernisation and expansion of the Saudi armed forces was greatly accelerated following the crisis with the PDRY at the end of 1972, when substantial quantities of Soviet arms reached the latter and Iraq. Probably related to the Iraqi–Kuwaiti crisis of March–April 1973 orders for an assortment of sophisticated weaponry worth about £250 million were placed with British firms, unknown quantities of arms were ordered from France and more than $500 million worth of modern weapons (including aircraft and missiles) were purchased from the United States.[176]

The decision to strengthen and modernise the Saudi armed forces was not taken without due consideration for the repercussions which it might have on internal security. Generally loyal to the government, the army could be neutralised in an emergency by the national guard. The modernisation, rather than the expansion, of the army, completely unsettled the balance between it and the national guard. With its light arms the national guard would no longer be a match for the regular armed forces with their tanks, modern war planes and other sophisticated weapons.

The king, as commander-in-chief of the armed forces, appointed members of his family, or families related to it, as commanders of the different units of the army. Other officers were usually recruited from dependable elements or came from the ranks. The expansion and modernisation of the army has forced the government in recent years to recruit officers and soldiers beyond the circle of traditionally loyal tribes and from among school graduates, many of whom were sons of townspeople whose loyalty was suspect. As the army became more professional and its weapons more sophisticated, the need for better-educated officers and soldiers constantly grew. Thus since the late 1960s the armed forces have been obliged to draw even more heavily on the educated élite and on 'commoners' who graduated from schools in the different towns. Naturally the loyalty of these elements cannot be compared with that of the majority of officers and soldiers of the ground forces, belonging to the nomadic and semi-nomadic tribes. Even officers of Bedouin origin, however, return to their country from military academies abroad 'contaminated' by new ideas, and their continued loyalty to the régime is in question.

The bulk of Saudi ground forces are nevertheless still loyal to the Saudi house and officers from the 'aristocratic families' still keep all the important positions in the Saudi army, navy and air force, albeit the same could not be said of other officers, especially those in the specialised branches of the armed forces. Like the technocrat-commoners in government service, these officers are gradually gaining importance and seniority and, due to necessity, are appointed in some cases to key positions. Through the extensive security network, the ruthless handling of subversion and the selective stationing of units of the national guard, the régime still succeeds in maintaining control of the situation. Nevertheless dissatisfaction with the archaic theocratic régime, which stubbornly refuses to undertake meaningful reforms, is constantly increasing. With more progressive officers and technocrats gaining key positions in the army and administration the question is how long the régime can maintain its power by suppressing the dissatisfied new élites.

Conclusions

Despite increasing internal tensions in Saudi Arabia it would be wrong to assume that the present régime is about to be overthrown and replaced by progressive or radical forces. As things stand, the ruling aristocracy is likely to retain its power in the near future despite the new circumstances.[177] It is still widely supported by the tribal forces and provincial rulers who have a vested interest in preserving the present system and is protected by their representatives in the armed forces and security services. Therefore, even if Faisal were to be deposed or to die, the progressive elements in the royal family would most probably assume power and accelerate reforms and modernisation, thus further consolidating their position. But there is always the possibility that civil war will break out and in such an event the kingdom could disintegrate into the four or five regions originally united by Ibn Sa'ud.

Nothing could be more wrong than to conclude that the new Saudi élites are mainly made up of extremists and radicals. Many are already integrated into the privileged ruling 'aristocracy', while the majority, in normal circumstances, could be considered the middle class of Saudi Arabia. Their dissatisfaction with the régime stems mainly from their objection to its theocratic and conservative character and the monopolisation of real power by Faisal and the traditional aristocracy (mainly of Bedouin origin). Radicalism among the Saudi intelligentsia, although claimed by some to be widespread, is in fact confined to a Marxist-oriented minority, the mainstay of the most militant and actively subversive organisations in the kingdom. These are vociferously supported by similar elements in the Arab countries and by the PDRY and Iraq. The majority of the dissatisfied intelligentsia however passively or actively sympathises with nationalist panarab revolutionary groups. But, having made its peace with Faisal and depending on his support, the mainstream of Arab nationalism, led by Egypt, is at present unwilling to support these elements. Although not in agreement with Saudi Islamic anti-communist policy, Egypt and its allies are opposed to the radical Marxist-oriented Arab governments and subversive organisations. The obvious change in the orientation of this group in recent years and the deterioration of its relations with the Soviet Union paved the way to even better relations and co-operation with Saudi Arabia. Yet this does not mean that the ultra-conservative Saudi monarchy is accepted by 'progressive' Arab nationalists. Traditionally loathed by the Arab republican régimes the monarchical system, as has been already demonstrated, is not a prerequisite for an Islamic-Arab nationalist and anti-communist policy (witness Libya). Presently tolerated, and to some extent even encouraged by Egypt, Faisal's relations with the West and Iran could, in certain circumstances, cause a renewal of the tension between Saudi Arabia and the Egyptian-led group. Despite the constant improvement of relations between Egypt and Iran a clash between the latter and the mainstream of Arab nationalism over Iran's policy in the Gulf is not unlikely.

Avoided so far mainly through the policy of Egypt, such a clash nearly occurred over the three islands which Iran occupied near the Straits of Hormuz. Iran's growing military power, her high-handed policy in the Gulf and her disagreement with the Arab oil-producing countries in OPEC have already caused a certain amount of antagonism between her and the Arab countries. Unless she broke her special relations with Iran, essential to both countries (and to the West), Saudi Arabia could find herself once again the main target of Arab nationalist propaganda and subversion. A nationalist military coup in Saudi Arabia, under such circumstances, would not only be welcomed (even at present), but probably even supported by other Arab countries.

Faisal's evolutionary reforms may have been suitable and sufficient for Saudi Arabia in the 1950s and early 1960s. But after the fundamental changes which the country's economy and society have undergone in the meantime, such a policy in the 1970s is an anachronism. Saudi Arabia's allies and some of his closest assistants occasionally try to impress upon Faisal the need for a new policy and extensive and far-reaching reforms. Too old, it seems, to comprehend the impact of the socio-political changes taking place in his country, Faisal is unwilling and unable to change his conservative theocratic concepts. Completely engrossed in his Islamic, anti-communist policy, he considers progress, constitutionalism and a change in Saudi Arabia's Wahhabi character a synonym for Marxism, atheism and other 'diabolic' ideologies.

The dramatic increase in Saudi Arabia's oil revenues in the coming years and the consequent expansion of her development programmes and educational system are bound to erode further the foundations of the country's traditional society. Moreover, Saudi Arabia's mini-war with the PDRY, the role she accepted in the Gulf and her fear of a Soviet presence in the area will undoubtedly increase the power of her armed forces. Circumstances in Saudi Arabia are different from those which existed in other Arab countries, whose monarchs were deposed by military coups. The Saudi régime enjoys the support of large elements of the population and the Bedouin-composed army and is allied with a powerful 'aristocracy'. However, the rapid and revolutionary changes in the country as a whole and in the army in particular, have completely unsettled the traditional balance of power. Given the right opportunity, the new generation of progressive officers commanding the specialised elements of the Saudi armed forces could easily overcome the traditional elements and the national guard supporting the régime.

A successful revolution in Saudi Arabia, led by progressive elements, will undoubtedly start a chain reaction leading to the overthrow of all traditional rulers in eastern Arabia. With tiny population and extensive oil revenues, the smaller Gulf states are closely watched by their larger neighbours, who would exploit any plausible opportunity to annex them. The situation in the different 'states' of eastern Arabia is, in most cases, even less stable than in Saudi Arabia. Having large immigrant communities and suffering from the activities of subversive organisations, they are all quickly developing their armed forces with Jordanian and British help. But, under the pressure of Arab countries and public opinion, the command of these forces is quickly being gradually arabised. Therefore these forces, supposed to preserve the power of the traditional rulers, may lead the revolutions against them in future. Revolution in eastern Arabia would undoubtedly win the support of the radical régimes on both sides of the Peninsula and possibly of the Soviet Union. It is unlikely that the British in Oman, the United States in Bahrain, or even Iran with its large armed forces, could stop such a process if the present Saudi régime were to be overthrown. The continued existence of a friendly moderate government in Saudi Arabia, at least in the present decade, is therefore essential to the West.

The West and the other industrial countries, realising the danger of their dependency on Gulf oil, are already trying to develop alternative sources of energy. But this is a lengthy process. The overthrow of the moderate régime in Saudi Arabia in the near future may, therefore, affect not only the whole Gulf, but the economy of many countries and possibly world politics as well. Economically, politically and strategically the Soviet Union stands only to gain from such a development. She may even exploit her treaty with Iraq as a lever to unsettle further the present *status quo* in the Gulf. Already taking a greater interest in the Peninsula, the United States, Britain and Iran, their strongest ally in the region, will probably do their utmost to prevent such a development.

Notes

1. Peck, M., 'Saudi Arabia's Wealth' *NME*, January 1972.
2. Ibid.; *FT*, 30.6.72.
3. See reports of the influence of Arab oil wealth on the intermittent international monetary crises since 1972. The impact of wealth and oil on the Arab–Israeli conflict and on United States and Soviet policy in the Gulf: *Ma'ariv* (Israel) 31.1.73, 30.3.73, according to *Wall Street Journal*; *Washington Post*, 21.1.73, 19.4.73, *Ha'aretz* (Israel). 12.2.73, 16.2.73; *IHT*, 21.3.73, 20.4.73; *DT*, 25.4.73.
4. *FT*, 30.6.72; Peck, *NME*, January 1972. Oil resources discovered in the North Sea until mid-1972 amounted to about 1% of Middle Eastern reserves. In addition to the technological complications of its extraction it is ten times more costly to produce than Middle Eastern fuel—*T*, 19.7.72, 8.8.72; *Ma'ariv*, 25.4.73; *Ha'aretz*, 14.12.72; *FT*, 31.5.73.
5. *FT*, 22.2.72; *T*, 25.2.72; *IHT*, 17.4.73.
6. Some experts envisage that Middle East sources will supply in the present decade up to one third of the United States fuel imports but the American government is determined not to allow fuel imports from the Gulf to surpass 15%—*T*, 20.4.72; *Sunday Times*, 28.5.72; *FT*, 25.9.72; *Ma'ariv*, 11.2.73, according to *Los Angeles Times* quoting United States Secretary of the Interior Morton.
7. See above p. 4. Also: *FT*, 13.6.72, 19.7.72, 24.4.73, 9.5.73; *T*, 18.7.72; *Observer*, 17.12.72; *Washington Post*, 21.1.73, 24.4.73.
8. *FT*, 16.3.72; *IHT*, 16.1.73 (the Tyumen field will supply by 1975 25% of Soviet production), 23.4.73; *Ha'aretz* (according to Novosti), 17.5.73.
9. *T*, 17.7.72; *Yediot Aharonot* (Israel), 25.4.72, according to Verner Gumpel, University of Munich (*East European Studies*); *FT*, 13.3.73.
10. Aziz Alkassas and Klaus von der Decken, 'Die politik Chinas im Nahen und Mitterlen Osten', *Orient* (Hamburg), March 1972; D. C. Watt, 'The Persian Gulf Cradle of Conflict', *Problems of Communism*, May–June, 1972; W. A. C. Adie, 'Peking's Revised Line', September–October 1972; *M* (weekly selection), 22.7.72, E. Rouleau; *INA*, 14.5.72, on China's intention to buy oil and oil byproducts in Kuwait; *Ma'ariv*, 31.5.73, on China's vast off-shore sources.
11. According to the *Washington Post* (21.1.73) Middle East oil producers will earn one trillion dollars in less than 30 years. Libya, Saudi Arabia and Kuwait already have a reserve of several billion dollars which they are unable to utilise locally. See also: *FT*, 25.9.72; *Time Magazine*, 2.10.72; *Ma'ariv*, 11.2.73 (according to the *Los Angeles Times*).
12. *T*, 14.4.72; *Washington Post*, 21.1.73; *IHT*, 21.3.73.
13. *FT*, 11.7.72, 9.5.73; *Ma'ariv*, 11.2.72 (according to the *Los Angeles Times*).
14. Nationalised about ten years ago.
15. Stephen Page, *The USSR and Arabia*, London 1971, chapters 2, 3, 4;

Geoffery Jukes, 'The Indian Ocean in Soviet Naval Policy', *Adelphi Papers*, No. 87, IISS, May 1972.

16. 'L'expansion Soviétique dans l'Océan Indien' in *International Problems*, June, 1971, Jack P. Mener, p. 95; *FBIS*, 9.12.71, radio Kuwait, 3–4.12.71; *FBIS*, 16.12.71, radio Hamburg 15.12.71; *FBIS*, 27.12.71, *INA*, Baghdad, 25.12.71. Establishment of relations with the Union of Arab Emirates (UAE)—*DT*, 28.12.71.

17. The Soviet–Iraqi treaty was already being negotiated at the end of 1971 during the visit of Marshal Gretchko to Iraq for talks on bases— *FBIS*, 16.12.71 radio Hamburg, 15.12.71.

18. Soviet aid to the PFLOAG—*ARR*, 1971, p. 516; Radio Aden, 29.9.71; BBC, SU/3810/AU/2, radio Moscow in Arabic, 10.10.71; *DT*, 18.4.72, John Bullock; *Al-Hayat* (Lebanon), 11.3.72; *Sunday Telegraph*, 5.3.72; D. C. Watt, 'The Persian Gulf', *Problems of Communism*, May–June 1972.

19. BBC, 1.2.72, radio Dubai, 31.1.72; *FBIS*, 3.2.72, radio Kuwait, 31.1.72; *EG*, 7.2.72; *JP*, 18.2.72; *Sunday Times*, 5.3.72; Radio Moscow (in Arabic), 11.3.72; *Al-Nahar* (Lebanon), 11.3.72; *INA*, Baghdad, 30.4.72; Radio Baghdad, 10.5.72.

20. See below, p. 20–26.

21. Tass, 10.4.72; *INA*, Baghdad, 2.4.72, 11.4.72.

22. *Al-Hayat* (Lebanon), 19.4.72; *DT*, 18.4.72; *Ha'aretz* (Israel), 19.4.72; MENA, 4.5.72. Despite Soviet and Iraqi attempts to water down the difference between this treaty and others Radio Moscow (in Russian), 10.4.72, (in Arabic) 11.4.72; *Al-Nahar* (Lebanon), 13–14.4.72; it is evidently different from agreements signed with Egypt and other Arab countries—*Al-Hayat* (Lebanon), 10.4.72.

23. FBIS, 1.2.72, *Ettelaat* (Teheran), 2.1.72; R. M. Burrell, *NME*, December 1972, p. 34; *Washington Post*, 23.4.73, 1.4.73.

24. D. C. Watt, 'The Persian Gulf', *Problems of Communism*, May–June 1972, pp. 32–40; *Al-Hawadith* (weekly, Lebanon), 14.4.72; *Al-Nahar*, 9.4.72; *M*, 13.4.72; *FT*, 25.2.72.

25. *JP*, 25.3.73; *FT*, 21.3.73, 5.4.73, 6.4.73; *IHT*, 2.4.73; *Ha'aretz*, 13.4.73.

26. MENA, 11.4.72; *DT*, 18.4.72, John Bullock; B. Lewis, 'Conflicts in the Middle East', *Survival*, June 1971, p. 197; *Al-Nahar*, 13–14.4.72, 16.5.72; *JP*, 17.7.72; D. Housego, 'Iran in the Ascendant', *The Round Table*, No. 248, October 1972, pp. 497–507; *IHT*, 23.4.73; *FT*, 10.5.73, 18 5.73.

27. Frauke Heard-Bey, 'The Gulf States, etc.', *Asian Affairs*, February 1972; D. Hopwood (ed.), *The Arabian Peninsula*, 1972, chapters 2 and 6.

28. Abu Dhabi's ruler was even ready to finance the expenses of the British garrisons in the Gulf—*Time Magazine*, 7.2.72.

29. See table page 10.

30. INA, Baghdad, 18.3.72; *Al-Nahar* (Lebanon), 20.4.72; FBIS, 4.5.72, radio Baghdad, 3.5.72; *Al-Hawadith* (Lebanon), 12.5.72. Events in March–April 1973 strengthen this claim.

31. *Dhofar, Britain's Colonial War in the Gulf*, edited and published by the Gulf Committee, London, January 1972.

32. During operations undertaken in the area of Ras Masandum facing the Hormuz straits the security forces uncovered large quantities of arms and bases prepared for wide-scale guerrilla operations—*EG*, 19.5.70, 30.7.70; *M*, 1.7.70, 27–28.5.71, Eric Rouleau; *DT*, 7.7.70; NCNA, 20.7.70; *T*, 28.7.70; *Sunday Times*, 2.8.70; *G*. 6.10.70; *NYT*, 19.1.71.

33. NCNA, 17.12.70; *FT*, 7.7.71, 23.7.71; FBIS, 21.12.71, radio Aden, 19.12.71; FBIS, 23.12.71, radio Baghdad, 22.12.71; FBIS, 31.1.72, radio Aden, 31.1.72; *Dirasat 'Arabiya*, January 1971, pp. 109–12; *Al-Nahar*, 31.5.72; *JP* (Reuters), 14.1.73; *Al-Hawadith*, 29.3.73; *FT*, 10.5.73.

34. *CSM*, 1.8.70; *G*, 2.9.70.

35. Weekly column of Hassanein Haykal, editor of *Al-Ahram*, MENA, 21.4.72; *al-Ahram*, 19.5.72, special symposium on American–Soviet talks in Moscow.

36. D. C. Watt, 'The Arabs . . . and the Future of the Gulf', *NME*, March 1971; *EG*, 23.9.70, 24.7.70; *DT*, 14.7.70, 12.2.71; *G*, 11.4.70; Numerous references in e.g. March–May 1971. On Egypt trying to convince Ras al-Khaima to join the federation see: BBC, 23.7.71, radio Cairo 21.7.71.

37. J. B. Kelly, *East Arabian Frontiers*, 1964, chapter 3. The more outstanding border problems with Kuwait were partly settled by the treaty of Uqair in 1922 and by later treaties.

38. Kelly, 1964, *op. cit.*, chapters 4–5; D. Hawley, *The Trucial States*, 1970. chapter 9; W. Phillips, *Oman—A History*, 1967, chapter 7.

39. Phillips, 1967, *op. cit.*, pp. 194–211; M. L. Heath, 'Arabian Extremities', *Royal Central Asian Journal*, 1960.

40. United States Assistant Secretary of State Sisco, 23.4.70.

41. *DT*, 3.7.70, 14.12.70; Press communiqué, British Foreign Office, following Prince Fahd's visit 8–14.12.70. See for instance, *T*, 26.9.70.

42. *NYT*, 29.11.70; *EG*, 8.7.70, 10.7.70.

43. *EG*, 8.7.70, 10.7.70, 15.7.70; *FT*, 15.7.70; A. J. Cottrell, 'Shah of Iran concerned . . .', *NME*, July 1970; Peck, *NME*, January 1972.

44. R. M. Burrell 'An Iranian Evaluation', MS. to appear in *The Indian Ocean, its Political and Military Importance*, edited by A. J. Cottrell and R. M. Burrell, Praeger 1972, p. 14; R. M. Burrell, *The Gulf*, Washington Papers Series (ed. W. Laqueur), p. 32. Burrell's work is extremely important for an understanding of Iran's policy in the Gulf. Also: Jan Nasmyth, 'The British leave the Gulf', *Interplay*, September 1970; A. J. Cottrell, 'A New Persian Hegemony', *Interplay*, September 1970, pp. 12–19.

45. 29% of Iran's revenues is alloted to its military budget—*Croissance de Jeunes Nations*, January 1972, L'Iran, p. 32; *NYT*, 18.11.70. *Ha'aretz*, 2.7.72, 13.4.73; *JP*, 13.7.72, 10.4.73; R. M. Burrell, *NME*, December 1972; *Ma'ariv*, 2.1.73; *IHT*, 5.3.73, on 28% increase in Iran's spending on arms; *Newsweek*, 21.5.73, on a substantial build-up of Iran's armed forces and the construction of bases in and out of the Gulf.

46. See for instance, BBC, 18.1.72, radio Teheran, 16.1.72; *T*, 14.3.72; *Observer*, 19.3.72; *Ha'aretz*, 30.6.73; also above, p. 17.

47. *Interplay*, September 1970, pp. 7–8; *Newsweek*, 21.5.73.

48. *DT*, 25.3.70; *M*. 31.3.70; A. J. Cottrell, *Interplay*, September 1970, p. 9; David Housego, *op. cit.*, *Round Table*, October 1972, pp. 497–507.

49. See for instance, *M*, 12–13.4.70; *EG*, 17.5.71; *CSM*, 18.5.71.

50. Most Gulf rulers also informed Luce that they were unwilling, or unable, to agree to a change in the British policy. A. Hottinger, *Swiss Review of World Affairs*, February 1971, p. 13; *Al-Hayat* (Lebanon), 17.5.71; Cottrell, *NME*, July 1970, p. 19.

51. On the history of the Iranian claims, see *Observer*, Foreign News Service, 14.8.70, No. 28001.

52. It is estimated that an oil tanker passes through Hormuz every ten minutes—*Croissances*, Iran, p. 32. On its importance see *Interplay*, September 1970.

53. Despite earlier agreements which Iran claimed were forced upon her by the British.

54. *DT*, 7.12.71; *T*, 29.2.72; *FT*, 2.6.72; *Al-Nahar*, 19.4.72.

55. *Al-Sayyad* (Lebanon), 25.3.71. Of Iraqi arms smuggled to Sharja—*ARR*, May 1971, p. 259. The case of the islands turns into a panarab issue—*G*, 6.7.71.

56. FBIS, 18.11.71, radio Baghdad, 6.11.71; FBIS, 11.11.71, Ettelaat (Teheran), 2.11.71; FBIS, 2.12.71, radio Baghdad, 2.12.71; *Al-Hayat*, 8.2.72; *Al-Hawadith* (Lebanon), 24.12.71; FAZ, 5.11.71.

57. *Observer*, Foreign News Service, 14.8.70; *ARR*, March 1971, p. 135.

58. *The Economist*, 'Arabian peninsula', 6.6.70, p. xxxiii.

59. Allegations that the British settlement concerning the islands was negotiated with the knowledge, if not the complicity, of several Arab countries, including Saudi Arabia and Egypt, appeared in the Arab press—FBIS, 10.12.71, INA, Baghdad, 9.12.71; Saleem Khan, *Economic and Political Weekly*, 4.3.72, p. 562; *G*, 6.7.71; *FT*, 8.12.71. On Egypt's role in the federation negotiations—*EG*, 4.6.71, 6.6.71; *EM*, 5.6.71. Many news items about the visits of Luce and the Gulf rulers to Egypt—*EG*, *EM*, June–July 1971.

60. *Al-Ra'y al-'Amm* (Kuwait), 10.11.70; *ARR*, May 1970, p. 548; *Daily Star* (Beirut), 3.10.70; *FT*, 15.10.71; *Al-Hawadith* (Lebanon), 16.4.71; *Review of World Affairs*, 52/2, July 1971; *EG*, 28.5.70.

61. *T*, 26.9.70, 12.2.71; *FT*, 15.10.70; *Al-'Uruba* (Qatar), 12.11.70; *DT*, 12.2.71; *NYT*, 18.4.71.

62. *T*, 12.2.71: *DT*, 19.1.71.

63. *G*, 16.4.70; *ARR*, May 1970, p. 291; *FT*, 21.5.70, 16.10.70.

64. *Al-Usbu' al-'Arabi*, 23.2.71; *DT*, 31.5.71.

65. *RWA*, 52/2, July 1971, p. 149; *FT*, 16.8.71; *NYT*, 13.8.71.

66. *G*, 20.11.70; RWA 52/1, April 1971, p. 35; *Al-Hawadith*, 7.5.71; BBC Arabic Service, 3.6.71; *DT*, 19.7.71; *Al-Usbu' al-'Arabi* (Lebanon), 6.12.71.

67. *ARR*, July 1971, p. 347; *ARR*, January 1972, p. 17; *NZZ*, 21.9.71.

68. *DT*, 19.7.71; *T*, 19.7.71; *Al-Hayat*, 28.7.71.

69. Sheikh Saqr's chief adviser, a Palestinian, is said to have been instrumental in fostering these relations. See also: R. M. Burrell,

'Problems and Prospects in the Gulf', *The Round Table*, April 1972, p. 216.

70. *DT*, 16.8.71, 8.9.71, 10.12.71; *Sunday Telegraph*, 15.8.71; *Observer*, 15.8.71; *FT*, 29.7.71; *RWA* 52/3, October 1971, p. 261; *T*, 14.2.71. On Egypt's pressure on Ras al-Khaima to join the federation—BBC 23.7.71, radio Cairo, 21.7.71; *EG*, 12.2.72. Britain terminating special relations with Ras al-Khaima—*G*, 7.12.71.

71. Union's army and tribal border warfare between Fujaira and Sharja—*T*, 12.6.72; *FT*, 18.7.72. There are numerous reports of expensive, unnecessary and often competing development projects undertaken by members of the UAE, Qatar, Bahrain and Kuwait.

72. Ras al-Khaima has agricultural potentialities. Sharjah will share Abu Masa's oil royalties.

73. David Ledger, 'Gulf Union,' *Middle East International*, December 1971; Burrell, *Round Table*, April 1972; *FT*, 15.6.71; *Al-Hayat*. 29.11.71; *Al-Mussawar* (Egypt), 1.10.71.

74. *FT*, 25.1.72, 14.6.72; *T*, 26.1.72; *Ma'rive* (Israel), 18.2.72, Burrell, *NME*, December 1972; *FT*, 8.6.73.

75. See for instance, *ARR* 1971, p. 259; *ARR* 1972, p. 55; *Al-Hawadith*, 7.1.72; *Sunday Telegraph*, 5.3.72; *Al-Hawadith*, 29.3.73; *FT*, 10.5.73, 8.6.73.

76. *Al-Nahar*, 17.2.72.

77. Burrell, 'The Gulf' (ms.), *op. cit.*, p. 54; radio Kuwait, 22.4.71; *INA*, Baghdad, 2.5.72; *Al-Hawadith*, 26.3.71. Jordanian officers are more extensively employed in the training and technical services of the UAE's and Abu Dhabi's armies. On massive arms purchases by the Gulf emirates—*JP* (Reuters), 2.2.73; Burrell, *NME*, December 1972.

78. *Arab World* (weekly, Beirut), 28.12.71, p. 8; *M*, 14.1.72; *Al-Hayat*, 15.2.72.

79. *FBIS*, 14.12.71, radio Kuwait, 13.2.71; *FBIS*, 15.12.71, radio Abu Dhabi, 15.12.71; *FBIS*, 22.12.71, radio Aden, 18.12.71; *T*, 16.12.71, 15.3.72; *FT*, 4.1.72; Radio Tunis, 13.3.72, according to the Saudi News Agency. The Americans are said to have been behind the negotiations between Saudia and Oman. On Saudi–American co-operation in Oman and elsewhere in the Peninsula—*Ma'ariv* (according to the *Los Angeles Times*), 8.1.73; *Al-Nahar*, 21.3.73; *IHT*, 24–25.3.73.

80. *JP*, 18.2.72; *Süddeutsche Zeitung*, 18.2.72; *Al-Nahar*, 17.2.72; Saudia's minister of defence—*Al-Hayat*, 17.4.72.

81. To some extent with the exception of Bahrain, where a representative parliament of a sort is functioning and where a modern constitution is partly implemented—*FT*, 8.6.73; Burrell, *NME*, December 1972. In the case of Qatar the constitution is still a dead letter and the ruling Al-Thani family constitutes about 12% of the country's population.

82. These agreements brought a flood of Egyptian experts, teachers and political representatives to the Gulf states. Most active is Abu Dhabi which, to counter the hostile Saudi attitude, is using her estimated £240 million oil revenue for 1973 (*FT*, 8.6.73) to foster her relations

with the other Arab countries and buy their good-will. See'
for instance, the grant of £10 million to Syria—*JP* (Reuters),
5.4.73.

83. With the exception of Bahrain.

84. *T*, 12.6.72; *FT*, 18.7.72; Burrell, *NME*, December 1972.

85. *T*, 3.12.71, 26.1.72; *IHT*, 2.12.71; *FBIS*, 31.1.72, INA, Baghdad,
29.1.72. On far more serious implications of the Sharjacoup —*Al-
Usbu' al-'Arabi* (Lebanon) 29.5.72.

86. *As-Siyasah* (Kuwait), 31.1.72; *Al-Hayat*, 8.2.72; *Al-Nahar*, 8.4.72;
Burrell, *NME*, December 1972; *Al-Hawadith*, 29.3.73; *FT*, 10.5.73,
8.6.73; *FT*, 4.1.74.

87. *T*, 23.2.72, 28.2.72, 15.5.72; *FT*, 23.2.72, 8.3.72; *EG*, 25.2.72; MENA,
Cairo, 24.4.72, on possible tie-up between revolution in Qatar and
Saudi Arabia—*EG*, 1.3.72.

88. *Economist*, 6.6.70, special supplement; *G.* 6.10.70; INA, Baghdad,
27.4.71, 18.8.71, 9.3.72, 15.3.72, 24.4.72; *Al-Hayat*, 9.3.72; MENA,
19.4.72; *FT*, 10.5.73. The Kuwaiti–Iraqi crisis of March–April 1973
again brought to the attention of the Kuwaiti authorities the problem
of the huge immigrant population in the country which includes tens
of thousands of Iraqis.

89. *FBIS*, 27.1.71, *INA*, Baghdad, 23.1.71, on a cell of the 'Front for the
Liberation of Eastern Arabia'; *Al-Hawadith*, 16.4.71, on the com-
munist 'Front for the Liberation of Bahrain' led by an Irani citizen.
Also: *Al-Hurriya* (Lebanon), 1.3.71; *Economist*, 6.6.70, p. XXII. On
PFLOAG in Bahrain—*FT*, 10.5.73 and other subversive elements—
JP, 22.4.73.

90. On basing agreement and criticism of American presence—*IHT*,
7.1.72, 11.1.72; *T.* 7.1.72; *Al-Nahar*, 20.11.71. The gutting of the
local refinery by fire—*JP* (Reuters), 1.12.72.

91. *INA*, Baghdad, 13.3.72, 19.3.72 (students' support for workers); *FT*,
14–16.3.72; *Al-Nahar*, 20.3.72; *Al-Siyasah* (Kuwait), 17.3.72.

92. *FT*, 10.5.73, 8.6.73.

93. Whether the Soviet Union is behind this policy is still an open question.
See: BBC, SU/3810/AU/2, radio Moscow (in Arabic), 10.10.71; *DT*,
18.4.72; *IHT*, 23.3.73; *Al-Hawadith*, 28–29.3.73; *Washington Post*,
24.4.73; *Newsweek*, 21.5.73; *JP* (AP), 24.5.73; *FT*, 8.6.73.

94. *FBIS*, 11.11.71; *Etteleaat* (Teheran), 2.11.71; *FBIS*, 23.12.71, radio
Teheran, 18.12.71; *Al-Hawadith* (Lebanon), 7.1.72, 12.4.72; *Al-Ra'i
al-'Amm* (Kuwait), 14.1.72, 29.1.72; *Sunday Telegraph*, 5.2.72; *ARR*,
February 1972, p. 55; *Al-Nahar*, 18.2.72; *DT*, 18.4.72; Burrell, *NME*,
December 1972, p. 55.

95. *Al-Hawadith*, 16.4.71, 7.1.72; Burrell, *Round Table*, April 1972, p. 216;
Al-Hayat, 8.2.72; *Al-Nahar*, 8.4.72; *DT*, 10.7.72; *JP* (Reuters), 14.1.73;
Al-Hawadith, 29.3.73; *FT*, 10.5.73.

96. Arnold Hottinger, *Swiss Review of International Affairs*, February 1971;
A. J. Cottrell, *NME*, April 1971; D. C. Watt *Problems of Communism*,
May–June 1971; *FBIS*, 16.12.71, radio Hamburg, 15.12.71; *FBIS*,
21.12.71, radio Baghdad, 17.12.71 (Marshal Gretchko's visit): *DT*,

28.12.71; *FBIS*, 9.12.71, radio Kuwait, 3.12.71; *FBIS*, 27.12.71, INA, Baghdad, 25.12.71.

97. See the Iraqi–Kuwaiti conflict of March–April 1973 and information in the world press in this period about the Soviet share in it and the naval base at Umm-Qasir.

98. Probably with British help.

99. British officers were seconded to the armies of the Gulf states as well. Since 1972 Oman has received military and other aid from Saudi Arabia, Jordan, Dubai and Iran. Of an attempt to revive NDFLOAG in Oman proper: *JP* (Reuters), 14.1.73; *FT*, 10.5.73, 8.6.73.

100. *Al-Hawadith*, 7.5.71, 21.4.72; *IHT*, 7.1.72; *FT*, 4.2.72; *JP*, 18.2.72; *T*, 15.3.72; *ARR*, 1972, p. 37; *Ha'aretz* (according to *NYT*), 9.4.72; *Al-Sayyad* (Lebanon), 10.8.72; *G*, 6.10.72. Also recent expansion of Diego Garcia base.

101. *INA*, Baghdad, 12.10.71, 24.4.72; *Al-Nahar*, 26.9.71, 9.4.72; *Ha'aretz*, 12.4.72; *Al-Anwar* (Lebanon), 3.5.72; *T*. 31.5.72. Sale of arms to Kuwait—*JP*, 18.2.72. Also on United States policy in the Gulf— *Al-Nahar*, 5.7.72; *Washington Post*, 25.4.73, 1.5.73; *JP*, 24.5.73. On negotiations for the sale of arms to other Gulf countries and Iran, see below p. 205.

102. *DT*, 9.12.71, 18.4.72; *Al-Usbu' al-'Arabi* (Lebanon), 7.2.72; *FT*, 2.6.72, 26.6.72, 13.7.72; *T*, 29.2.72, 29.3.72; *Al-Nahar*, 19.4.72; *Ma'ariv*, 11.10.72 (on another island near Hormuz captured by the Iranians). Innumerable reports appeared in world press on arms purchases of Iran from the end of 1972. On a 28% increase in her budget for the armed forces—*IHT*, 5.3.73; *Newsweek*, 21.5.73; *JP* (AP), 24.5.73.

103. See for instance, *IHT*, 24–25.3.73; *FT*, 13.4.73; *Washington Post*, 1.5.73.

104. Hence the West's willingness to sell large quantities of modern arms to Kuwait and other Gulf countries—*FT*, 30.3.73; *IHT*, 2.4.73; *JP*, 1.4.73; *Washington Post*, 23.5.73. Also: On Arab attitude concerning Iran, D. Housego, *op. cit., Round Table*, October 1972; *JP* (OFNS), 11.4.73; *Washington Post*, 1.5.73; *FT*, 10.5.73; *Newsweek*, 21.5.73; Burrell, 'The Gulf Pot Begins to Boil', *NME*, May 1973.

105. As it is already doing in Oman, and as the Shah has declared that he should do if the necessity should arise.

106. Average annual rainfall in Saudi Arabia is 3 inches. However, most of the rain falls in the agricultural centres of Assir and Al-Hassa.

107. Contributing only 6% of the country's GNP. However, those who are pure nomads constitute less than 20% of the population.

108. *FT*, 3.10.72. All figures concerning proven oil reserves should be treated with reservations.

109. *T*, 29.11.71—special supplement, 14.3.72; *G*, 14.3.72; *FT*, 6.7.72; Peck, *op. cit., NME*, January 1972, p. 7. It is estimated that by 1980 Saudi Arabia will export 500 million tons of crude oil annually compared to about 175 million in 1971/72. See also: *Washington Post*, 4–5.12.72; *IHT*, 20.4.73.

110. Common market countries are already becoming increasingly dependent on Saudi oil, not to mention the growing dependence of the United States on the same source—*FT*, 4.2.72.

111. A conservative estimate of Saudi Arabia's oil revenues in 1975 is fifteen billion United States dollars. Further revenues may arise from the 'participation agreement' and the expansion of Saudi oil production encouraged by the United States—*Washington Post*, 4–5.12.72, 19.4.73; *Ma'ariv*, 11.2.73, according to *Los Angeles Times*; *IHT*, 20.4.73. Already flexing its muscles, Saudi Arabia is using its newly gained power in relation to the Arab–Israeli conflict and Gulf politics.

112. At present estimated at about 5,000.

113. On Faisal's policy, see: Ahmed Assah, *Miracle in the Desert Kingdom*, London 1969, pp. 140–7.

114. Compare Egypt's attitude to an Islamic conference in March 1970 with her more co-operative attitude in 1972. *Pakistan Horizon*, 2nd quarter 1970, pp. 181–4; *EG*, 19.2.72, 25.2.72; *Observer*, 5.3.72.

115. *G*, 14.3.72; FT, 7.3.72, 20.7.72. *Al Ra'ya al-'Am* (Beirut), 16.8.71, on the extradition of Saudi political refugees by Egypt.

116. Many thousands of Egyptian teachers, administrators and technicians are replacing the less desirable Palestinian, Iraqis and other Arab 'radicals' in eastern Arabia and Saudia. See for instance, *Al-Hadaf* (Lebanon), 19.6.71. Of 100,000 Palestinians in Saudi Arabia—*Interplay*, July 1970, p. 18. Of 30,000 Palestinians in Saudi Arabia—*FT*, 5.3.73. Of their role in subversive activities—*FT*, 8.6.73.

117. Fred Halliday, *New Left Review*, September–October 1970, pp. 17–9; J. J. Malone, 'Yemen Arab Republic's "Game of Nations"', *World Today*, December 1971, p. 543.

118. The subject material on pp. 38–43 below is treated more extensively in chapter 2, 'Crisis in Southern Arabia.'

119. On this subject see chapter 2.

120. Bell, *World Today*, 1970, p. 80; *ARR*, November 1969, pp. 493, 514.

121. A good part of the members of FLOSY were North Yemenis who settled in Aden. Many North Yemenis have left Aden for the YAR in recent years, finding themselves out of favour and out of work.

122. Mainly 'Awlaqis and Yafi'is, later joined by some Dathina, the most warlike tribes, from which the British recruited their soldiers.

123. Halfhearted negotiations were going on during this period for the unification of the two Yemens.

124. The bases frequently mentioned as the centres for activities against the PDRY are Najran, Sarura, Khamis-Mushait and Jaizan, MENA, Cairo, 10.3.70; *FBIS*, 11.3.70, radio Aden, 10.3.70; BBC, 14.3.70, radio Aden, 11.3.70; *ARR*, March 1970, p. 182; *CDL*, 8.4.70; *ARR*, February 1971, pp. 115, 123; D. C. Watt, *op. cit.*, *NME*, March 1971, p. 25. *ARR*, September 1971, pp. 479–480; Amman Radio 15.9.71 on 'Military Towns in the South'.

125. The PDRY always claimed that the United States was the instigator of the Saudi activities.

126. Radio Kuwait, 6.4.71.
127. BBC, 5.7.71, radio Riyadh, 26.6.71, 28.6.71; RWA 52/3, October 1971, p. 26; *EG*, 10.11.71.
128. On the dissatisfaction of the republican intelligentsia with this policy and attempts at subversion and sabotage—BBC, 12.8.71, ANA, Aden 10.8.71; *M*, 7.9.71; *FBIS*, 8.12.71, radio Baghdad, 6.12.71. For more recent developments and sources, see below, chapter 2, 'Crisis in Southern Arabia'.
129. *Al-Bilad* (Jedda), 9.11.71, 14.1.72; *Ath-Thawra* (San'a), 10.11.71, 19.1.72, 31.1.72; *MENA*, Cairo, 2.11.71; *FBIS*, 4.11.71; ANA, Aden, 4.11.71; BBC, 29.12.71, radio Peace and Progress, 25.12.71; *Al-Ra'y al-'Amm* (Kuwait), 14.1.72; *FBIS*, 28.1.72, radio Aden, 26.1.72; *Akhbar al-Yaum* (Egypt), 16.11.71.
130. See chapter 2, 'Crisis on Southern Arabia'.
131. *G*, 16.3.72.
132. This decision, if true, was no doubt connected with a similar step taken earlier by Egypt and with Saudi Arabia's influence—*T*, 5.8.72. See also: *Al-Hawadith* (Lebanon), 13.4.72; Radio Aman, 22.5.72; MENA, Cairo, 1.6.72; *T*, 15.3.72, 3.7.72 (recognition of United States); *G*, 16.3.72. *Izvestia* (24.2.72) does not mention the YAR among progressive Arab countries. See Libyan support to the YAR in this connection—*CSM*, 9.8.72.
133. See below.
134. *G*, 14.3.72, 16.3.72; ANA, Aden, 30.3.72; *FT*, 4.1.72; *Morning Star*, 4.4.72; *ND*, 4.4.72.
135. See for instance, *The Economist*, 6.6.70, p. xxii.
136. 'Saudi Arabia's Dilemma', *Interplay*, July 1970, p. 18; Ahmed Assah, pp. 123–8; *Handbook*, pp. 138–43, 158–9, 321, 325.
137. See the case of Sa'ud.
138. Estimated to be about 5,000 strong.
139. Ahmed Assah, *op. cit.*, p. 123; Muhammed J. Nadir, *op. cit.*, p. 2; *Handbook*, p. 134.
140. According to a law passed in 1963.
141. See for instance radio 'Aman, 9.4.71; Radio Cairo, 15.4.71; *Handbook*, p. 146.
142. *Handbook*, pp. 145–6, 157–8; Ahmed Assah, *op. cit.*, pp. 129–31; *G*, 16.3.72.
143. Although he had never had more than the four wives permitted by the Shari'a.
144. Previously already related to Abdul Aziz.
145. Khalid al-Sudairi, the amir of Jaizan, for instance, co-ordinated the operations against the PDRY and is described as tribalistic in his outlook—*G*, 16.3.72.
146. *Interplay*, July 1970, p. 18. He is also said to be pressing for more extensive reforms.
147. *Handbook*, p. 157, Peck, *NME, op. cit.*, January 1972, p. 7; Tom Little, *Forum World Futures*, WF/1811, 30.10.71; *T*, 29.11.71, special supplement (Paul Martin).

148. Despite rumours of his death.

149. *Ha'aretz*, 21.8.70; *Ma'ariv*, 4.1.71.

150. *Corriere della Serra*, 3.1.72, 4.1.72; *T*, 29.11.71; *G*, 14.3.72.

151. Compared to 7% in 1960. See also: Muhammad J. Nadir; United States State Department, *Background Notes*, Saudi Arabia, March 1971; *Interplay*, July 1970, p. 18.

152. The 1973–4 budget authorised by Faisal is 22,810 Rials or over five billion dollars—*ARR* 16–31, July, 1973, p. 326; Peck, *NME, op. cit.*, January 1972, p. 7.

153. About 30% of Saudi Arabia's imports consists of foodstuffs—*T*, 29.11.71, special supplement (Wallace).

154. 7% of 1970–71 budget for agriculture. In actual figures 130 million dollars compared to less than 95 million dollars in 1969–70—Middle East and North African Europa publication 1971, p. 600; *T*, 29.11.71. On projects in this field see: Ahmed Assah, *op. cit.*, pp. 232–42.

155. Ministry of Agriculture, Government of Saudi Arabia, 'Saudi Arabia offers a rich potential for water development', Saudi Arabia Embassy, Washington 1967; Hopewood (ed.), *Arabian Peninsula*, pp. 292–3, 296; Overseas Business Report, United States Department of Commerce, *OBR* 67–78, December 1967; *Al-Bilad*, 24.2.71.

156. *The Middle East* (Europa), p. 597; Muhammad J. Nadir, p. 9; Hopewood, pp. 291–8. Petromin is encouraging foreign capitalists to take part in the industrial development of Saudi Arabia—*al-Hayat*, 17.3.72; *Washington Post*, 16.1.73; *G*, 9–10.5.73.

157. *Handbook*, pp. 144–5. Many of Saudi Arabia's officials in the 1940s and 1950s were non-Saudis. Egyptian teachers and experts, for instance, spread seditious propaganda against the Saudi government in 1957.

158. *Economist*, 6.6.70, p. xxi; Ahmed Assah, *op. cit.*, pp. 291–322; *The Middle East* (Europa 1971), p. 602; *Handbook*, pp. 92–104; Muhammad J. Nadir, pp. 7–8; *Interplay*, July 1970, p. 18.

159. *Corriere della Serra*, 3.1.72; United States State Department, *Background Notes*, Saudi Arabia, March 1971.

160. In 1970 about 250,000. *Al-Ahram*, 12.9.71; *Al-Hawadith* (Lebanon), 26.5.72—the number of Egyptian teachers in Saudi Arabia will grow from 6,000 to 12,000.

161. Especially the private sector with the exception of the oil industry, which employs only a limited number of people.

162. Only 4·7% of a projected five-year budget was allocated to 'education and training' (*T*, 29.11.71, special supplement, Ashford) possibly because the government wishes to adjust education to the rate of growth of the economy.

163. Not counting slaves, belonging to all classes and despised groups.

164. Naturally the ones affected most were the townspeople of the Hijaz and to some extent al-Hassa who previously looked down on the Bedouins, and the first graduates of the schools.

165. See 'Emergence of a New Middle Class in Saudi Arabia' by W. Rugh, *Middle East Journal*, 1973, No. 1.

166. *Handbook*, p. 154. Page, *op. cit.*, p. 92. It is claimed that 17 people were executed.

167. The attempted coups in June and September were probably connected.

168. It is alleged that hundreds were executed and even the few who escaped were later prosecuted or captured by the Saudi security forces. See for instance, *Al-Nahar*, 8.4.72. Also report in *Al-Raya* (Lebanon, 16.8.71) of extradition of refugees by Egypt, although it could relate to the next wave of arrests in 1971. Nevertheless, there were hints that another plot was uncovered in the beginning of 1970· *Interplay*, March 1970, p. 19; *Sunday Times*, 5.4.70; *Middle East* (Europa 1971), p. 595; *Haaretz*, 21.8.70; *G*, 14.3.72; Saleem Khan, pp. 262–3; *Al-Nahar*, 8.4.72.

169. The Arab and non-Arab communist press claims that SAP members arrested in 1971 and at the beginning of 1972 were tortured and executed. Thousands are alleged to be in detention in special national guard camps in most inhuman conditions. See: *INA*, Baghdad, 29.3.72; *ND*, 4.4.72 and footnote below.

170. *Al-Hurriya* (weekly, Lebanon), 1.3.71; *Al-Ra'ya* (Lebanon), 16.8.71; *Al-Hadaf* (Lebanon), 19.6.71. Expulsion of Palestinians working in oil industry; *INA*, Baghdad, 29.3.72; *ANA*, radio Aden, 30.3.72; *ND*, 4.4.72; 14 October (newspaper, Aden), 30.4.72. On relations with extremist Palestinian organisations—*DT*, 10.7.72. On sabotaging ARAMCO's installations in Saudi Arabia and other Palestinian guerrilla activities—*Ha'aretz*, 11.7.72; *IHT*, 23.1.73; *FT*, 24.1.73.

171. *Handbook*, pp. 321–8; Peck, *NME*, January 1972, p. 7.

172. Although intended mainly to serve its politics, the arming of Saudi Arabia could also contribute to the United States balance of trade. On new American experts in Saudia—*Washington Post*, 6.3.73. On sale of modern warships, aeroplanes and other sophisticated weapons worth hundreds of millions of dollars—*Washington Post*, 27, 28, 29, May 1973; *FT*, 28.5.73; *IHT*, 27–28.5.73.

173. *Handbook*, pp. 326–7; *Interplay*, July 1970, p. 18; *Military Balance 1972–1973*, p. 34; *Middle East* (Europa) 1971, p. 600; *T*, 29.11.71; Ahmed Assah, *op. cit.*, pp. 192–9; United States State Department, *Background Notes*, Saudi Arabia, March 1971; ARR, 16–31 July, 1973, p. 236; MEEP, 24.8.73, pp. 967–70.

174. *T*, 29.11.71, special supplement.

175. *The Military Balance 1972–1973*, p. 34; *Al-Kifah* (Lebanon), 29.3.71; *EG*, 12.7.71; *M*, 16.12.71; *Ha'aretz*, 14.1.72; *T*, 29.11.71 (special supplement), 18.1.72; ARR, 1972, p. 37; *Al-Hayat*, 17.4.72; *JP*, 13.4.72; *Al-Hawadith*, 28.4.72; *Al-Mussawar* (Egypt), 21.4.72.

176. Not to mention 19 vessels of war promised by the United States. *DT*, 4.12.72; *JP*, 21.12.72; *FT*, 11.5.73; *JP* (AP), 11.5.73, 17.5.73; *IHT*, 16.5.73.

177. For my reservations concerning this statement see below p. 62.

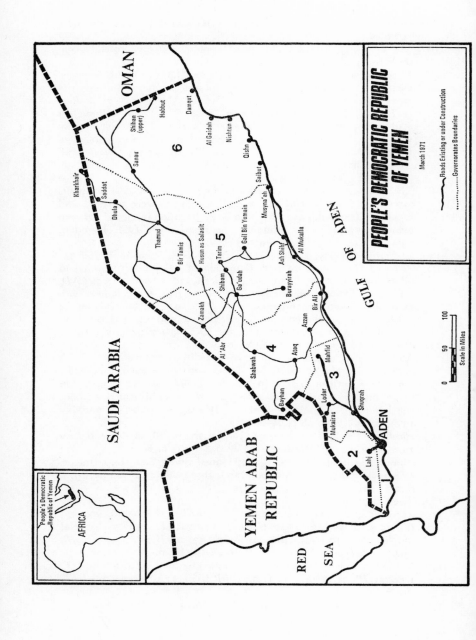

PEOPLE'S DEMOCRATIC REPUBLIC OF YEMEN

March 1971

——— Roads Existing or under Construction
········· Governorates Boundaries

OMAN

Habbut
Damqut
Shihan (upper)
Al Gaidah
Nishtun
Sanau
Qishn
Saibut
Kharkhair
Saddat
Musyna'ah
Dhula
Gail Bin Yumain
Thamud
Husun as Salasit
Bir Tamis
Tarim
Ash Shihr
Shibam
Al Mukalla
Ga'udah
Zamakh
Burayyirah
Al' Abr
Bir Ali
Azzan
Shabwah
Ataq
Mahfid
Bayhan
Lodar
Shuqrah
Mukairas
ADEN
Lahj

GULF OF ADEN

SAUDI ARABIA

YEMEN ARAB REPUBLIC

RED SEA

AFRICA
People's Democratic Republic of Yemen

Scale in Miles
0   50   100

6
5
4
3
2

II

Crisis in Southern Arabia

With a population of only 1·5 million and area of about 114,000 square miles, mostly desert of several kinds, the People's Democratic Republic of Yemen (PDRY[1]) ranks among the poorest countries of the Arabian Peninsula. Yet because of its strategic position and its proximity to the world's major oil sources, the aggressive radical policy of the National Liberation Front (NLF), its ruling party, is viewed with apprehension by its neighbours and the West. Moreover, as a most outspoken supporter of the Palestinian cause, the PDRY, for ideological as well as internal reasons, threatens the fragile peace of the Middle East. In the closing months of 1972 the constant guerrilla warfare along the PDRY's borders (in which the Great Powers were indirectly involved) briefly intensified into a full-scale war between the two Yemens, a condition that could in the future ignite the whole area. Ignoring the basic problems which sparked off these hostilities and following the mediation of some Arab governments an agreement was signed in November 1972 concerning the future unification of the two Yemens. Undoubtedly the tense situation in the southern part of the Peninsula will persist in view of the disparity in the revenues of countries in this extremely important region and as long as the PDRY continues to follow its 'revolutionary' policy.

Physical and Historical Setting

Average annual rainfall in the PDRY is about three inches, only 1 % of its land is cultivable, and there is little hope of any significant expansion. Beyond the narrow and relatively dry coastal plain rise a series of parallel ridges which merge into a rugged plateau. In its western part this plateau is an extension of Yemen's tableland but otherwise it gradually falls northwards into the Rub' al Khali desert. Even in areas of sufficient precipitation, the rugged terrain, broken by many wadis, prevents extensive cultivation. The exceptions are some areas in the west, the Abyan delta on the coast and Wadi Hadramaut in the east.

Following the rise of Islam the southwestern periphery of the Arabian peninsula (with the exception of some coastal towns) was in most periods cut off from the mainstream of Arab development and often in a state of anarchy. The poverty and physical characteristics of the region were not conducive to the development of large cohesive socio-political structures, but led rather to units based on the tribe, whose leaders, in most cases, were *primus inter pares*. Several coastal and Hadramaut sultanates occasionally gained some importance but the power of their rulers was relatively limited and usually short-lived. The Ottomans extended their authority to Yemen in the second quarter of the sixteenth century. Their hold over the south, however, was even more precarious than their government in the north. When Yemen's heterodox Zaidi imams regained their independence at the beginning of the seventeenth century the orthodox Shafi'i south was theoretically considered under their jurisdiction. Hardly able, in most periods, to uphold their authority in central Yemen, they paid little or no attention to the poverty-stricken southern borders of their country.

The British home government developed an interest in a short route to India via the Red Sea only after Bonaparte's invasion of Egypt. Thereafter Britain gradually assumed a more active role in the politics of the Red Sea and its environs and in 1839 occupied Aden. A great emporium in the past due to its excellent harbour and advantageous position, Aden had declined in the last centuries and when captured by the British was but a dilapidated village under the sultan of nearby Lahj. Following the British occupation Aden gradually regained its commercial importance and its population began to grow. The opening of the Suez Canal naturally contributed to the development of the town. Yet the full impact of this factor has become evident only in recent decades as a result of the dramatic expansion of Persian Gulf oil exportation. After World War II, therefore, Aden's port facilities were considerably enlarged and a refinery was built near it by British Petroleum. In the early 1960s, still playing the role of a major power, Britain decided to use Aden as its central military base in the region. Hence substantial funds were invested in the colony for building military installations and facilities.

A most cosmopolitan and sophisticated community of Indians, Somalis, Jews, Europeans and Yemeni Arabs, Aden's population numbered by the early 1960s nearly a quarter of a million. The Arab majority in the town was preserved by the continuous inflow of North Yemeni labourers, attracted by employment opportunities. Some, together with indigenous Arabs, profited from the general prosperity and, becoming merchants, entrepreneurs and government officials, provided the backbone of the town's sizeable middle class. A substantial part of this middle class was, however, non-Arab and the town as a whole was more strongly linked to the Indian Ocean than to its hinterland.

After seizing Aden the British were forced to pacify the nearby area in order to guarantee their hold over the town. Gradually they found it prudent to sign protection and friendship agreements with the rulers and tribes of Southern Yemen, similar to ones signed with rulers in the Gulf. This policy was accelerated after the Turks re-established themselves in Yemen and tried to undermine the British position in the south. Thus, by World War I the British had protectorate agreements with all the rulers and tribes of all the area which came to be known as South Yemen.

Unlike in Aden, the British had no direct interest in their protectorates. The latter preserved their independence and did not come within the sphere of British activities. Unaffected by Aden's dynamic economic and social development they remained poor and backward. Indeed, the protectorate agreements may have been responsible for the gradual halting of the traditional socio-political mobility within tribal society. Profiting from the new circumstances, the ruling houses, sometimes with British help, consolidated their authority. Together with the Sayyids, the powerful Adnani[2] religious aristocracy, they exploited the population and monopolised the country's meagre economic resources.

During the 1920s and early 1930s Yemen's ruler Imam Yahye, who considered himself the true master of the south, constantly harassed the western protectorates. In 1934 Yahya

signed an agreement with the British meant to preserve the
status quo until the settlement of dispute over the future of South
Yemen. But while the imam, preserving his claim to the whole
region, considered the agreement a temporary measure, the
British interpreted it as a recognition of their hegemony over
the protectorates. After declaring Aden a crown colony in
1937[3] they began to consolidate their position in the protectorates by persuading their rulers to sign 'advisory agreements'
with them. This partial extension of British authority to the
interior further consolidated the power of the ruling classes but
did not produce meaningful improvements and was not
conducive to greater cohesion in the protectorates.

The wave of Arab nationalism which followed World War II
did not bypass South Yemen. Organised with the blessing of
the British, the strong local trade union council, led by Abdallah al-Asnaj, became a channel for the dissatisfaction and
aspirations of the Adeni masses. The South Arabian League
(SAL), the first political movement in South Yemen, was
founded about 1950 by the Jifry brothers who served the Sultan
of Lahj and had his support. This movement[4] represented the
more activist element among Aden's Arab middle class, which
was opposed to British domination. After 1953 and inspired
by Nasser's leadership, it identified itself with the mainstream
of Arab nationalism and led the opposition to British plans to
establish a South Yemeni federation.

Concerned about their future position in the area, the British
launched in 1954 the 'South Arabian Federation' plan but
quickly shelved it in the face of the opposition it aroused. The
British plan was revived in 1958 by the rulers of several
western protectorates who suffered from Imam Ahmad's
aggressive policy. Nevertheless, that policy accelerated after
Yemen 'joined' the UAR and the revolutionary nationalist
wave which swept many Arab countries in 1958 prompted
several rulers of the western protectorates to revive the British
plan. Established in 1959, the South Arabian federation
gradually expanded in the coming years. Britain, which
welcomed this development, took steps to suppress the SAL,
which strongly opposed the plan. Some of its leaders were
arrested and the Sultan of Lahj was deposed.[5] Ironically, the
British action against the SAL moderate nationalists probably

helped pave the way for the final victory of the radical elements. Moreover, the expansion of the federation and the inclusion of Aden in 1962, despite strong opposition, proved a pyrrhic victory for the British. The new federation was far weaker and more loosely organised than envisaged and its establishment triggered off a process which completely eroded the authority of the British in Aden and of the ruling classes in the protectorates.

The government of Imam Badr of Yemen was overthrown on the day following Aden's merger with the federation. Thereafter the opposition to the puppet federal government continued to grow with the support of Yemen's republican régime as well as of Egypt. Founded in 1962 by Abdallah al-Asnaj and other leaders of Aden's TUC, the 'People's Socialist Party' (PSP) drew its support mainly from Aden's North Yemeni workers. Although at first only political, its activities gradually spread to urban guerrilla warfare. Events in Aden, constantly publicised due to the town's accessibility and its press, had overshadowed development in the hinterland since the early 1950s. The availability of transistor radios made the inhabitants of the smaller coastal towns and rural areas aware of profound social, economic and political changes in the Arab countries; it exposed them to propaganda broadcast from Arab and other stations, helped widen the gulf between rulers and subjects and intensified the dislike of foreign imperialists. Moreover, for political and economic reasons since the late 1940s the British had given preference in employment in Aden to subjects of their protectorates. Offspring of these labourers and youngsters from the hinterland educated in Aden and elsewhere found it difficult to integrate into Aden's cosmopolitan society and enter the ranks of the colony's administration. Personal frustration, the condition of their kinsmen in the protectorates and contacts with the South Yemeni diaspora all affected their social outlook and political thinking. Thus the new tribal intelligentsia, in contradistinction to most of the Adeni proletariat, was attracted by radical socio-political ideologies rather than merely by pragmatic Arab nationalism.

The revolution in Yemen provided the opportunity and incentive for South Yemen's rural intelligentsia to unite. Despite ideological differences ten different organisations, together numbering several thousand members, merged in 1963 with Egyptian help and formed the National Liberation Front (NLF). From its inception the NLF was dedicated to armed rebellion against the British and their 'lackeys', the ruling classes, and was motivated by a socialist ideology. By providing inspiring leadership the NLF General Command, a politburo of about forty members, soon managed to transform a typical tribal uprising in the Radfan mountains into the nucleus of a popular war of liberation. With Egyptian and Yemeni Republican help this rebellion gradually expanded into all the protectorates, despite the frantic efforts of the federal government to crush it.

In 1965, following the British decision to evacuate South Yemen by 1968, the Egyptians became determined to unite all the nationalist factions in an effort to overthrow the puppet South Yemeni federal government. As a result, the PSP, SAL and several smaller organisations merged into the Organisation for the Liberation of the Occupied South (OLOS). Soon afterwards negotiations were opened between OLOS leaders Abdallah al-Asnaj and Abdul Qawi al-Makawi,[6] and the NLF's General Command leader in Yemen (YAR), Qahtan Ash-Sha'abi.[7]

Although a convenient framework for different progressive nationalist movements the NLF was soon considered an off-shoot of the Qawmiyyun al-'Arab. Originally a socialist pan-arab pro-Nasserite movement, the Qawmiyyun represented a spectrum of opinion. By the mid-1960s its Palestinian-dominated mainstream was not only inimical to the Ba'th ideology but had become progressively more critical of Egypt's pragmatic nationalism.[8] It was this branch of the movement which mostly influenced the NLF ideologists. Despite their unquestionable social radicalism Qahtan Ash-Sha'abi and his followers in the General Command—considered the moderate faction—still respected Nasser's leadership and were willing to co-operate with other nationalist movements. Thus an agreement was signed at the beginning of 1966 which merged the NLF and OLOS into the Front for the Liberation of Southern Yemen (FLOSY). A son of a North Yemeni labourer, the party's ideologist Abdul Fattah Isma'il, was the leader of the Field Command representing the extremists in the NLF politburo. As Britain announced its intention of discontinuing support of the federal government after independence the NLF militants refused to accept an agreement which could jeopardise their chances of establishing a truly socialist régime in South Yemen.

Because it was mainly active in the rural area, the NLF's power was underestimated and at the end of 1966 it finally broke away from FLOSY, President Nasser, enraged by its 'ingratitude' and suspicious of NLF radicalism, pledged Egypt's support of FLOSY. During 1967, nevertheless, the NLF's carefully built military organisation gained control over most of the protectorates. Reinforcements were also moved into Aden for the final struggle for power with FLOSY. As the NLF was gaining the upper hand and the Federation was clearly collapsing, its army, made up of tribal elements, joined the NLF. After a most vicious battle in Aden what remained of FLOSY's members escaped to the Yemen Arab Republic (YAR). Hence the British had no alternative but to hand over the government to the NLF.[9] Thus when the British evacuated Aden in November 1967 the NLF formed the government of the unitary People's Republic of Southern Yemen (PRSY).

Reforms and the Struggle for Power

The short history of the PDRY is dominated by growingly radical internal and external policies, accompanied by an endemic financial crisis and a ruthless struggle for power within the NLF. With the power of all their rivals broken before independence it seemed that nothing could curb the revolutionary Marxist zeal of the NLF leadership. Made over-confident by their success on the battlefield, a majority of the young radicals wished to bring about an immediate upheaval of the country's socio-economic structure, regardless of conditions and consequences. Indeed, in accordance with the NLF's ideology (influenced by the Palestinian Marxist offshoots of the Qaumiyyun al-'Arab) they considered themselves bound as well to take an active role in the struggle against Israel[10] and to support 'world revolution'. Surprisingly, the NLF's moderate wing, rather than the extremists, formed the government of Aden at the end of 1967. Qahtan Ash-Sha'abi, the oldest and most respected member of the General Command, became president and his cousin, 'Faisal Abdul Latif, prime minister.

Although ideologically Marxists as well, Ash-Sha'abi and his supporters advocated a more realistic and pragmatic policy than did their adversaries. South Yemen's service economy suffered a disastrous blow from the closure of the Suez Canal and the departure of the British in 1967. Government revenues declined in the years after independence to about £8 million, a third of the Federation's budget, or about £3 million beneath minimal expenditures. The British stopped their small subsidy when requested in 1968 to withdraw their military advisors and the communist countries' aid was still limited and not in the form of cash. Despite the NLF's ambivalent attitude towards 'Arab bourgeois chauvinism', Ash-Sha'abi turned to 'progressive' Arab countries for help. In order not to antagonise these countries and because PRSY's government was convinced that the backward population was still unprepared for far-reaching socio-economic reforms, it was considered prudent to delay, or at least limit, such measures. Ash-Sha'abi moreover feared that indiscriminate implementation of reforms at this stage would completely unsettle the tottering economy and exacerbate the divisive factors in the country.

Contrary to the Federation plans PRSY was established as a unitary state. For administrative purposes it was divided into six provinces. In accordance with the NLF's policy of centralisation and integration, the provincial governors, high-ranking party members appointed by the president, held at first full legislative, administrative and judicial authority in their respective provinces. But, whereas it had easily eliminated the previous ruling classes, the régime experienced great difficulties when it tried to overcome the individualism and traditional socio-political fragmentation of the population. The backwardness of the population, lack of resources and the inaccessibility of most of the country made the task of governing even more difficult. Hence in the first years after independence control by the central authorities over most of the rugged countryside was nominal. The provincial governors maintained their authority only through the special relations which the NLF had maintained with the tribes and by their ability occasionally to 'show the flag'. This was especially true in the eastern provinces. Traditionally oriented towards Zanzibar, Indonesia and Oman rather than to the rest of the PRSY,

Hadramaut and Mahra were literally cut off from it by the absence of roads. For a time semi-independent, these provinces were ideally suited for the activities of NLF radicals and conservative separatists.

Steps to establish the authority of the government and to overcome tribal allegiances were taken by the PRSY's government from the end of 1967. Above all, the tribally oriented ex-federal army was gradually purged of conservative elements, especially Aulaqi officers considered friendly to FLOSY. Always jealous of the Aulaqis, members of other warlike tribes in the army, especially the Dathina, eagerly suppressed rebellions which broke out among the former. Consequently many Aulaqi soldiers and tribesmen escaped to the YAR and Dathina influence in the army began to grow.[11] Limited social and economic reforms were also carried out by Ash-Sha'abi's government. But generally speaking President Ash-Sha'abi and his cousin Faisal Abdul Latif tried to walk a tightrope between capitalist *laissez faire* and socialist étatism and were careful not to harm the country's economy by unrealistic dogmatism. Some consideration was paid to Aden's middle class and the administrative economic framework left by the former government was on the whole still functioning.[12]

The hesitant reforms and pragmatic policy of the government was strongly criticised by the NLF's militants. Their discontent and power were manifested during the party's congress held in Zanjibar in March 1968. Despite Ash-Sha'abi's opposition, the congress adopted a most radical socialist programme meant to bring about an immediate upheaval of the socio-economic structure of the country and a reorientation of its foreign policy. The government was to draw its power from a coalition of intellectuals, poor farmers, workers and soldiers and lead the country towards 'scientific socialism' through a process of continuous revolution.[13] The army was to be re-organised and politicised and a people's militia established to protect the revolution against 'opportunistic elements' and help bring it into the countryside.

A direct challenge to Qahtan Ash-Sha'abi's authority, the Zanjibar resolutions constituted as well a threat to the traditional army and its British-trained commanders. Ignoring the government, though it may have had its sympathy, the army set out to crush the power of the militants. Many were arrested, some were killed but the majority sought the protection of their tribes or escaped from the country. Although President Ash-Sha'abi exploited the situation to shelve the Zanjibar resolutions he still preferred his NLF comrades to the conservative army commanders. In the year following the army's *putsch* he continued to purge its ranks of traditional and disloyal elements. Because of personal and tribal jealousies his policy met with little resistance and further strengthened the Dathina in the armed forces. While soldiers and officers from other tribes preferred to seek refuge across the border NLF radicals were pardoned and, seemingly willing to accept Ash-Sha'abi's policy, were allowed to resume their previous positions in the party and administration. The breach between the radicals and the moderates was, however, irreparable, especially after Ash-Sha'abi's pragmatic government made some overtures to western countries in order to secure badly needed economic aid.

Careful not to arouse the suspicion of the government, the militants, led by Abdul Fattah Isma'il and Salim Ruba'i Ali, gradually managed to rebuild their power in the capital and the provinces. In the middle of 1969 Ash-Sha'abi dismissed his Dathina Minister of Interior, Muhammad Ali Haytham,[14] and thereby alienated the army. Their popularity eroded in the General Command and among the tribes, President Ash-Sha'abi with his cousin Faisal Abdul Latif was forced by the radicals to resign in June 1969. Haytham became Prime Minister while Ruba'i 'Ali was appointed president. Abdul Fattah Isma'il, in addition to his key position as the NLF's Secretary General, became, together with the two others, a member of the newly formed Presidential Council.[15]

The coalition which brought Ash-Sha'abi's downfall, although undoubtedly Marxist in its ideology, represented a spectrum of opinions and interests within the NLF. Prime Minister Haytham, still supporting Ash-Sha'abi's 'Arab policy', could be classified as a moderate and was one of the leaders of the strong 'tribalistic' element in the party.[16] A link between the important tribes and the régime, this element's participation in the country's power structure was considered by the tribes a safeguard of their interests. On their part the 'tribalists' fostered contacts with their areas of origin and endeavoured to reward their supporters. As the power base of this faction was the army Haytham, although he readily integrated the NLF's cadres in the army, was reluctant to develop the people's militia.[17]

The party's hard-core ideologists, especially Abdul Fattah Isma'il and the small North Yemeni group in the NLF, were critical of tribal allegiances which they felt were detrimental to national integration. Dedicated to unification, on their own terms, of both Yemens, they were partly responsible for the growing tension between the two countries.[18] Instrumental in fostering relations with the Soviet Union and expanding the aid obtained from her, Isma'il and his supporters were, by the end of 1970, described as the pro-Soviet faction in the NLF. President Salim Ruba'i, still in Isma'il's shadow in this period, represented another group of radicals made up solely of South Yemenis. This faction, possibly less committed to Marxist–Leninist ideology, was even more militant about acceleration of the pace of socio-economic reforms and reorganisation and politicisation of the armed forces. In disagreement with Isma'il concerning relations with North Yemen and progressive Arab countries, this group, among whom were many Hadramautis, began, for obvious reasons, to foster relations with the People's Republic of China (PRC). As rivalry was generally more personal than ideological both factions were themselves made up of elements of varying opinions. Isma'il's and Ruba'i's supporters were, however, united in their opposition to Haytham's moderate tribalists and to any aspect of pragmatism in the country's internal or external policy.

The aftermath of the June 1969 coup is termed by the NLF 'The Corrective Period'. No mercy was shown to Ash-Sha'abi's supporters and those who did not succeed in escaping the country were imprisoned or executed. In its foreign relations the new régime unequivocally placed itself in the revolutionary socialist camp and, in accordance with the Zanjibar resolutions, made determined efforts to foster its ties with the communist countries. Relations with the West, on the other hand, sharply deteriorated when the PRSY took a most vociferous aggressive stand concerning the need to fight Western colonialism and its 'lackeys'.[19] Not only was 'World Revolution' preached, but

Aden, becoming an important centre for revolutionary movements, intensified its subversion of 'reactionary' governments.[20] Devoted to Marxist–Leninist ideology and hypnotised by dogmatic interpretations of socialism, the NLF radicals completely ignored South Yemen's economic realities and were determined to transform, in the shortest time possible, their country's backward and still largely capitalist economy into a progressive socialist one. Foreign assets and several branches of the PRSY's economy were immediately nationalised[21] and an agrarian reform was introduced and implemented in 1970. Still dissatisfied with the pace of reform the ultras initiated 'revolutions' of poor peasants, fishermen and workers against employers and tried to enforce collectivisation in different sectors of the economy.

Already in 1970 it looked as if the NLF's radical reforms and dogmatic policy were leading the country towards bankruptcy and isolation. Aden's service economy further stagnated and unemployment constantly grew. Many skilled labourers and a large part of Aden's middle class left the country legally or illegally with whatever assets they could salvage. Happy to rid itself of the bourgeoisie and potentially dangerous elements the régime purposely closed its eyes to this exodus. Generally unsympathetic to Aden's service economy, the NLF cared little about the economic repercussions of this migration and the future of this sector. But even in the countryside the agrarian reforms and 'peasant revolutions' for a time bred chaos and damaged agricultural production. Hence despite heavier taxation government revenues declined and the salaries of the bureaucracy and the army were not only repeatedly reduced, but constantly in arrears.

Critical of these radical socio-economic reforms which disregarded its theory concerning the gradual advance of developing countries towards socialism, Russia was unwilling to expand its aid to the PRSY.[22] The symbolic Chinese aid was mainly meant for the Dhofari rebellion and a £16·5 million development loan granted by China, following President Ruba'i's visit there in August 1970, took long to materialise and further antagonised the Russians. Relations with the Arab countries deteriorated following the rise of the radical regime, which was considered communist and atheist.[23] Saudi Arabia, now seriously worried about the radicalisation of Aden's régime and policy, began to take steps to overthrow the NLF's government in Aden. Tension between the two Yemens grew steadily after Isma'il's group, which became influential in the south with the help of radical political refugees from the north, began to subvert the YAR's government, which was steadily moving towards moderation and better relations with Saudi Arabia. Moreover, constantly reinforced, the elements inimical to the NLF who found refuge in YAR stepped up their guerrilla warfare against the PSRY, causing the latter further financial and political difficulties.

Badly in need of economic and political assistance, but unwilling to compromise over its ideology, the NLF leadership tried to manipulate the Arab–Israeli conflict in order to win over the 'progressive' Arab countries. Dedicated to the Palestinian cause in any case, South Yemen repeatedly argued the advisability of a new Arab strategy against Israel in the southern parts of the Red Sea, a strategy it was willing to spearhead. To gain the support of Arab public opinion for its plans, Aden issued innumerable reports of Israeli bases near Bab al-Mandeb, part of a 'diabolic' imperialist plan against the Arab countries.[24] During this period Haytham travelled extensively between Arab capitals trying to gain the sympathy of his hosts for the NLF's régime and to get financial aid. He even negotiated with nationalist South Yemeni exiled leaders the possibility of their participation in his government. At home, Anis Hassan Yahya, a Ba'thist, and later Abdallah Badhib, leader of a small pro-Moscow communist party previously made legal, joined his cabinet.[25] Consequently, relations with several Arab countries, notably UAR, Algeria, Syria and Iraq, were somewhat improved and Libya even granted the PRSY £6.5 million in order to help solve its immediate budgetary crisis. But, from ideological, military and economic points of view and partly because of the still-lukewarm attitude of most Arab countries to its régime, it was more important for the NLF radicals to win the support of the Soviet Union.

Despite the closure of the Suez Canal Russia was trying to acquire new military facilities in the countries of the Red Sea and the Gulf of Aden, in addition to those it already had in Yemen.[26] The proximity of the area to the oil-rich

Arabian/Persian Gulf as well as East–West rivalry were no doubt major considerations. But so too was the development of the American Polaris A-3 missile, ideally deployed from the north western corner of the Indian Ocean.[27] In 1968 the Soviet Union began to maintain a permanent, though modest, naval presence in the Gulf of Aden and shortly afterwards began to take advantage of South Yemen's naval and other facilities. Nevertheless, until 1970 Soviet military and economic aid to the PRSY remained quite limited and, it seems, was given reluctantly. Afterwards the Soviet Union, although still dissatisfied with the NLF's policy, began to increase its commitments in South Yemen.

China's expanding presence and influence in South Yemen, part of its efforts to undermine the Soviet position in the Middle East and Africa, could not be ignored for long by the Russians. But the NLF did not benefit only from Sino–Soviet rivalry. The pressure, although ineffective, on the PRSY's border and exaggerated reports about 'Saudi–CIA–British plots' against the PRSY (originating in Aden), also helped change Russia's attitude. Moreover, with the YAR gradually moving towards the West and the British withdrawal from the Persian Gulf approaching, the NLF régime was turning out to be an asset rather than a liability for Russia. In fact, after the erosion of its position in the Sudan following the abortive communist coup in July 1971, the Soviet Union could no longer ignore the ideological orientation of developing countries it supported. As its interests in any case gradually shifted from Egypt to Iraq and the Gulf, Russia was bound to be even more concerned about the security of the Marxist régime in Aden. Once committed to support the NLF government, Russia endeavoured to undermine China's presence in South Yemen and to establish its influence there. In view of its involvement and interests in the PDRY it tried to convince the NLF leadership of the advisability of moderation and of expanding the power base of their régime. It also pressed them for bases in addition to the facilities it already had.

After 1970 Soviet (and East European) assistance became even more essential for the PDRY as an outcome of constantly growing external pressures and of its economic plight. Indeed, Russia's presence and aid was also emerging as a major factor in the factional struggle within the NLF. It was no coincidence that Moscow's friends in the NLF were led by the party's secretary-general and ideologist 'Abdul Fattah Isma'il, the North Yemeni chief of security Muhsin Sharjabi, and the army commander, Ali Antar. Accepting the Soviet Union's leadership of the socialist camp and appreciative of its military, financial and technical capabilities, they considered the entrenchment of its interest in South Yemen a safeguard for the NLF régime and a lever to implement their policy. The NLF's ultras, although they welcomed Russia's assistance, were critical of its pragmatic and opportunistic policy. Suspicious of its growing influence in the army and security services they refused to comply with the Soviet Union's requests and supported Ruba'i's policy of fostering relations with the PRC. This conflict between the NLF's pro-Russian and pro-Chinese factions reached its climax in 1972. More immediate, however, was the struggle within the party over the attempt to build a constitutional framework for the régime, expand its foundations and strengthen its control over the different parts of the country.

In 1970 all authority in South Yemen still emanated from the NLF's General Command, which carefully guarded the party's monopoly of power. Through its Executive Committee and Presidential Council it ruled the country by decree and supervised the government's policy. The outcome of the new circumstances in 1970, a constitution drawn up by East German experts, provided for a certain democratisation of the country's power structure and the expansion of the base upon which the régime rested beyond the few thousand NLF members. A new 'mass' political movement to be comprised of all progressive elements in the country was to elect provincial councils and the 'People's Supreme Council'. A parliament of 101 members, the People's Supreme Council, was to take over the functions of the NLF's General Command and especially of legislation. Thus it was hoped to mobilise more popular support for the régime and to accelerate national unity. Significantly, the country's name was changed from the People's Republic of Southern Yemen (PRSY) to the People's Democratic Republic of Yemen (PDRY).

Although proclaimed at the end of 1970, the implementation of the constitution was constantly delayed because it met with opposition from two directions. NLF extremists feared that it would enable moderates to gain power and that pragmatism once again would replace ideology. On the other hand, tribal elements in the party and other power factors in the provinces were apprehensive that the constitution and the new 'mass' movement, in addition to other reforms, might gradually erode their power. A people's Supreme Council was appointed, nevertheless, in March 1971 and met for the first time two months later. But the new parliament became to a very large extent a guise for the old General Command, and the NLF's Executive Council remained the source of all power in the PDRY. Even when implemented in the following year the new constitution remained a dead letter, only causing an intensification of the bitter struggle for power within the NLF.

Forced upon the militants by circumstances, Haytham's policy was only temporarily tolerated. In the beginning of 1971 he purged his government of its more radical members and, in view of the catastrophic financial situation of his country, expressed willingness to accept aid from non-communist sources.[28] Added to his reluctance to implement some of the Zanjibar resolutions and the matter of a constitution, Haytham's pragmatic policy drove his opponents to form a united front despite their differences. In July 1971, probably with Moscow's blessing,[29] the NLF General Command Executive Council and the cabinet were reshuffled and Haytham and his supporters were left out of both. Ali Nasir Muhammad, Haytham's Dathina Minister of Defence, became prime minister and power rested thereafter solely in the hands of Isma'il, the party's secretary general, and President Ruba'i. The latter immediately accelerated the pace of socio-economic reforms and the process of politicising the armed forces. Greater progress was achieved in collectivisation and the development of the people's militia. By 1973 all private enterprise of consequence in Aden and other urban centres was nationalised.[30] Abdul Fattah in the meantime reorganised and gradually expanded the NLF, reinforcing it by developing various militant Marxist organisations. Instead of collaborating with other progressive elements as prescribed by the new constitution he suppressed them. Those who argued the need to improve relations with the West in view of the communist countries' inability to solve the PDRY's grave economic problems were persecuted. Despite the intention to bring about some democratisation within the structure of the régime the NLF policy was now geared to achieve greater centralisation in every field and to strengthen its control over the provinces by reorganising the administration and the party branches. Most ruthless methods were used by the highly efficient security services to overcome opposition to the party's new policy, and revolutionary courts established in the different provinces severely punished those who erred.[31]

Greatly strengthened during 1972 the NLF seemed to be in complete control of the internal situation in the PDRY. Disregarding the ring of enemies surrounding the country, the only serious threat to Aden's régime emanated from the struggle for power within the ruling party. It is generally accepted[32] that the NLF's radicals were divided ideologically into two main camps. The first (Maoist in its orientation and pro-Chinese) was led by President Ruba'i. The second, (conservative Marxist and pro-Russian) was led by Abdul Fattah Isma'il. In fact, although seemingly motivated by ideology the connections of the two leaders with China and Russia respectively were to a large extent a matter of tactics and the outcome of personal rivalry enhanced by difference in origin, background and outlook. Both men believed in the PDRY's brand of 'scientific socialism' and even Isma'il never wished the PDRY to become a Russian client. Disregarding Moscow's displeasure he pressed for the implementation of the Zanjibar socio-economic reforms and undermined the position of 'Abdallah Badhib, the leader of the pro-Soviet communist party. Salim Ruba'i 'Ali, on the other hand, rejected China's doctrine concerning possible co-operation with the petit bourgeoisie, and is critical of the PRC's policy of respectability and betrayal of 'World Revolution'.[33]

Although after Haytham's disgrace it was assumed that the radical wing had overcome tribalistic elements within the NLF, tribal allegiances are still exceedingly important in the PDRY.[34] In a climate of endless personal rivalries, tribal support, especially if accompanied by influence in the army, is crucial. Manoeuvring within such a framework, Isma'il, was at a disadvantage because of his northern origin. During the NLF's fifth congress in March 1972 it appeared that he was losing ground to President Ruba'i when the latter was appointed the party's deputy secretary-general. In the second part of 1972 it was already evident that Ruba'i had emerged victorious from the struggle with Abdul Fattah Isma'il. Always pragmatic in its relations with its overseas allies, Moscow quickly made overtures to the victor. The latter was not unwilling to take advantage of this turn of events and by the end of the year was warmly received in Moscow.[35]

The coalition of progressive intellectuals, poor farmers, workers and soldiers envisaged by the Zanjibar congress to serve as the government's source of power never materialised. The PDRY's totalitarian régime is monopolised by the progressive intellectuals, or more exactly by the NLF old guard. In a society such as that of South Yemen with a ruling party as militant and rigidly dogmatic as the NLF, a constant struggle for power within the government is inevitable. The predominant position of the régime is nevertheless completely secure and time only further helps its entrenchment. Yet, without special circumstances and the communist countries' support in different fields' it is doubtful if the NLF radical régime could have carried out its revolutionary reforms and survived to this day.

Communist Aid and NLF Achievements

A South Yemeni identity did not emerge before independence despite the period of British rule and the British-sponsored federation. After 1967, the combination of fragmentation, backwardness and poverty typical of the area's society, together with NLF extremism, was not conducive to integration and stability. Matters were further complicated by the ruggedness of the country and the near absence of a road network. In normal circumstances the PDRY might have disintegrated, or as happened in some other developing nations degenerated into a state of permanent chaos with one government rapidly following another. Ironically, the constant pressure of the NLF's enemies on the PDRY has helped the régime to survive and to keep the country together. Yet it was, and still is, mainly the communist assistance which has enabled the Aden government, despite its unrealistic dogmatism, to overcome the centrifugal forces in the country and its many enemies, and gradually to assert its authority over the whole territory. Similarly, the development of most government services and the economy and the régime's experimentation in creating a revolutionary socialist society have to a large extent been made possible by continuous, although not over-generous, aid of the communist bloc.

Organised with East German financial support and by East German experts, the PDRY's security services are known for their efficiency, power and ruthlessness. Commanded by Muhsin Sharjabi, they are nominally under Muhammad Salih Mut'i,[36] Minister of the Interior, but in fact the infamous 'Muhsin' is directly responsible to the NLF's Executive Committee. With headquarters in Aden and branches in every important urban centre, the security services have successfully suppressed every plot, real or imaginary, against the régime and are considered an important safeguard of the NLF's hegemony. Partly responsible for the present internal stability of the country, this fear-inspiring organisation has enabled the NLF to carry out its reforms and nationalisation policy with hardly any opposition. But although most effective in the towns and occasionally employed against NLF's enemies across the border, the security services are unable, and were never meant, to defend the nation against external threat and to establish the government's authority among the tribes. The army, more powerful and loyal since 1969,[37] is far better suited for this purpose, but its deployment was initially greatly hampered by the near absence of a communications infrastructure in the PDRY and the inaccessibility of most of the countryside.

The cost of developing a communications infrastructure is so prohibitive that although essential for economic progress its construction would have been delayed were it not for its military-political importance. A substantial part of the PDRY's budget is annually allocated to 'communications', but considering the size of the budget the funds available from this source are ridiculously small.[38] Influenced by the increasing threat to the NLF's régime since 1970 and its inability to establish its authority in some vital and remote border regions, the communist countries granted the PDRY substantial assistance for this purpose.[39] Hence a road network is emerging, a telephone, telegraph and radio system has been developed and airfields in different parts of the country now exist. Even more impressive, however, is the aid rendered by the Soviet Union and its East European allies for building up the PDRY's armed forces.

As an outcome of several military assistance agreements signed by Russia and Aden's government between 1970 and 1973, substantial quantities of relatively modern arms were given or sold on long-term credit to the PDRY.[40] While South Yemeni officers, technicians and pilots were trained in Soviet academies, Russian experts built military installations in the PDRY and trained its army. By 1973 this army had expanded from 11 to 21 battalions organised in brigade groups and with its small but efficient air force,[41] it was alleged to be the best in the Arabian Peninsula. Its soldiers, 'sons of farmers and workers' (the NLF's officials claimed) were drawn from many tribes. Officer material was carefully selected from among educated party cadres. Special attention was paid to the political education of the soldiers, and for this purpose a new department was created in the Ministry of Defence and political officers responsible for indoctrination were appointed to every unit.[42]

Even purged of disloyal elements and with its British-trained officers replaced by Russian-trained NLF members, the PDRY army is still far from being detribalised. Notwithstanding the appointment of political officers, ideology has not replaced traditional allegiances[43] and 'bourgeois' panarabist nationalism is still widespread under the surface in the army (as it is among the masses). Obviously, the army cannot be separated from general socio-political developments in the country. Thus despite official claims to the contrary, most soldiers and officers still belong to the tribes which traditionally monopolised the armed forces (especially the Dathina). Even though described in 1969[44] as one of the leading NLF 'tribalists', Ali Antar, the army's CIC and deputy Minister of Defence, survived all purges and government reshuffles. He did not lose ground and his power and that of his Dathina and Fadhili associates was consolidated by the growth of the army's strength. Alleged Soviet influence in the army served only to enhance the suspicion of Ruba'i's radicals of professional soldiers and this faction's determination to build up the power of the people's militia.

The development of para-military organisations subordinated to the party was advocated by the NLF's ideologists immediately after independence. Qahtan ash-Sha'abi, however, dispersed the NLF's *feda'iyyun* and ignored the Zanjibar resolutions concerning development of a people's militia. After the fall of his government steps were taken to establish the militia. Impressed by the Chinese example and wishing to counter Soviet influence, President Ruba'i entrusted its organisation to the PRC. Quantities of Chinese arms and a Chinese military delegation had already reached Aden at the beginning of 1971.[45] But the militia, although its size slowly increased, remained embryonic throughout the period of Haytham's government; after July 1971, however, its development was immediately accelerated.[46]

A representative of the army command and of 'tribalist' elements in the NLF, Ali Antar continued to resist the development of the militia even after Haytham's dismissal. Now supported by Isma'il, who opposed measures which could strengthen his rivals, Antar argued that the undisciplined tribesmen might turn the arms entrusted to them against the régime. But the existing state of the militia was unacceptable to Ruba'i's faction. These militants considered the militia necessary for establishing the NLF's authority in the provinces and for implementing its programme in the countryside. With external pressures still increasing and military expenditure already consuming nearly half the country's budget, expansion of the militia, they reasoned, would be far cheaper than that of the army. Following the NLF's fifth congress in 1972 and the consolidation of Ruba'i's dominant position in the General Command it was inevitable that the militia's power would grow in the future.[47] Yet even the most militant NLF leaders intend it to supplement rather than supplant the army.

Financed by the PRC, militia training centres were established during 1971 in different parts of the PDRY with the help of Chinese experts.[48] Young men from all tribes were brought to these camps in relays for a duration of three months. The recruits, mostly illiterate or semi-literate, underwent on arrival a crash programme in reading and writing. In addition to military training they were given elementary courses in Marxism, 'political economy', leadership and organisation and new methods of farming. When they terminated their training the majority of the new militiamen were sent back to their respective villages. But the most talented were kept in the camps for a period of higher-level ideological and organisational training. After graduating from the militia's 'academies' these men provided cadres for militia commands which co-ordinated the activities of the militia units on the district level. In their turn, the district commanders were subordinated to senior NLF members, appointed by the militia's headquarters to command the militia in each province.

Back in their homes, ordinary militiamen are responsible for the indoctrination and education of the population and the administration, development and defence of their villages. They organise village councils and co-operatives and attempt to create peasant communes, although their success in the last is admittedly limited. Finally, through the militia chain of command, they serve as a link between the village community, the party and the government. If in fact functioning on these lines, the militia organisation should prove an invaluable asset for economic development, national integration and the consolidation and protection of the régime's authority.[49]

Despite the much-publicised successes of the people's militia in border clashes as well as in other fields, it is too early to evaluate its true contribution. Evidently, illiterate and semi-literate tribesmen are not the most suitable vehicle for the diffusion of Marxist–Leninist doctrine or modernisation and revolutionary socio-economic reform. Aspects of collectivisation may benefit the PDRY's rural population—some were practised anyway by the tribal society. But the principle as a whole (especially the Chinese-type peasant communes so cherished by NLF radicals) is incompatible both with the individualism and backwardness of the population and the physical characteristics of the land. What may be successful in rich but limited areas such as the Abyan delta, or among fishing communities, is not necessarily applicable to the dry majority of the country with its poor soil and broken terrain. It is also still questionable whether the militia's loyalty to the régime is absolute (as claimed by NLF officials) or whether (as in the past) it is conditional on tribal representation in the party and government. The militia's superficial indoctrination can hardly be expected to succeed in overcoming tribal and other loyalties. Evidently members of provincial supreme councils and the People's Supreme Council, 'elected' by the party's branches and the militia cadres, still reflect the traditional power structure and the socio-political *status quo* in most rural areas. Yet the régime can now rely on the support of many thousands of militiamen in addition to the NLF old guard. Even if conditional, this support is to some extent enhanced by external pressures and by the fact that the somewhat privileged militiamen have a vested interest in the continued existence of the NLF government. Above all, time and education are undoubtedly working in favour of the NLF's interesting experiment.

As a tool to combat illiteracy and promote political indoctrination, even the militia's limited contribution to education is not to be looked down upon. Despite an illiteracy rate of about 90% the NLF government is unable to allocate more than 9% of its tiny budget to education.[50] In real terms the sum involved is ludicrously small and the Ministry of Education is forced to decide on priorities and rely on foreign aid. As future development of the national economy is expected to take place mainly in the agricultural and fishing sectors,[51] higher education is regarded by the régime not only as a luxury it is unable to afford but, if uncontrolled, as potentially dangerous. The country's need of university graduates in specific fields is amply supplied through the many scholarships offered to South Yemen by the socialist governments.[52] This does not mean that higher education is neglected altogether; technical institutions, teacher-training colleges, military and police 'academies', and secondary schools have been opened in different parts of the country. Still, most of the education budget as well as the communist assistance is channelled into the development of elementary, intermediate and vocational schools.

Completely secular, the state education system in the PDRY is generally geared to produce a new generation of South Yemenis loyal to the party and its ideology and better able to contribute to the socialist development of their country. *Inter alia* it exposes the students to Marxist doctrine and provides them military training. Still there are signs that the PDRY's experimentation in education, especially its strong anti-religious aspects, is meeting some resistance.[53] Moreover, surrounded by relatively affluent Arab countries which, although 'reactionary', are quickly developing their own higher education systems and exciting employment opportunities for school leavers and university graduates, the PDRY is bound to come under pressure from its quasi-intellectuals. Emigration temporarily served, to some extent, as a safety valve against such a danger. Economic development, one of the régime's most cherished goals, will it is hoped in the long run solve this problem as well as many others.

To the present day, no minerals of economic value have been found in the PDRY, although it is claimed that there is oil in the eastern provinces.[54] Despite its decline Aden's much-criticised service economy is still contributing most of the PDRY's revenue. Indiscriminate nationalisation in the last several years and heavier taxation have resulted in a further decline of the local economy and increased unemployment. Many of the town's entrepreneurs and skilled labourers escaped to the YAR[55] and the town's population has declined by about 30–40%. Even if the Suez Canal were reopened it is doubtful whether Aden would flourish again, as the NLF's government is determined to reorient the country's economy from services to production.[56] Lip service is constantly paid to the importance of industrialisation; but, realising that the PDRY does not have the necessary preconditions for this, the NLF régime has allocated in recent years only about 10% of its budget for the purpose. With communist aid the PDRY embarked on a three-year industrial development plan in 1971. This plan has a relatively limited target and cannot significantly change the present tiny contribution of the industrial sector to the country's economy.[57] Despite the fact that 80% of the population are engaged in farming and animal husbandry, the PDRY still imports food, and in view of its limited resources and options, the government has given first priority to the development of agriculture.[58]

South Yemen's largely primitive agriculture contributes less than one-fourth of the country's GNP. With modern techniques and relatively modest means the government is trying to expand the cultivable land, develop new water resources, produce better and larger crops and improve pastureland and cattle breeds. Moreover, the Arabian Sea, exceedingly rich in fish, offers nearly unlimited opportunities for the development of fishing and the fish-canning industry. Yet in its primitive state in the past it supported only a few thousand fishermen whose standard of living was among the lowest in the country. In recent years therefore about a third of the government's budget has been devoted to the development of agriculture, animal husbandry and fishing. It was hoped (with some justification) that this preferential treatment would have an immediate impact on the country's GNP, balance of trade and the standard of living of the majority of the population, and the Soviet Union concentrated its non-military aid programme mainly in these fields. Soviet experts are engaged, for instance, in a large number of projects, seemingly minor but important to the PDRY, such as the building of secondary roads and small dams, digging artesian wells and developing model farms. Special attention is devoted as well to the modernisation of South Yemen's fishing industry.[59]

The involvement of the People's Republic of China in the PDRY was at first indirect and mainly within the framework of its revolutionary anti-colonialist policy. Together with the NLF it began in 1968 to support the rebellion in Dhofar. Involving only small quantities of light arms and training of guerrillas, this type of aid was extremely cheap and seemed noticeably rewarding. Direct aid to South Yemen consisted mainly of a medical team and a number of experts in other fields. As a result of growing competition with the Soviet Union and of the radicalisation of Aden's régime, China's aid to the PDRY increased significantly after 1970. Her most costly project is the construction of strategically important roads in the outlying provinces and the Aden–Mukalla arterial road.[60] Far less expensive are several agricultural projects and her much appreciated assistance to agrarian reforms (especially in the field of collectivisation).[61] Although relatively inexpensive her involvement with the people's militia enabled the PRC to expand her influence and presence in the PDRY greatly. Several industrial development projects are also financed by

China but, like the Russians, she realises that conditions in the country are more conducive to agriculture and fisheries than to industrial development.

Carefully selected and supervised, the PRC aid programme has been most successful and welcome. The amount is said to be rapidly approaching that of Soviet aid and was valued in 1972 at about £22 million.[62] However it took a long time to materialise and came mainly in the form of labour and Chinese-made goods. Reports on the amount and character of Soviet assistance are confusing; it seems that between 1968 and 1972 South Yemen received over £25 million in aid from Russia and in 1971–72 alone about £12 million.[63] Soviet assistance is far more diversified and sophisticated than China's and includes large quantities of arms[64] either given or sold at a great discount on long-term credit. Moreover, Russia's East European allies shoulder a good part of the burden of sustaining Aden's Marxist régime and their collective assistance may equal that of the Soviet Union. In addition to economic and military aid the Soviet bloc occasionally grants the PDRY's government low-interest loans essential to the survival of the NLF régime.[65] In sum, the Russians may not be over-popular in the PDRY but, the NLF militants, aware of the Soviet Union's technical and economic superiority over the PRC, show surprising pragmatism in their relations with Russia. Ideologically justified by China's 'betrayal' of 'World Revolution', the Ruba'i faction's improved relations with the Soviet Union, were justified by an £18 million development loan granted by Russia following President Ruba'i's visit there in November 1972.[66]

Evidently the NLF attempt to impose modernisation and revolutionary socio-economic reforms on a backward society is meeting with tremendous difficulties despite 'popular enthusiasm'. NLF claims notwithstanding, some reforms have completely failed because they ignored the social realities of the country. Other reforms were unsuccessful because the PDRY lacked the economic infra-structure for their implementation. Still others have not had time to bear fruit but may prove justified in future. Nevertheless, a good part of the rural population which had been extremely poor and barely self-sufficient has benefited to some extent from development and reforms in agriculture, animal husbandry and fishing. This achievement is however off-set by the growing plight of the rest of the rural population and especially of the townspeople.[67] But for ideological, historical and political reasons the régime cares little about the latter. Unless ready to accept the situation and await better days the many South Yemenis who disagree with the NLF policy, left with no legal outlet to express their opposition, are forced to join the enemies of the régime across the border. Saudi Arabia determined to overthrow the 'communist-atheist' NLF government, and probably encouraged by allies, has exploited their frustration, thus contributing to the explosive situation in Southern Arabia.

The upheaval in the PDRY's economy and society is largely responsible for the sharp decline in the country's production and its endemic financial crisis. This of course limits the ability of the NLF régime to implement its social reforms and economic development plans. Unless oil is found in the PDRY, it will remain utterly dependent on foreign aid, mainly that of the Soviet Union. Apart from the repercussions of such a situation, the growing disparity in revenue and development between South Yemen and most other countries in the Peninsula enhances the frustration of the NLF radicals. In addition to their inflexible dogmatism and relative isolation in the Arab world, this no doubt influences their aggressive foreign policy and is a good deal responsible for the increasing tension in the Arabian Peninsula.

Revolution and Counter-Revolution

Among the most backward and poorest in Arabia, Dhofar's population of less than 100,000 is divided mainly between Arabic-speaking tribes and speakers of dialects of what may have been the ancient indigenous language.[68] Remote and virtually isolated from the world, Dhofar was annexed by Oman in the second part of the nineteenth century. But Omani authority in the Qarra mountains beyond the narrow coastal strip, if recognised at all, was nominal. The fact that in the twentieth century the Omani sultan moved his residence to Sallala, Dhofar's capital, did not noticeably change his relations with the province's population, and at most he was recognised as a supra-tribal power. This did make him however in a better position to exact taxation by force of arms and, even more effectively, to impose a blockade on the mountain-people who depended in certain seasons on supplies from the coast.[69]

Tyranical and conservative, Sultan Sa'id ibn Taymur, who ruled Oman until 1970, intentionally preserved the backwardness and isolation of Dhofar. The Ibadhi sultan hoped that by closing Dhofar (and Oman) to the world he would preserve his authority. But developments in nearby countries since the 1950s, and the oil boom in the Persian Gulf, began to have an impact even in Dhofar. At first dissatisfaction with the sultan's régime was limited to the young educated Dhofaris from well-to-do families in the coastal towns. In 1958, with the wave of panarabism sweeping the Arab countries, Dhofari labourers in the oil fields in the Gulf formed a political party opposed to the reactionary isolationist government of Sa'id ibn Taymur.[70] Yet it is doubtful whether their activities would have led to an armed struggle against the sultan, had it not been for Saudi intervention.

Never cordial after the Buraimi incident, relations between Saudi Arabia and British-controlled Oman were further aggravated by the discovery of oil in Oman in 1963 in an area claimed by the Saudis. It was not accidental, therefore, that the Dhofar Liberation Front (DLF) was formed in 1964 and that armed rebellion broke out in Dhofar after its leader, Muhsin ibn Nuffel, visited Saudi Arabia.[71] Frustrated by Sultan Sa'id's refusal to allow them to work in the newly discovered oil fields in Oman, many mountain tribesmen joined the uprising. The traditional strategy of blockading the mountains backfired and drove into the rebel ranks many more tribesmen who would otherwise have remained neutral in the struggle between the sultan and 'nationalists'. But Riyadh completely misjudged the outcome of the rebellion; the original middle-class founders of the DLF were gradually replaced by elements influenced by the Marxist ideology of the radical Palestinian organisations in the Gulf or by their NLF counterparts active in Hadramaut. Trained in China, probably during 1967, their leaders gradually infiltrated the command of the DLF, while the remnants of its middle-class founders were gradually purged.

At the end of 1968 the DLF held a congress at Hirmin.[72] A

new revolutionary Marxist programme similar to that of the
NLF was adopted and the movement dissociated itself from its
previous policy of pragmatic nationalism. Significantly, the
DLF also changed its name to the Popular Front for the
Liberation of the Occupied Arab Gulf (PFLOAG). 'The
vanguard of world revolution', PFLOAG considered the rebellion in Dhofar only a phase in the battle against reactionary
régimes in the Gulf and the Western-controlled oil companies.
An extension of the NLF (at this stage especially of its radical
elements in Hadramaut), PFLOAG formulated its programme
partly with reference to the new British 'East of Suez' policy,
and partly to Dhofar as an ideal springboard for the Gulf
principalities.

Notwithstanding Qahtan Ash-Sha'abi's pragmatism, the
NLF's dedication to world revolution was not shelved altogether. Although limited, Aden's support for the Dhofari
rebellion was crucial, especially as its eastern provinces were
used by China to supply PFLOAG with arms and train its
cadres in guerrilla warfare. Once Ash-Sha'abi's government
was overthrown, the NLF régime became far more committed
to the policy of supporting revolutionary, anti-reactionary,
anti-imperialist movements. Hence, by the beginning of 1970
seven different revolutionary organisations maintained offices
in Aden and the NLF government was actively and openly
supporting subversion, both in Arab and in non-Arab countries.

Ethiopia, a short distance from Aden, was considered by the
NLF to be a reactionary ally of Western imperialism. With a
coastline crucial to the PDRY-supported 'new Arab strategy
against Israel' and her complicated minority problems, she
became one of the main targets of PDRY subversion. During
1970 and 1971 the PDRY systematically helped build up the
power of the Eritrean Liberation Front (ELF) and, as with
the DLF, attempted to gain control of it. The PDRY also
encouraged and supported the activities of two anti-Ethiopian
Somali 'liberation fronts' but, due to circumstances, with far
less success. Within the Arab camp it opposed any attempt to
reach an understanding with Israel on the basis of Security
Council Resolution 242 and vociferously supported the radical
Palestinian guerrilla organisations.[73] Considered the arch-
reactionary in the Arab world, Saudi Arabia was constantly

attacked by PDRY propaganda and every attempt, real or imaginary, to overthrow her régime was supported by the NLF. Despite the cherished principle of uniting the two Yemens, or because of it, the Aden régime did not hesitate to subvert the YAR government. For this purpose Abdul Fattah Isma'il and his North Yemeni group in the NLF constantly exploited Marxist and other Shafi'i refugees from the north. Yet the PDRY government devoted most of its efforts after 1969 to supporting the Dhofari rebellion and subversion in the Gulf.

By the second half of 1970 PFLOAG virtually controlled Dhofar, with the exception of a few coastal towns. Ultra-conservative and increasingly senile, Sultan Sa'id ibn Taymur was utterly unable, and to some extent unwilling, to cope with the new situation. It looked therefore as if the NLF's revolutionary policy was about to win its first major victory. In itself unimportant, the fall of Dhofar the West realised—could spark off a chain reaction leading to the collapse of the weak conservative governments of the Gulf which controlled immense oil wealth. In fact signs of such a development appeared in several parts of the Gulf and in June 1970 the National Democratic Front for the Liberation of Oman and the Arab Gulf (NDFLOAG) began to operate in Jabal Akhdar in Oman's hinterland.[74] Greatly alarmed, the British quickly suppressed this uprising and in July 1970 engineered a palace coup, which replaced Sultan Sa'id with his Sandhurst-educated son, Qabus.

After coming to power Qabus, with the help of British advisers, began to use Oman's relatively modest oil revenues[75] to modernise his country. But even more attention and funds were devoted to the reorganisation and modernisation of the Sultan's Armed Forces (SAF) and to building up its small air force and navy. By the end of 1970 the SAF, commanded by British officers, launched a limited offensive against the rebels. Aimed at lifting the siege from the few Dhofari coastal towns still in the sultan's control and establishing footholds in the Qarra mountains. This expedition convinced the British that the Marxist rebels were stronger than originally expected. Moreover, it was realised that any attempt to overcome the rebels would require Saudi co-operation and support.

Until June 1969 the NLF's Marxist polemics were not taken too seriously by Riyadh. Although the defunct sultans and members of SAL who had found refuge in Saudi Arabia were allowed to operate from its territories against the PRSY's régime, they enjoyed little or no Saudi assistance. King Faisal also seemed indifferent to the fact that the NLF had gained control over the previously Saudi-oriented DLF. Bitter about British treatment of Saudi Arabia in the 1950s, he watched the developments in Dhofar with a certain glee and possibly hoped for an opportunity to press forward his country's territorial claims on Oman. But after June 1969 Saudi Arabia was seriously concerned about the NLF's determination to export its ideology to the whole Peninsula, and the increased Russian and Chinese presence in South Yemen; she thus dedicated herself to the overthrow of the 'Marxist-atheist' régime in Aden. In view of the PDRY's internal instability and grave economic difficulties, Riyadh was convinced that the NLF régime would collapse if South Yemeni refugees were supplied with the means to fight it. Based on this assumption, Saudi Arabia's policy thereafter was to encourage all the conservative elements inimical to the NLF to unite and harass its régime.[76]

Socially quite heterogeneous and politically disunited, the South Yemeni refugee community in Saudi Arabia and the YAR grew steadily after 1967.[77] Originally composed of ex-rulers, members of SAL and remnants of FLOSY, it was supplemented by officers and soldiers of the ex-federal army, tribesmen who opposed the régime, supporters of Qahtan ash-Sha'abi and a sizeable part of Aden's middle class and proletariat. The YAR, especially its Shafi'i southern part, was preferred by the 'progressive' elements, who used it as a base of operations against the PDRY's second province. From 1970 the most active of the 'progressives' was Colonel Hussein Othman Ashal, who as the PDRY's army CIC had been instrumental in the victory of the NLF's radicals. Ironically Ashal and many other officers were afterwards considered untrustworthy and cashiered from the army. Together with soldiers and tribesmen who followed them they crossed to the YAR and joined FLOSY and ash-Sha'abi's supporters, whom they had previously helped persecute. Saudi Arabia distrusted

South Yemen 'progressives', and at first supported only conservative elements, such as the force commanded by Sayyid
Abdul Rahman al-Jailani, called the Army of National
Salvation (ANS). Its aim was the independence of Hadramaut
and Mahra, the PDRY's fifth and sixth provinces respectively.[78]
Another force supported by the Saudis was commanded by
Colonel Nasir Buraiq Aulaqi, the South Arabian federal army
ex-CIC and composed mainly of Aulaqis, Audhalis and the
followers of various sultans; it operated against the fourth
province. Further to the west the Saudis gave assistance to
Baihan's ex-sultan, Hussein al-Habili, who since 1968 has
constantly fought the NLF's authorities in the third province.
Aware of the ineffectiveness of sporadic raids by the different
anti-NLF groups, Saudi Arabia unsuccessfully tried to co-
ordinate their efforts in 1970.[79] In most cases, jealousy and
rivalry between the refugee factions proved stronger than their
hatred of the NLF régime. Consequently, Riyadh's efforts led
finally to the creation of a loose framework called the Army
of National Unity (ANU) which, with the notable exception of the ANS, theoretically co-ordinated the activities of
most elements—mainly conservative—fighting the NLF régime.[80]

By early 1971 Saudi Arabia had begun to sense that far more
than the raids of South Yemeni refugees was required to
overthrow Aden's government. Washington, becoming more
concerned about the future of the Gulf, advised King Faisal to
co-operate with his neighbours to isolate the PDRY and curb
its revolutionary activities. Hence when Sultan Qabus visited
Riyadh he was received with open arms. With nearly 60% of
his limited oil revenues absorbed by the Dhofari rebellion, and
dissatisfaction and disappointment growing in Oman, Qabus
was badly in need of Saudi support, political, financial and
military. At his meeting with Faisal Qabus agreed to the Saudi-
proposed settlement of the border problem and undertook to
support Faisal's policy in the Peninsula and the Gulf, and since
1971 Saudi Arabia has helped Oman financially as well as
militarily.[81] The YAR remained the only loophole in the
Saudi-planned *cordon sanitaire* around the PDRY, and its
involvement was essential to the success of any plan against the
NLF régime because of its geographical position.

The most populous country in the Arabian Peninsula,[82] the YAR is also among the poorest and most problem-ridden. The revolution of 1962 swept away Yemen's medieval régime and many of its antiquated socio-political institutions. For a time it broke the monopoly of power of the Zeidi tribal confederations and gave a fair share in the government of the country to the somewhat advanced Shafi'i population. With massive aid from Egypt, as well as communist and non-communist countries, a relatively modern government and administration began to emerge. Steps were taken to achieve greater social cohesion and national integration, to modernise the economy and to lay the foundations for a badly needed communications infra-structure. But even before the Egyptians left the country at the end of 1967, the larger part of the republican camp was reconciled to the fact that it was impossible to overcome overnight the backwardness and conservatism of the population and the strong centrifugal forces. In order to preserve as many of the achievements of the revolution as possible and keep the country together it was ready to compromise many of its ideals. Thus, once General Sallal was out of the way the YAR's policy became extremely pragmatic. Close relations were maintained with the 'progressive' Arab countries; the Soviet Union continued to train and supply the army and together with the PRC carried out development projects in different fields. At the same time the need for financial aid, to terminate the civil war and to curb the power of the tribes drove the 'third force' republican leaders to seek aid from the West and peaceful co-existence with Saudi Arabia.

Relations between the YAR and Saudi Arabia were somewhat improved after the power of a Marxist wing of the republican movement was crushed in 1968 by General Hassan al-'Amri.[83] Although adamantly opposed to the re-establishment of the imam's dynasty, the republican leaders were willing to allow the imam's supporters to participate actively in the government. A settlement between the two rival camps was facilitated by the Saudi decision to phase out her support of the imam's dynasty and the royalists. A milestone in Saudi–YAR relations, the Jedda Islamic conference of 1970 provided both sides with the opportunity to iron out their remaining differences. No longer worried about communist influence in the

YAR, Saudi Arabia thereafter was willing to help her neighbour overcome economic difficulties. She realised that such a
policy was bound to strengthen the hand of the YAR's conservatives and limit the country's dependence on Russia and Chain.

Unwilling to put a strain on its relations with the powerful
tribes, the republican government did not enforce its policy of
greater centralisation and national integration. Tribal leaders
were given key positions in the government, parliament,
administration and army, in order to gain their confidence and
win their support. By gradually developing the country's road-
network and extending government services to tribal areas it
was hoped to bring them to accept the authority of the central
government and surrender the vast quantities of arms accumula-
ted during the long war. Any Saudi attempt to involve the
YAR tribes in a conflict with the PDRY would have eroded
the central government's authority and set back its policy of
national integration. Although tempted, Riyadh refrained so
as not to harm rapprochement with the Yemen Republic.

Her increasing economic crisis and internal difficulties in
1971 made the YAR more vulnerable to Saudi pressures.
Indeed many North Yemenis, hostile to the PDRY because of
either kinship ties with South Yemeni refugees or political
motives, were critical of their government's passive policy
toward its southern neighbour. As a result the YAR's government subsequently closed its eyes to the activities of Saudi agents
in its southern provinces and to the mini-war carried on
against the PDRY from the area. Abdallah al-Asnaj, FLOSY's
leader was requested in September 1971 to join General Al-
Amri's short-lived cabinet and remained in the government
even when Muhsin al-Ayni, the veteran Ba'thist republican,
became premier. Devoted to the principles of socialism, progress
and national unity Al-'Ayni was unable to curb the growing
power of the conservative elements, Zaidi tribes and Saudi
influence. He resigned himself to watching the dissipation of
much of the progress achieved up to and shortly after 1968 and
the rapid deterioration of relations with the PDRY.[84]

During 1971 it was becoming increasingly evident that the
NLF revolutionary policy was losing momentum and slowly
grinding to a halt. Across the Red Sea Ethiopia curbed, at
least for a time, the activities of the ELF, while the Somali

'liberation fronts' became impotent. Despite Iraqi co-operation, the PDRY's subversion in the Gulf principalities turned out to be largely ineffective and they achieved independence in the last months of 1971 without serious incident. In Dhofar the SAF, reinforced by British élite units and allegedly supported by the RAF, gradually succeeded in establishing itself in the Qarra mountains. In the meantime the Soviet Union had become involved in the Dhofari rebellion[85] as a result of her rivalry with China, her aspirations in the Gulf and her growing commitment in the PDRY. At the end of 1971 she was probably partly instrumental in the merger between PFLOAG and NDPFLOAG.[86] As the erosion of PFLOAG's power was inevitable, this merger really indicated that the Saudi–Omani–Western counter-action was proving successful; by the beginning of 1972 Qabus's 'authority' was re-established by the SAF in most of Dhofar's central and eastern districts.

The pressure on the PDRY during 1971 caused the Soviet Union to increase its aid and verbal support to South Yemen considerably,[87] but she was cautious about committing herself to defend such an irresponsible and unpredictable ally. Threatened by 'Western imperialism and Saudi reaction', uncertain of Russian assistance and isolated in the Arab camp,[88] the PDRY tried again to mobilise Arab public opinion and break the Saudi encirclement. In the last months of 1971, while its news media repeatedly attacked the American–Israeli–Saudi–Irani 'plots' in the Red Sea and the Gulf,[89] South Yemen's armed forces overwhelmed guerrilla strongholds along its northern border. Simultaneously, to prevent or deter the YAR from joining the Saudi camp, subversive and terrorist activities against her were stepped up.[90] By adopting this policy, for which Abdul Fattah Isma'il was largely responsible, the PDRY in fact played right into Saudi hands.

In March 1972 Sheikh Naji al-Ghadir, an ex-royalist leader of the Khawlan tribe,[91] and his retinue were assassinated by the PDRY's authorities whose guests they were. Shocked by this treacherous act the powerful Zaidi, Bakil and Hashid confederations as well as the YAR's Shafi'i tribes (the main victims of the PDRY raids), determined to act against the NLF government. Alarmed by this alliance between the tribal interests of Saudi Arabia and the YAR, Muhsin al-'Ayni accepted the mediation of Algeria's president. With the support of most of the army commanders, who feared the revival of tribal strength and were aware that the YAR army was inferior to that of the PDRY, in April he reached an understanding of sorts with the NLF government; by this time, however matters were completely out of his hands.

Despite her success in curbing the PDRY's revolutionary activities, Saudi Arabia began in 1972 to doubt the effectiveness of her tactics against the NLF régime. Moreover, in the light of the growing Russian interest in the Gulf and the Soviet–Iraqi treaty of April 1972 it became even more imperative for King Faisal and his allies to overthrow the NLF régime or at least to render it powerless. He therefore determined to exploit the assassination of Sheikh Naji in order to precipitate a crisis in southwestern Arabia and to create, if possible, a direct confrontation between the two Yemens. Reinforcements for the tribal 'white army' were sent to the Saudi–PDRY–YAR border and construction of military installations there was accelerated. Not by accident, the SAF chose this time to press on its attack in Dhofar to the very gates of the PDRY and its air force bombed the PFLOAG's training centres across the border.[92]

Pursued more vigorously in 1972, negotiations between the anti-NLF refugee factions, although inconclusive, led to the establishment in the YAR in July of the 'United National Front of South Yemen'. Directed by Abdul Qawi al-Makawi, the political bureau of this organisation—meant to facilitate the formation of a provisional government-in-exile—controlled the 'Popular Liberation Army', commanded by Colonel Ashal.[93] The conservatives based in Saudi Arabia formed their own 'League of the Sons of the South' which controlled the ANU, commanded by Colonel Awlaqi. But the two organisations, as well as the NSA, intensified their attacks all along the PDRY's border with the YAR and Saudi Arabia. Meeting in Taʿiz at the end of July, the YAR's most prominent tribal leaders decided to join the campaign against the NLF government.[94] Large quantities of arms and substantial sums of money were subsequently sent from Saudi Arabia to the YAR and presumably distributed among the tribes. Supported now by Iran in addition to Saudi Arabia, the Omani sultan began to reinforce his SAF units along the PDRY's border.[95]

Following the PDRY's 'pacification' policy which had led to the invasion of North Yemen's territory, the YAR's army joined the tribal forces and in October a full-scale war broke out between the two Yemens. Alarmed by the possible repercussions, some Arab countries, notably Libya, offered to mediate between the PDRY and the YAR. Previously, NLF attempts to gain Arab sympathy and support generally had met with a lukewarm reception.[96] The exception, Libya, was emotionally and financially involved in the PDRY's anti-Israeli Red Sea strategy and anti-Irani policy in the Gulf, and even willing to overlook the NLF ideology.[97] The Soviet Union, finding herself in the unenviable position of having both interests and military experts in each of the Yemens, also used her influence to convince the PDRY and the YAR to reach an understanding.[98] With the support of powerful elements in North and South Yemen (which originally opposed the conflict and feared its outcome), the persuasion of the Arab countries brought about a cease-fire agreement at the end of October. Dramatically, a month later, under Libyan pressure the presidents of YAR and the PDRY signed an agreement for the unification of their countries. Although unrealistic, since it disregarded the basic factors which had given rise to the crisis, this agreement temporarily defused the tension between the two Yemens. For a time at least the YAR abandoned its policy of *laissez faire* concerning South Yemeni refugees while the PDRY lessened subversive and terrorist activities in the north.[99]

The deterioration in relations between the two Yemens was to some extent the outcome of the activity of Abdul Fattah Isma'il's North Yemeni group in the NLF. Bitter at the 'betrayal' of the Republic's ideals and possibly at the revival of Zeidi hegemony, they were determined to overthrow the YAR's pragmatic régime and create a united and progressive Yemen. Although they paid lip-service to the principle of uniting historical Yemen, President Ruba'i's supporters were in fact indifferent, if not hostile, to the plan. Partly motivated by the factional struggle in the NLF, they were also apprehensive that the more populous and pragmatic (if not reactionary) YAR would submerge the PDRY, annul its socio-economic achievements and reverse its revolutionary ideology.[100] Ironically, it was Ruba'i's policy rather than Isma'il's which

coincided with the Soviet Union's interests. She feared that
Isma'il's aggressiveness towards the YAR would only serve the
interests of Russia's enemies by creating a dangerous confrontation in this sensitive region. Generally opposed to traditional
panarabism, the Soviet Union was also unsympathetic in
principle to the unification of Yemen, which could lead to the
erosion of her influence and the loss of facilities she had in the
PDRY.[101]

Apprehensive that unity with the PDRY would strengthen
the Shafi'i element and that the central government might
revive the power of the Marxists crushed in 1968, the YAR
Zeidi confederations and other tribal elements were strongly
critical of the unification agreement. Supported by Saudi
Arabia their pressure led to the resignation of Premier Muḥsin
Al-Ayni, considered the main architect of the unification
agreement.[102] To appease the tribes and Saudi Arabia, the
YAR's President, Qadi Iryani (himself instrumental in
persuading his parliament to agree to unification) appointed a
relatively unknown conservative politician to replace Al-Ayni.
Despite occasional mentions of the intention to unite the two
countries, no one today takes the agreement seriously.[103] The
new prime minister is further fostering relations with Saudi
Arabia and the YAR treasury has become completely dependent on its rich conservative neighbour.[104]

Even if Saudi Arabia intended to intervene at a suitable
moment in the conflict between the two Yemens, she was
taken aback by the strong reaction of Arab public opinion to
the 'reactionary conspiracy against the PDRY's progressive
régime'. Moreover, far from evoking a popular uprising,
the invasion of the PDRY by different guerrilla forces and the
foreign threat to its territory mobilised (with the help of the
strong security services) the support of South Yemen's population behind their government. As early as the middle of October
1972 it was clear that a stalemate had been reached and that
the NLF régime could not be overthrown without direct Saudi
intervention. Riyadh, however, was both unwilling and unprepared to take such a step. While fully convinced now of the
ineffectiveness of its previous policy, the Saudi government and
its allies cannot remain indifferent to the revolutionary policy
of Aden's government. They realise that because of the common

border between the PDRY and Dhofar it is almost impossible to suppress PFLOAG altogether and stop its and the NLF's revolutionary activities in the Gulf. At present Saudi Arabia, now joined by Iran and other conservative régimes in the Gulf, is biding her time and continues to support Sultan Qabus and similar forces inimical to the NLF.[105] Yet if all the funds dedicated to the overthrow of the NLF government were to be diverted to the development of the YAR the latter, with its far larger and more advanced population, could in the long run submerge its problematic sister state. Such a policy however would take long to materialise and the oil-rich conservative régimes of the Gulf have little time to spare.

Circumstances may bring occasional changes in the NLF's General Command and government in the future. But as long as the PDRY is supported by the communist countries there is little likelihood of a meaningful reorganisation of the present régime. Throughout the years of the PDRY's existence the general trend has been rather towards the entrenchment of NLF government authority and a gradual radicalisation of its policy. In spite of appearing more pragmatic in its relations with the communist powers and seemingly seeking the friendship of 'middle class chauvinistic Arab nationalism', the NLF leadership remains as dogmatic as ever concerning its ideology and revolutionary policy. The tense situation in Southern Arabia and its environs will, therefore, persist and may, in special circumstances, even lead to a far wider conflict.

Notes

1. Until December 1970 the People's Democratic Republic of Southern Yemen—PRSY.
2. South Yemen's population is Qahtani.
3. Previously it was governed by the Indian authorities.
4. Later identified with conservative or moderate nationalism.
5. Several rebellions broke out in Lahj, one of which was led by the radical leader Qahtan Ash-Sha'abi, the future leader of the NLF.
6. After becoming prime minister he was dismissed from his post for refusing to co-operate with the British.
7. The middle-aged NLF's leader was previously a member of SAL.
8. This faction gave birth to the Popular Front for the Liberation of Palestine (PFLP) and the Marxist–Leninist Popular Democratic Front for the Liberation of Palestine (PDFLP).

9. It is claimed that the British preferred the NLF to FLOSY because of the former's anti-Egyptian attitude.

10. The island of Perim was captured by the NLF before the evacuation of Aden by the British. Shortly afterwards Abdul Fattah Isma'il declared the NLF's intention to use its against Israeli shipping in the Red Sea—*IHT*, 16.11.67; *T*, 16.11.67; *Economist*, 25.11.67, p. 838.

11. *NYT*, 7.8.69; *Al-Hayat* (Lebanon), 28.1.68; J. B. Bell, *World Today* 1970, p. 80; *Al-Nahar* (Lebanon), 3.12.69.

12. *M*, 5–6.4.70; *MD*, February 1971; *L'Humanité*, 10.1.72, 12.1.72.

13. J. P. Viennot, 'Aden, de la lutte pour la libération', pp. 5–30 of the Zanjibar programme, *Orient*, 1967; *MD*, February 1971, p. 2; *L'Humanité*, 12.1.72.

14. Haytham was previously the NLF's liaison with the army.

15. At first made up of five members, but later reduced to three.

16. *Al-Hayat*, 23.6.69, 27.6.69; *Al-Nahar*, 6.12.69; *EG*, 6.12.69, 27.3.70; *CDL*, 8.4.70; *Unita*, 12.9.70.

17. *NYT*, 7.8.69; J. B. Bell, *World Today*, February 1970, pp. 81–2; *FAZ*, 5.5.72.

18. In addition to the many South Yemeni refugees in the North. See below. At the end of 1970 the PRSY was renamed the People's Democratic Republic of Yemen—PDRY.

19. Relations with West Germany, for instance, were broken and its aid was phased out whereas East Germany was recognised and later became one of the PRSY's staunchest supporters.

20. Both directly (see below) and indirectly by broadcast propaganda from Aden's radio, made far more powerful with East European and Soviet aid.

21. With the outstanding exception of BP's refinery, the source of most of the country's earnings of foreign currency.

22. *Pravda*, 14.9.67; Ben Dak, *Current History*, September 1970, p. 150.

23. A point taken up by Libya as well as to Saudi Arabia.

24. The attack on the Israeli tanker *Coral Sea* in 1971 by Palestinian guerrillas was organised with the complicity of PDRY authorities. BBC, 1.6.70, radio Aden, 29.5.70; *EG*, 2.7.70; *Al-Hadaf* (Lebanon), 26.6.71; BBC, 9.11.71, radio Aden, 27.10.71; *FBIS*, 28.12.71; ANA, 26.12.71; *Al-Anwar* (Lebanon), 5.4.72; INA, 15.4.72.

25. *EG*, 27.11.70, 9.1.71; *G*, 5.1.71; *T*, 14.1.71.

26. See Chapter 3.

27. G. Jukes, The Indian Ocean in Soviet Naval Policy, *Adelphi Papers* No. 87, The Institute for Strategic Studies, London 1972.

28. *G*, 5.1.71; *EG*, 9.1.71, 1.2.71; *T*, 14.1.71; *Al-Hayat*, 14.3.71. In May 1971 Ruba'i warned in his speech against co-operation with reactionaries—*M*, 18.5.71.

29. The reshuffle took place immediately after Abdul Fattah Isma'il returned from Moscow.

30. Once again with the exception of BP's refinery. *MD*, February 1971, p. 4; *ARR*, 1971, p. 224; ANA, 25.4.71; *L'Humanité*, 11.1.72; BBC

Economic Report, 15.2.72, ANA, 3.2.72; *FBIS*, 1.3.72, radio Aden 29.2.72; *FBIS*, 10.3.72, radio Aden, 9.3.72; *G*, 15.3.72, 6.10.72.

31. *ARR* 1971, p. 423; *Al-Hayat*, 10.10.71; BBC, 10.12.71, radio Aden, ·7.12.71; *FBIS*, 15.12.71, FYSR, 14.12.71; BBC, 3.1.72; FYSR, 30.12.71; *Al-Nahar*, 6.1.72; *ND*, 1.2.72; BBC, 18.2.72, INA, 2.2.72. The government took control of every non-political organisation, including the trade unions.

32. Numerous reports to this effect of Arab and Western origin.

33. Eric Rouleau, *M*, 31.5.72.

34. See below.

35. *Al-Hayat*, 13.11.72; *JP*, 22.11.72; *New Times* (Moscow), No. 49, December 1972, p. 16; INA, 10.12.72, of a new aid agreement.

36. Sharjabi, North Yemeni by origin, is considered a supporter of Isma'il, whereas Mut'i, a militant radical, is said to be a supporter of Ruba'i.

37. See below.

38. Only 0·1% of the sixth province and parts of the fifth are cultivable. Nevertheless, the most costly development projects are the Aden and Mukalla road and the road network in the fifth and sixth provinces— CDL, 26.6.71; *MD*, February 1971, p. 2. One third of the £40 million. 1971–72 budget allotted to the communications—*CDL*, 7.7.71. On Soviet built road from Mukalla to Hadramaut—*Pravda*, 25.12.71.

39. The major part of China's £16·5 million development loan granted in 1970 is for the building of roads and bridges. A good part of East German and Soviet aid is also in the field of communications.

40. In addition to artillery of different kinds the PDRY received over 50 T-34 tanks, 20 Mig-17 and Mig-19 fighter-interceptors, several transports-bombers, helicopters and a number of small patrol boats. Unconfirmed reports claim that the PDRY was given a squadron of Mig-21s and other more sophisticated weapons—*DT*, 9.5.72.

41. A five-year development plan for the armed forces was prepared by Russian experts and arms shipments were accelerated in 1971 and 1972 in view of the British evacuation of the Gulf and the growth of pressure on the PDRY's borders.

42. Nevertheless, the 22nd brigade, intensively indoctrinated and commanded by officers most loyal to the party, is stationed near the capital ready to crush any attempt against the régime. BBC, 15.6.70, radio Aden, 11.6.70; BBC, 16.7.70, radio Aden, 14.7.70; *T*, 2.1.71; *FT*, 13.1.71; *ARR*, February 1971, p. 124; *Al-Hayat*, 14.3.71; *Observer*, 9.1.72; *Sunday Telegraph*, 5.2.72; *Al-Hayat*, 11.3.72; *G*, 15.3.72; *FAZ*, 17.4.72; *M*, 30.5.72.

43. David Hirst, *G*. 15.3.72.

44. *Al-Nahar*, 2.12.69.

45. *T*, 2.1.71; *FBIS*, 29.1.71, FYSR, 28.1.71; *ARR*, February 1971, p. 95; *Sunday Times*, 7.2.71; *NYT*, 14.3.71.

46. BBC, 2.7.71, FYSR, 30.6.71; NCNA, 31.8.71; *FBIS*, 1.9.71, FYSR, 28.8.71; Radio Cairo (Sawt al-Arab), 15.10.71; *FBIS*, 2.11.71, radio Aden, 1.11.71; *FBIS*, 20.12.71. FYSR, 16.12.71; *FBIS*, 28.12.71, radio Aden, 23.12.71.

47. MENA, 29.3.72; *FAZ*, 5.5.72.

48. *DT*, 9.5.72. The spokesman of the anti-PDRY's national forces claims that 200 of the 700 Chinese experts active in South Yemen are involved in the organisation of the militia.

49. *L'Humanité*, 10–12.1.72; *M*, 30.5.72.

50. *CDL*, 7.7.71, concerning 1971–72 budget. Nearly half of the budget is earmarked for defence and about one third for agricultural development.

51. See below p. 100.

52. See, for instance, *Morning Star*, 4.4.72 on 150 PDRY's students in Moscow university. FBIS, 1.5.72, INA, 27.4.72 of 40 new scholarships offered by the Soviet Union.

53. *ARR* 1969, p. 562; *Al-Bilad* (Saudi Arabia), 7.12.69; *ARR* 1971, p. 567; A. Yodfat, *New Outlook*, March 1971, p. 47; BBC, 9.9.71, FYSR, 7.9.71; BBC, 27.11.71; FYSR, 20.11.71; INA, 1.2.72; *DT*, 18.5.72. On further politicisation of school curricula in the decisions of the NLF's fifth congress, see: MENA, 6.3.72.

54. Algerian, Iraqi and Soviet teams have been drilling in the PDRY's eastern provinces for oil without results.

55. Of the positive impact of this immigration of the Shafi'i part of the YAR, see: D. Hirst, *G*, 15.3.72.

56. *G*, 15.3.72; *FAZ*, 2.5.72; *DT*, 18.5.72; *M*, 30.5.72; *Ma'ariv* (Israel), 17.1.73, according to *Los Angeles Times*.

57. *CDL*, 26.671, 7.7.71; *FBIS*, 4.4.72, radio Aden, 1.4.72; *FAZ*, 2.5.72. Of the 10% contribution of this sector to the GNP, 80% comes from BP's refinery.

58. *DT*, 18.5.72; 'Ali Husain Halaf, *Dirasat 'Arabiya*, March 1971, pp. 134–58.

59. See for instance: BBC Economic Report, 15.2.72, Tass, 8.2.72, SU/3911/A4/3; *Ma'ariv*, 17.1.73, according to *Los Angeles Times*.

60. All within the framework of the £16·5 million aid agreement signed in August 1970.

61. For instance, BBC, 10.1.72; FYSR, 7.1.72; BBC, 25.2.72; FYSR, 25.2.72.

62. *M*, 31.5.72, E. Rouleau.

63. *M*, 10.2.72; *ARR*, 1972, p. 69; *FAZ*, 2.5.72; INA, 10.12.72.

64. Obsolete in the USSR but quite modern in the Arabian Peninsula.

65. Much of the badly needed financial aid comes from this source. See: BBC Economic Report, 22.2.72, ANA, 16.2.72; *CDL*, 26.2.72; *FAZ*, 2.5.72.

66. INA, 10.12.72. Of 600 Soviet experts transferred from Egypt to the PDRY after the July 1971 crisis—see *Ha'aretz* (Israel), 2.2.73, according to Reuters (Beirut).

67. *CDL*, 27.10.71; *L'Humanité*, 11.1.72; *FAZ*, 2.5.72; *DT*, 18.5.72; *M*, 28–29.5.72, 30.5.72; *Ma'ariv*, 17.1.73, according to *Los Angeles Times*.

68. Known as Ahl al-Hadara. B. Thomas, *Arabia Felix*, London 1932, pp. 8–9, 12, note 1, 24–5; W. Thesiger, *Arabian Sands*, London 1959, pp. 29, 33. There is also the mixed coastal population, including many of African origin. There is no way of knowing the exact number of Dhofar's people. Estimates range from 50,000 to 300,000.

69. Thomas, *op. cit.*, p. 13.

70. *L'Unità*, 14.2.70; *Daily Express*, 3.8.70; *L'Humanité*, 30.12.70; *Observer*, 6.6.71.

71. The Saudis are said to have given him arms which he smuggled into Dhofar with help of Kathiri tribesmen. *Observer*, FNS, 12.8.70; *Observer* 6.6.71.

72. *Dhofar, Britain's Colonial War in the Gulf*, edited and published by the Gulf Committee, January 1972; on PFLOAG's programmes—*Dirasat 'Arabiya*, December 1971, pp. 144–52, March 1972, pp. 143–54.

73. In June 1971 a faction of the NLF General Command enabled Palestinian guerrillas to use Perim island against the Israeli tanker *Coral Sea*.

74. Founded by the Syrian Ba'th it later become a tool of Iraq. Even more serious were the preparations of the PFLOAG discovered by the TOS to operate from Ras Masandum facing the Hormuz straits.

75. Estimated at about £50 million annually.

76. A clash between Saudi and PDRY troops in the area of Wadeya at the end of 1969 was an outcome of an unmarked borderline in the area and the possibility of finding oil along it. Bell, *World Today* 1970, p. 88; *ARR*, November 1969, pp. 493 and 514.

77. By 1973 it seems that there were about 300,000 South Yemeni refugees in the YAR and Saudi Arabia. *G*, 6.10.72; 300,000 in the YAR *MD*, February 1971, p. 3. Half a million, according to *DT*, 18.5.72.

78. The NLF accused Saudi Arabia of using this force to annex Hadramaut and Mahra and isolate the Dhofari rebellion.

79. The services of the SAL's veteran leaders Muhammad Ali Jifry and Shaykhan al-Habashi were used.

80. Bulletins about the operations of the ANU and ANS were broadcast by a 'clandestine' radio established in 1970, called 'Free Yemeni South Radio', probably from Jazan (Saudi Arabia).

81. Mainly by interfering with the supply routes between the PDRY and Dhofar.

82. Population about seven million.

83. *Dirasat Arabiya*, Vol. 8, No. 4, February 1972, pp. 51–6; F. Halliday, Counter Revolution in Aden, *New Left Review*, No. 63, September–October 1970, pp. 3–25.

84. BBC, 14.9.71, radio Aden, 12.9.71; *L'Orient le Jour* (Beirut), 5.11.71; Akhbar al-Yaum (Cairo), 6.11.71; *FBIS*, 14.11.71, ANA, 4.11.71; BBC, 17.11.71, ANA, 15.11.71; J. Malone, *World Today*, December 1971, pp. 541–8; *Ra'y al-'Amm* (Kuwait), 14.1.72.

85. *ARR*, September 1971, p. 516; BBC, 30.9.71, radio Aden, 29.9.71; *Sunday Telegraph*, 5.3.72; *Al-Hayat*, 11.3.72, 14.3.72.

86. On the political programme and merger of the two movements and of the PFLOAG's congress at Ahlish in December 1971—*Dirasat 'Arabiya*, Vol. 8, No. 2, December 1971, pp. 144–52; *Ibid*, No. 5, March 1972, pp. 143–54.

87. *CSM*, 6.6.71; *Pravda*, 3.8.71; BBC, 2.10.71, FYSR, 30.9.71; BBC, SU/3879/A4/4, 29.12.71, radio Peace and Progress, 25.12.71; *Pravda* 25.12.71; *Observer*, 9.1.72; *Sunday Telegraph*, 5.3.72.

88. With the outstanding exception of Iraq. *FBIS*, 3.11.71, MENA, 19.11.71; *Al-Hayat*, 7.3.72; *Al-Nahar*, 4.5.72; *M*, 31.5.72. NLF militants are well aware of the Soviet Union's pragmatism concerning its supporters in the Arab world.

89. *FBIS*, 8.11.71, ANA, 7.11.71; *FBIS*, 23.11.71, MENA, 19.11.71; BBC, 29.11.71, radio Aden, 27.11.71. It became the champion of the cause of the three islands in the Hormuz straits which Iran claimed and later captured. But with the exception of Iraq and Libya there was little response to its efforts.

90. BBC, 12.8.71; ANA, 10.8.71; *Al-Hawadith* (Lebanon), 3.9.71; *T*, 4.9.71; INA, 6.12.71; *G*, 16.3.72; *FAZ*, 16.3.72.

91. Of the Bakil confederation, *G*, 16.3.72; *FAZ*, 16.3.72.

92. *FBIS*, 14.2.72, radio Cairo, 12.2.72; *T*, 15.3.72, 12.5.72, 26.5.72; *DT*, 2.5.72, BBC, 11.5.72, INA, 9.5.72; *Ha'aretz*, 3.10.72, according to UP, Beirut; *G*, 6.10.72.

93. *Al-Ra'y al-'Amm*, 14.1.72; *FT*, 4.5.72, 6.10.72; *Al-Muharir* (Lebanon), 21.7.72; *Al-Sayad* (Lebanon), 10.8.72.

94. *Al-Siyad*, 10.8.72; *Kul Shay* (Lebano), 12.8.72; *G*, 6.10.72; *Ma'ariv* (Israel), 25.10.72. YAR's government was granted 44 million Saudi riyals.

95. *FT*, 3.1.73, 13.4.73; *Al-Nahar*, 21.3.73.

96. *Al-Nahar*, 4.5.72; *Al-Gumhuriyya* (Cairo), 25.5.72.

97. Libya granted the PDRY financial aid and supported the ELF and Palestinian guerrillas active from bases in the PDRY such as their camp on Kamran islands. *Al-Nahar*, 4.5.72; *FBIS*, 15.5.72, ANA, 6.5.72; *M*, 31.5.72; *Al-Ahram al-Iqtisadi* (Cairo), 1.7.72; *JP*, 18.10.72, according to UP, Beirut.

98. It was repeatedly alleged that Russia was requested to withdraw its experts from the YAR. *T*, 5.8.72; *Al-Anwar* (Lebanon), 3.10.72.

99. *Al-Hayat*, 20.11.72; MENA, 3.12.72. Both sides still hold territories captured during the war, and border incidents are occasionally reported.

100. *FT*, 4.5.72; *FAZ*, 5.5.72; *T*, 13.7.72; *Al-Sayad*, 10.8.72; *Al-Hawadith*, 3.9.72; *G*, 6.10.72; *Al-Hayat*, 12.11.72. It is claimed that because Ruba'i succeeded in further entrenching his position and began to gain control of the party's administration Abdul Fattah Isma'il hoped to win popularity by creating a confrontation with YAR.

101. *Al-Hawadith*, 8.1.73.

102. *G*, 6.10.72; INA, 14.11.72.

103. *Al-Hayat*, 12.11.72; Ma'riv, 21.12.71 (Reuters, San'a); *Ha'aretz* (Israel), 29.12.72, AP Beirut; *JP*, 31.12.72, UP (Beirut).

104. *Ma'ariv*, 21.12.72 (Reuters San'a); *FT*, 3.1.73; *Ha'aretz*, 10.4.73, of demonstrations of Yemeni students in Cairo against the YAR government's policy.

105. *FT*, 3.1.73, 13.4.73; *Al-Nahar*, 21.3.73. Although occasional clashes occur between the Saudi armed forces and those of the PDRY it is careful not to allow them to develop into a major incident—Radio Voice of Israel (in Hebrew), 23.3.73; *IHT*, 23–24.3.73.

III

Red Sea Politics

Historical Background

From a purely geopolitical point of view the Red Sea could be ironically termed an extension of the Suez Canal connecting the Mediterranean with the Indian Ocean. Yet long before the Suez Canal was completed in 1869 the Red Sea had been an exceedingly important avenue of trade and communications between the Far East, the Middle East and Europe. From the seventh century onwards the Muslim world, and especially Egypt, derived substantial benefits from control of this important waterway. Indeed, some Italian city-states made their fortunes by participating in the transit trade between Egypt, the Levant and Europe during the medieval and post-medieval period.

Even before their appearance in the Indian Ocean at the turn of the fifteenth century the Portuguese were aware of the economic-strategic importance of the Red Sea. Their search for a new way to the Indian Ocean was motivated to a great extent by their wish to outflank their Muslim enemies and to deprive them of an important source of revenue and power. For this purpose they attempted in the last decades of the fifteenth century to ally themselves with the legendary Prester John. But once in the Indian Ocean, Albuquerque, by far the greatest of Portuguese admirals in this region, insisted that success would be achieved only if the Portuguese effectively blocked the entrance of the Persian Gulf and the Red Sea. The Portuguese succeeded in closing the straits of Hormuz and, though having at first misjudged the importance of Sokotra and later failing to take Aden, they constantly harassed Muslim shipping in the Gulf of Aden and the Red Sea in the first decades of the sixteenth century. Consequently, the volume of trade passing along this ancient route greatly declined and therefore

Egypt and the other Red Sea littoral countries began to stag-
nate. Contrary to common belief, however, the trade of the Red
Sea revived in the second half of the century, even surpassing its
volume of the past. By this time, most of the Red Sea littoral
was already controlled by the new Muslim world power—the
Ottoman.

Following their capture of Egypt and the Hijaz in 1517 and
realising the strategic-economic importance of the Red Sea and
the Gulf of Aden, the Ottomans gradually extended their hold
over most of the Red Sea countries. In order to expel the
Portuguese from the Indian Ocean they organised several major
naval expeditions. But the Ottomans never excelled on the seas;
their admirals in the area were unfit for their duties and the
expeditions turned into costly failures. By the third quarter of
the century, with the Portuguese having stretched their meagre
resources to the limit, a balance emerged by which the Portuguese retained their control of the Indian Ocean whereas the
Ottomans were left as the masters of the Red Sea. By the second
quarter of the seventeenth century Ottoman authority in the
area had declined and was gradually replaced by that of powerless indigenous rulers, who abused their authority and were
unable to keep law and order. Once again the Red Sea passed
into historical obscurity.

A new era in the history of the Red Sea area was opened when
the government of India, under the inspiring leadership of
Warren Hastings, tried in the 1770s to open direct communications between India and Britain by way of the Red Sea and
Egypt. The short-sightedness of the home government in
London and pressure from Constantinopole brought this
interesting attempt to a close. The French, Britain's rivals in the
Indian Ocean in the eighteenth century, were also aware of the
strategical importance of the Red Sea and Egypt. French
archives contain numerous reports from the second part of the
eighteenth century on the strategic-economic value of the Red
Sea and of plans for its conquest. It was in fact the French
invasion of Egypt by Bonaparte at the turn of the century
which finally convinced the British government of this. Yet only
the ambitions of Egypt's ruler, Muhammad Ali, who planned
in the 1810s to turn the Red Sea into an Egyptian *mare nostrum*,
prompted the British government to ensure its control over this

important waterway. His gradual success in Yemen, for instance, was one of the main reasons for the British conquest of Aden in 1839. Thereafter the British viewed the Red Sea and Egypt as essential for imperial communications; hence their conquest of Egypt in 1881–1882.

In spite of French and Italian competition and the rise of Arab nationalism in the twentieth century the Red Sea remained under British control virtually until the 1950s. During this period its strategic-economic importance grew immensely as a result of the opening of the Suez Canal and the discovery of enormous oil resources in the Persian Gulf region. From the 1950s the Red Sea could already be termed a vast oil pipeline between the Persian Gulf and Europe. How crucial the Canal had become to Europe was clearly demonstrated when it was closed for several months in 1956, thereby bringing the whole economic structure of Europe nearly to a standstill.

Since the rapid erosion of Britain's power after World War II, her evacuation of the Canal Zone in 1955 and the Suez fiasco of 1956, the politics and strategic balance of the Red Sea area have become far more complex. Though in many ways the stakes have become more narrowly regional than previously, in others the situation is growing more intricate, in part because of the tendency of the Arab–Israeli conflict to overflow into the Red Sea and in part, and more recently, because of the interest many countries have in Gulf oil and consequently in the northwest Indian Ocean area. Further, Britain's old dominance has gradually been replaced by a multiplicity of influences. Britain herself has become in many ways the least significant of the major powers interested in the Red Sea since her withdrawal from Aden in 1967 and from the Persian Gulf in 1971. Now the area responds to many pressures, some regional, such as Arab radicalism and Israel, and others from much further afield including not only the super-powers but China and France, though possibly the strongest pressures of all today are the host of local nationalisms.

The first lineaments of the post-imperial patterns, as they emerged in the middle 1950s, suggested that the Middle East would become one of the major non-European theatres of the cold war and in many ways the most dangerous one of all. The

United States, as the leader of the West, and the Soviet Union, as its arch-challenger not only in the Middle East but in the world, rapidly became involved as the faction-leaders and would-be controllers of local conflicts, seeking to shape them to their global ends.

The United States

During the Dulles era, the United States was primarily concerned to create a *cordon sanitaire* around the growing Middle Eastern power of the Soviet Union through bilateral and regional alliances. Egypt which, after 1956, controlled the Suez Canal and became the leader of Arab nationalism, was, as a 'non-aligned' country, opposed to such alliances. In fact, she was moving closer to the Soviet Union, because her aspirations clashed with Western interests in the Middle East and with America, also because of the latter's special relations with Israel. But the Canal was still crucial to America's allies and the United States herself had interests and obligations in the Red Sea. She led the 'maritime nations' which guaranteed Israel's freedom of passage through the Straits of Tiran after 1956. She had oil interests in Saudi Arabia, was committed to an aid programme to Ethiopia and maintained the important communications base Kagnew near Asmara, in Eritrea.

Kagnew base was leased from the British in 1943. In 1953, after Eritrea became federated with Ethiopia, the United States signed a 25-year economic and military aid agreement with Ethiopia to secure the use of the base until 1977. As a result of the cold war and military, technical and political developments Kagnew's importance to American communications, space and other defence programmes gradually grew during the 1950s and 1960s. When Wheelus base in Libya was evacuated in 1970 some of its functions, it is claimed, were transferred to Kagnew. In 1971 Kagnew became the terminal of a communications network stretching from the Philippines through the Indian Ocean.[1] In return for the base at Kagnew the United States undertook to equip, train and help maintain an Ethiopian army of some 40,000 soldiers. Between 1953 and 1971 Ethiopia received from the United States about $170 million in direct military aid and some $23 million in economic aid. In addition, the Ethiopian treasury benefits annually to the extent of several million dollars from the expenditures of the American training mission (MAAG) and the several thousand servicemen and their dependants at Kagnew.

At the end of 1970 when the activities of the Eritrean Liberation Front (ELF) reached their peak, the ELF purposely initiated an anti-American propaganda campaign. As expected, politicians and journalists in the United States clamoured for the evacuation of Kagnew and the termination of military aid to Ethiopia in order to avoid an involvement in a Vietnam-type situation in the Horn of Africa.[2] Even before the 'Eritrean scare' the United States was re-evaluating her commitments in Ethiopia and Kagnew's importance, in relation to Ethiopia's request to modernise her army and review and renew the 1953 agreement. By the end of 1970 the importance of Kagnew and its location to the United States was greatly reduced by the development of satellite communication with submarines. In general, American policy regarding overseas military bases and commitments was undergoing a change as the outcome of the tremendous progress in the development of submarine missiles, and the reaction to the Vietnam war. The United States decided, therefore, gradually to phase out her military aid to Ethiopia and, if necessary, to replace Kagnew with a base on an island in the Indian Ocean. It seems that Diego Garcia was leased from Britain in 1971, possibly for this purpose among others.[3] Although at present unlikely, the possibility that Ethiopia might be driven to seek Soviet aid did not escape the Americans, but Washington continued to turn a deaf ear to Ethiopia's requests for military aid. Ethiopia received in 1972, nevertheless, $31·8 million in economic assistance and a total of $169·1 million is projected for the five years 1973–77. Ghana and Nigeria, however, are now forging ahead of Ethiopia as the primary focus of United States' non-military aid in Africa.[4] The United States tendency to withdraw from Ethiopia stands in marked contrast to her renewal of the basing agreement in Bahrain as soon as Britain left the Gulf in 1971 and to the sale of a large quantity of arms to Iran and Kuwait and Saudi Arabia (all of whom, unlike Ethiopia, have no difficulty in footing the bill). Only in 1973, in view of new developments in the region and the renewed flow of more sophisticated arms to Somalia, did the United States become, it seemed, more willing to consider a limited modernisation of the Ethiopian armed forces, a matter which Emperor Haile Selassie discussed in Washington during his visit there in May 1973. It is still unresolved.

The Soviet Union

The growth of a Soviet naval presence in the Mediterranean provided the Russians with important political-strategic advantages and entrenched their position in the region. With the Suez Canal closed and its narrow straits controlled by NATO members, the Mediterranean is considered a fatal trap for the Soviet surface navy. Had the Suez Canal been re-opened it would have enabled the Russians to rotate their fleets between the Mediterranean, the Indian Ocean and the Pacific as they are presently doing in the Atlantic and the Black Sea.

Until her recent discomfitures in the Sudan and Egypt, the Soviet Union, as so often seeming to act as a kind of mirror-image of the United States, gave the impression of advancing as rapidly in the area as the other withdrew. Towards the end of World War II, the Soviet Union, whose interest in the Red Sea area began to develop as early as the 1920s,[5] proposed that the Italian colonies in the Horn of Africa should be placed under Soviet trusteeship. Soviet interest in the Red Sea, however, really grew in the latter half of the 1950s. In 1957, despite the medieval character of the imam's régime, the Soviet Union signed military and economic aid agreements with Yemen. By 1960, several hundred Russians were employed in industrial and agricultural aid programmes there and in training the Yemeni army.[6] A beginning was made in dredging a deep water port at Hodeida. After the 1962 revolution, Soviet aid to the Yemen was substantially increased and by 1965 amounted to $95 million in total.[7] The construction of Hodeida's harbour and of roads and the extension of pre-existing airfields was greatly accelerated. To some extent the Soviet Union may have been following the initiative of the UAR, which wanted to undermine British authority in Aden. But installations such as Hodeida could also serve 'wider strategic interests; landing and refuelling facilities, could prove useful in extending Soviet access to, and activities in, East Africa'.[8] Even following the withdrawal of Egyptian troops from the Yemen in 1967, Soviet pilots flew combat missions against the Royalists and the Republican régime was saved by massive Soviet shipments of tanks, guns and other military equipment.

Aden was always considered the gate to the southern entrance of the Red Sea while South Yemen as a whole acts as an ideal springboard into the Gulf. Thus the predominant influence which the Soviet Union gained in South Yemen could be considered an important victory for Russian policy in the region. In reality, the Soviet position of strength in that country was mainly the outcome of internal developments in Aden rather than of Soviet initiative. In 1967 the Marxist government of South Yemen, later renamed People's Democratic Republic of Yemen (PDRY), dispensed with British aid and turned to the Soviet Union for military, technical and financial assistance. The links were tightened further when the more radical wing of the ruling National Liberation Front (NLF) came to power in 1969. Thereafter, the PDRY became the focus of Soviet activity in the area. Though details have not always been made public, it is evident from Arab, Western and Communist sources that the Soviet bloc is providing relatively large aid to the PDRY in the military, internal security, communications and economic fields.[9] The Economic Counsellor of the Soviet embassy in Aden claimed recently that Soviet aid to the PDRY exceeds $29 million annually.[10] It is unlikely, however, that this figure includes military aid and it ignores, of course, aid channelled through smaller East European countries.[11] The PDRY's government categorically denies that it has granted bases to the Soviet Union, or to China.[12] It has never denied, however, that the Soviet Union has the right to the use of Khormaksar and other airfields and that Aden, with its Soviet harbour-master, marine engineers and technicians, has become an important servicing port for Soviet warships[13] and for a Soviet 'fishing fleet'[14] active in the Indian Ocean. Soviet experts are to be found in all the military installations in PDRY, and since 1971 there has been a growing Soviet presence and activity in the eastern governorates of PDRY and the port of Mukalla.[15]

On the west coast of the Red Sea, in 1962 the Soviet Union, unable to gain a foothold in Ethiopia, signed military and technical aid agreements with the Somali Republic. These were accompanied by a loan which, with later additions, has been estimated at $55 million. Funds were allocated to various development projects, but most of the Soviet aid was in the military field. The Soviet Union undertook to equip, train and help maintain the Somali armed forces, and to build a naval base at Berbera (suitable for ships up to 10,000 tons total draught weight) with radar installations, communications systems, an airfield in the hinterland and SAM-2 missile sites around it.[16] According to reports in the Western press, the Soviet navy has been granted facilities in Berbera and other Somali ports.[17] Still less is known of Soviet undertakings concerning the closely guarded port near Kismayu which, because of its natural advantages, was used during World War II by Italian submarines.[18]

Whether the Soviet Union supported the 1969 coup which deposed the Egal Government is still an open question.[19] Soviet aid to Somalia certainly increased substantially after the revolution either directly or through East European governments.[20] In November 1971, President Siyad went to Moscow to discuss among other matters further Soviet aid to Somalia. His government seemed dissatisfied because the Soviet Union was supplying factories (e.g. fish canning) and military equipment and developing the ports but not providing cash.[21] After the visit, however, Somali's Defence Minister and Vice-President, General Samatar, expressed satisfaction with the results achieved.[22] Then, in February 1972, the Soviet Defence Minister, Marshal Gretchko, came to Mogadishu for talks about which, understandably, little is known. According to Radio Mogadishu, he and the Somali leaders, discussed 'questions relating to Somali–Soviet military co-operation and its further development.[23] Following this visit large quantities of relatively modern arms reached Somalia and the *New York Times* reported in April 1973 the existence of an extensive Soviet 'communications centre' in Somalia and of the facilities which the Soviet air force and navy have in that country. Whatever the outcome of the Gretchko–Siyad talks, the military installations built in different parts of the Somali Republic seem to be out of all proportion to the needs of the tiny Somali navy and air force.[24] In general the Somalis, dependent on Soviet military and economic aid since they were turned down by the West in 1961 in favour of Ethiopia and Kenya, are in a poor position to refuse the Soviet Union any co-operation she may want.

The limitations of the influence bought in such ways has however, been dramatically illustrated of late in the countries more to the north. The Soviet Union's influence began to grow in the Sudan from 1968. She sold large quantities of relatively modern arms on credit to the Mahgub Government, which closely co-ordinated its policy with the UAR. Her influence grew dramatically following General Numeiri's revolution of May 1969. General Numeiri was brought to power mainly by panarab and communist officers, intellectuals and trade unionists. Although a minority, the communists were disciplined, determined and exceptionally well organised. They were instrumental in the creation of closer ties with the Soviet Union and the adoption by the Sudanese government of a relatively radical socialist policy. In spite of the constant tension between the panarabists and communists in the government, the Soviet Union continued to increase her financial commitments in the Sudan. Overestimating the power of the local communists, she seemed to hope to establish in the Sudan an important centre for future activities in the region.

Sudanese delegations, which visited the Soviet Union in 1969 and 1970, signed with the Soviet Government a number of financial, technical and military aid agreements (valued at over $100 million). The number of Soviet officers and experts in the Sudan increased to more than a thousand by 1971.[25] Soviet and East European pilots and navigators were alleged by the Western press to be flying combat missions against the rebels in the southern provinces.[26] In 1970 it was reported that the Soviet Union was building a naval base or a port near Port Sudan, usually confused with the existing harbour at Port Sudan, which was also undergoing expansion and modernisation at the time. These reports claimed that the new harbour was protected by SAM-2 missiles, a radar system and a military airfield.[27] Here again and assuming the reports to be correct, the installations seem far greater than the inconsequential Sudanese navy could require, especially at a time when the country's economy was under tremendous strain.[28]

All these links broke in July 1971 following the abortive communist coup in Khartoum. General Numeiri's régime has since been critical of the Soviet Union, and has been rebuilding bridges to the West and, even worse from a Soviet point of view, has been strengthening relations with China. The Sudan, however, still receives some Soviet aid, her army depends on Soviet arms and spares and there is still a Soviet presence in Sudan.[29] In spite of the persecution of local communists, the Soviet Union is trying to improve her relations with the Sudan, helped by Syria, Somalia and, before July 1972, Egypt.[30]

These efforts were partly successful when relations between the two countries were re-established in October and the Soviet Union agreed to supply the Sudan with badly needed spares.

In 1972, the Soviet experience in the Sudan was repeated on a still larger and more damaging scale in Egypt. Egypt, in view of Israel's ability to strike at her Red Sea naval installations at Safaga and Ghardaka and targets beyond Luxor during the war of attrition in 1968–69, had special reasons to transfer part of her air force to Wadi Sayyidna (north of Khartoum) and other Sudanese air bases. Egyptian naval units were also moved temporarily to Port Sudan,[31] Hodeida and Aden. In March 1972, *The Times* (London) reported that Egypt had refused a request by the Soviet Union (who already have several air and naval bases in the country) for a naval base on her Red Sea coast.[32] In May, the same newspaper reported that 'Gretchko is understood to have pressed the Egyptians for additional facilities for the Soviet Indian Ocean fleet along Egypt's Red Sea coast . . . The Russians already have refuelling and refitting facilities on the Red Sea coast. This is supported by a string of 'special' facilities at several military airports.[33] An Israeli newspaper alleged in February 1972[34] that the Soviet Union had begun to build as early as 1970 a base at Ras Banas on the Egyptian coast, north of the Sudanese border. In March 1972 Egyptian sources announced that a new port was being built at Berenice (sheltered by Ras Banas), to be connected by a new road (through most difficult terrain) to Aswan. It would serve as an outlet for the produce of the area and for pilgrims to Saudi Arabia (a most unlikely route).[35] Several airfields and the sites of the more sophisticated SAM missiles controlled by the Soviet Union were located near Aswan.[36]

Although the Suez Canal had been closed since 1967, the

Soviet Union continued to build naval and other installations along the coasts of the Red Sea and the Gulf of Aden, in which she had probably acquired facilities. The cost of building these installations in each country has been relatively small, but cumulatively Soviet investment in the whole region in recent years has been quite impressive, and parallels the general rise in Soviet maritime activity in the Indian Ocean[37] and the increase of Soviet interests in the Gulf. The number and dispersion of their installations provided the Soviet Union with flexibility and independence so that the loss of one, or several, would not cripple her position. The débâcle they suffered in the Sudan, nevertheless, caused the Soviet Union to question her policy of indiscriminately supporting 'progressive revolutionary régimes' of developing countries, and to consider giving preference to governments more ideologically acceptable and politically dependable. In the last months of 1972, for instance, when the doctrinal revolutionary policy of People's Democratic Republic of Yemen (PDRY) provoked armed pressures from its neighbours, the Soviet Union training and supplying both Yemeni armies, sided with the PDRY against the Arab Republic of Yemen (YAR). Consequently, relations between North Yemen (anyway moving closer to the West) and the Soviet Union further deteriorated.

Neither the change in the character of the YAR's régime, nor even the deterioration of relations with the Sudan could drastically affect the Soviet position in the region. However, although the Soviet Union's interest began to shift away from Egypt to Iraq, the former remained a key-stone for Soviet policy in the Middle East and Soviet strategy in the Mediterranean, the Red Sea and the western Indian Ocean. The Soviet Union, it seems, was not unaware of the possible threat to her position in Egypt when she refused President Sadat's request for new offensive weapons needed to reopen the war against Israel, or cause her to agree to the Arabs' peace terms. When asked to leave Egypt in July 1972, the Soviet Union was, nevertheless, shocked and her policy and strategy in this whole area were gravely undermined. Even gains in Iraq and the prospect of using Syrian bases could not provide a substitute for Egypt's support in the Arab world and her strategic importance to the Soviet Union.

Developments in Soviet–Egyptian relations since the last months of 1972 and what seems a partial re-establishment of the Soviet presence and influence in Egypt are generally viewed with some reservations, as an outcome of Egypt's military-economic dependence on Russia and its inability to gain Western support. But many political analysts forget that despite the blow to her prestige, the persecution of her friends and the unreliability of Sadat's régime, the Soviet Union was willing to resume her role in Egypt (although probably on different terms and on a more limited scale than before). Whether the facilities which she previously enjoyed in Egypt were completely or partially withdrawn after July 1972 is still unknown.[38] What is clear is that, realising the inadequacy of other arrangements, the Soviet Union was quick to exploit the opportunity opened to her by Egypt's difficulties.[39] She can thus repair the damage to her former Red Sea, Indian Ocean and Gulf strategy, but *inter alia* she may reconsider its viability. Be that as it may, it is doubtful if Russia wishes at present a new eruption of hostilities between Egypt and Israel. Russia hopes for an Israeli withdrawal from Sinai and the re-opening of the Canal; this would clearly serve her interests and would deprive her current main rival, China (CPR) of an important factor in her attempt to gain Arab favour.

Sino–Soviet Rivalry

Some scholars and politicians believe that the Soviet build-up in the Indian Ocean and Red Sea is due in large part to Soviet–Chinese rivalry.[40] The West is phasing out its presence in the area and has hardly tried to counter the Soviet Union's efforts to establish herself in the region. So long as Gulf oil continues to flow freely, Western states are unlikely to resist Soviet efforts to participate in the exploitation of oil. China, on the other hand, competes with the Soviet Union for the leadership of the communist camp and the favours of the Third World. She is dynamic and aggressive and has succeeded in out-manoeuvring the Soviet Union in Tanzania and Zambia. In recent years she has become interested in the Arabian/Persian Gulf and the Red Sea areas and expanded her aid to several countries there.

China began to compete with the Soviet Union in Africa and

the Arabian peninsula following the growing ideological rift between the two countries. Soon after the collapse of her subversive Marxist revolutionary policy in Africa in the early 1960s, China became involved in the Cultural Revolution. Nevertheless, through limited, but carefully selected, aid programmes to developing countries, China achieved several successes and was able to build a reputation for reliability and efficiency. However, she lacked the capital and technology to compete seriously with the Soviet Union. Accordingly she tried to gain influence in 'progressive countries' by supporting revolutionary and subversive movements. Such activities, in line with the Cultural Revolution, were far cheaper than technical or military aid. In co-operation with PDRY, China has, since 1967, supported the Popular Front for the Liberation of the Occupied Arab Gulf (PFLOAG), which is active in Oman, the ELF and, in co-operation with Somalia, the Fronts for the Liberation of Western Somalia and the Somali Coast (FLWS, FLCS).

With the echoes of the Cultural Revolution fading away, China opened a new phase in her relations with developing countries. Wishing to gain recognition as a world power, she strove to normalise relations with the governments of developing nations, whatever their character or ideology, rather than revolutionary movements with dubious futures. From the end of 1970 she discontinued her support of the ELF and Somali 'fronts' and gradually reduced her commitments to PFLOAG,[41] while expanding aid programmes to friends old and new.[42] In July 1971 and 1972, despite the Arab Republic of Yemen's recent 'moderate' orientation, China signed a new and probably more comprehensive aid agreement with its government.[43] Even more dramatic was the change in Ethiopian–Chinese relations which led to China's aid to the ELF and culminated in a $85 million interest free loan granted to Ethiopia.[44] Chinese aid to PDRY was relatively limited until 1970 and began to grow only following the visit of President Ruba'i to Peking in that year. A $40 million interest free loan was granted to PDRY to finance several essential projects, the most important of which was the construction of a strategic road network. Characteristically, much of the loan was in the form of goods, machinery, experts and labour. Such aid, apart from economising on foreign exchange, makes the most of opportunities to establish China's presence and diversify her activities in PDRY. Following agreements reached in 1971 and 1972 the volume of Chinese technical and military aid (for the people's militia) to the PDRY seem now to approach that of the Soviet Union.[45] Moreover, unlike the Soviet Union, China neither seeks nor is it interested in military facilities in the country.

Across the Gulf of Aden, Chinese aid to the Somali Republic, although limited at first, has been selective and most successful. Following the radicalisation of the Somali régime, China signed a new aid agreement with Somalia in 1970 to the value of about $125 million. The agreement covered projects connected with agriculture, light industries and fisheries; the most costly, however, was the building of an arterial road connecting southern and northern Somalia and running in many areas parallel to the border with Ethiopia.[46] Less publicised was the project for a road network in the region of Hargeisa in northern Somalia oriented towards the Ethiopian plateau, an area suitable for mechanised invasion of the latter. But although construction of the arterial road began in 1972, the future of the road complex around Hargeisa is doubtful in the light of China's present friendly relations with Ethiopia. In 1972 President Siyad visited Peking and in addition to the undertaking to implement the previous agreement the Chinese promised additional financial and economic aid to the Somali Republic.

As for the Sudan, China offered a $40 million interest free loan for development projects following Numeiri's revolution.[47] The abortive coup in 1971 gave a new impetus to the Sudan's relations with China. A Sudanese delegation, visiting Peking at the end of 1971, announced that it had signed an aid agreement with China valued at over $189 million. The size of the loan, if this is true, China's readiness to write off previous Sudanese debts and supply Sudan with arms and spares for Soviet weapons, indicate how anxious she is to supplant the Soviet Union in Arab countries. Chinese experts are already studying various development projects in the Sudan, including the re-habilitation of the southern provinces.[48] and an agreement was signed in 1972 for the training of the Sudanese army by the Chinese.[49]

Until recent years Chinese trade with the UAR and its aid to it were insignificant. Relations between the two countries

rapidly improved and Chinese aid to Egypt has grown substantially since the end of 1970. Several important Egyptian
missions visited the PRC during 1971 and the first half of 1972,
and a new trade agreement was signed in Cairo in 1972. The
Soviet Union has frequently been criticised by the Chinese
for 'betraying her Arab friends—mainly Egypt' and China
gives the Egyptians her unreserved political support in their
struggle against Israel. A new era in Sino–Egyptian relations
was opened after the Russian reverse in Egypt in 1972, and
high-ranking Egyptian military and economic delegations often
visited Peking during the following year. Yet both countries
were aware of the fact that China was unable and unwilling to
assume Russia's role in Egypt.[50]

Israel recognised the People's Republic of China as early as
1950 and made several unsuccessful attempts to establish
diplomatic relations with her. Following the Bandung Conference in 1955 China's attitude towards Israel, influenced by the
former's relations with the Arab world, gradually became more
hostile. Since 1967 China has repeatedly condemned Israel as
'an agent of Western imperialism' and has supported the
PDRY and the radical Palestinian guerrilla organisation's
negative attitude to a settlement with Israel on the basis of
United Nations Resolution 242. At the same time she delicately
repudiated Egypt's willingness to accept Secretary of State
Rogers' peace initiative and the Great Powers' mediation
efforts. Her policy in this matter remained consistent even after
she replaced Nationalist China in the Security Council in 1972.

The Arab–Israeli Conflict

Chinese activities in the Red Sea and the Gulf of Aden are
probably partly an outcome of China's determination to prevent
the Soviet Union from gaining a predominant position in the
Third World. They are bound, however, to increase the risks of
the Arab–Israeli conflict, since the Chinese are inciting the
Arabs to renew the war of attrition of 1968–70 and increasing
pressure on the Soviet Union herself. The Arab–Israeli conflict
is in any case an important factor in Red Sea politics, just as the
Red Sea has in its turn been a major factor in the Israeli–
Egyptian wars of 1956 and 1967. There has been considerable
discussion in the Arab press of the need to hit Israel's soft

underbelly through the Red Sea (especially in the area of Bab al-Mandeb), Eilat and the increasingly important oil pipeline with its terminal there. As for Israel, the pre-emptive attack of 1967, following Arab threats to annihilate Israel, was partly undertaken to maintain the viability and prestige of her warnings that a renewal of the blockade of Sharm al-Sheikh would be considered a threat to the existence of Israel and would mean war.

Historians will argue whether President Nasser's plan to turn the Red Sea into an Egyptian lake was part of his panarab policy or was Egyptian nationalism in the guise of panarabism. Nasser's (or Neguib's) first step towards 'Arab unity' and control of the Red Sea was the attempt to 'convince' the Sudanese to unite with progressive Egypt on the grounds of common culture, destiny and economic inter-dependence. When the Sudan opted for independence in 1955, Egypt declared that she would respect this decision, but secretly fomented rebellion there. Then followed the Suez crisis of 1956 and unity with Sudan became a side-show compared to the ideal of a united and powerful Arab nation controlling strategic assets such as Suez, Bab al-Mandeb and most of the world's proven oil reserves. This implied turning the Red Sea into an Arab lake.

Even before the 1956 Suez war President Nasser, aware of the strategic importance of Aden, was determined to dislodge the British from this stronghold, and the Suez war only hardened his decision. Having become the hero of Arab nationalism he encouraged the strong Aden TUC to foment political and labour unrest in the colony and later helped organise the NLF which fought the authorities in the South Yemen's protectorates.

In spite of the medieval character of the Yemeni régime he supported the imam in his dispute with the British. Secretly, however, he had helped build the power of the Free Yemeni Movement. In the meantime, following the collapse of the UAR in 1961 Egypt moved from pragmatism to ideology. Thereafter Arab nationalism, led by Nasser, was dedicated to 'Arab socialism' and 'unity of purpose'. Among other things this meant that Egypt undertook to support, and if necessary, to provoke, revolutions in Arab countries aimed at changing the character of their régimes and facilitating true and lasting unity.

Accordingly when revolution broke out in Yemen in 1962 Egypt was bound to support the new Republican régime. Nasser hoped that the Yemeni revolution would start a chain reaction, topple the reactionary oil régimes of the Arabian Peninsula and force the British out of Aden and the Arabian/ Persian Gulf. But by 1965 the Yemen adventure had turned out to be a costly failure. Nasser had lost much of his prestige among the Arab masses and many small nations considered Egyptian intervention in Yemen to be 'neo-imperialism'. The hoped-for chain reaction in the Arabian Peninsula did not materialise and only Saudi Arabia's obstinacy and the British declaration of intent to grant independence to Southern Yemen induced Nasser to postpone evacuation of his troops. Even the independence of Southern Yemen turned out to be a pyrrhic victory as the Marxist NLF defeated the Egyptian-backed Front for the Liberation of Occupied South Yemen (FLOSY) and established a new government in Aden. Although Egypt's hopes of controlling the Red Sea disappeared long before the collapse of her army in Sinai in 1967 and the departure of her expeditionary force from Yemen following the Khartoum Conference, by then most Arab states had come to recognise the importance of the Red Sea to the Arab strategy against Israel.

Immediately after her war of independence (1949), Israel became interested in developing trade relations with East African and Asian countries. In the early 1950s she tried to implement the right of 'innocent passage' through the Suez Canal, according to the Rhodes armistice agreement. Her attempts were foiled by Egypt whose embargo on Israeli shipping gradually came to include all Israeli-produced goods, or merchandise destined for Israel, shipped on non-Israeli vessels passing through the Suez Canal. Egypt went even further and declared a blockade of the straits of Tiran (Sharm al-Sheikh) leading to the Gulf of Aqaba and Eilat. The coast of this Gulf is divided among four countries. Saudi Arabia owns its eastern side as well as the tiny Coral islands at its entrance. The Hashamite Kingdom of Jordan controls a relatively small part of its northeastern corner on which the town of Aqaba is situated. Israel has only a few miles of the northwestern corner of the Gulf, where she had built the port-town of Eilat. The whole of the western part of the coast of the Gulf of Aqaba, being part of the Sinai peninsula, belongs to Egypt. But whereas the countries owning most of the Gulf littoral have no positive interest in it, the narrow strip of coast belonging to Jordan constitutes her only outlet to the sea and is of extreme economic importance because her trade by way of Syria and Lebanon is frequently interrupted by upheavals in these countries or strained relations with the Syrian Ba'th régime. As for Israel, although she has access to the Mediterranean her inability to use the shorter route from Eilat to the Indian Ocean prevented development of commercial relations with Asia and part of Africa. Founded in 1949, the town of Eilat therefore stagnated until 1956.

When Israel was constrained by America and Russia to relinquish all the territories captured in the 1956 war she was left with one important asset: the presence of a small contingent of United Nations soldiers stationed at Sharm al-Sheikh which symbolised the 'maritime powers' guarantee' of free passage through the straits of Tiran. Thereafter, Israel's relations and trade with East African and Asian countries were gradually developed, and a 12-inch oil pipe-line constructed between Eilat and Haifa provided for all the country's needs in oil. The violation of freedom of passage through the straits of Tiran by Egypt in May 1967 was probably the catalyst for the Six-Day War.

Since the Straits of Tiran were reopened after the Six-Day War, Israel's maritime trade, through Eilat and the Red Sea, has grown at a rate of about 15% a year. Several African and Far Eastern countries have begun to use the 'land bridge' between Eilat and the Mediterranean[51] and in 1970–71 about 9% of Israel's exports and 5% of her imports passed through Eilat. More important, in 1967 a 42-inch pipe-line was built between Eilat and Askelon on Israel's Mediterranean coast. Israel was able in 1972 to control a transit trade of some 30 million tons of oil, mainly, it is claimed, from Iran.[52] Several pumping stations under construction should soon enable Israel to exploit the full capacity of the pipe-line which is 60 million tons of oil per annum; in addition to the expansion of the oil refinery in Haifa the constructions of the Ashdod refinery (near the Askelon terminal) is nearing completion and another refinery is to be built in Sinai.[53] The Israeli pipe-line has

obvious attractions for European customers. It has been functioning for several years and proved itself economic, whereas the
proposed terms of the international concession for the planned
Egyptian pipe-line (which will be longer and more expensive
to build) have already met with serious opposition in Egypt.[54]
Barring a new war, the Israeli pipe-line will not be affected by
local politics and seasonal upheavals as in the Arab countries.[55]
It had been argued that if the Suez Canal is reopened the
Israeli pipe-line will lose its value. But the very fact that international companies and the Egyptian government are interested
in a similar pipe-line shows the fallaciousness of this claim.
Moreover to rebuild the Suez Canal so as to enable passage of
average supertankers would cost, it is estimated, more than a
billion dollars, take several years and present the planners with
tremendous engineering problems. Supertankers have made the
long route around the Cape as economical as the passage
through the old Canal. However, such a long route is most
vulnerable and apart from the problems of pollution and safety
of traffic in certain areas, supertankers necessitate the building
of suitable terminals and pipe-line networks in the consuming
countries. This of course does not mean that shipment of oil in
this way is not the cheapest and best method. The Israeli
pipe-line has, however, the extra advantage that its Askelon
terminal is very near to southern Europe and the Black Sea and
it enables oil to be reshipped by small and medium-size
tankers which can unload their cargo in every port through
existing facilities. Be that as it may, her entry into the international oil market, though still modest, has given Israel both
a means of action and a hostage to conflict which she cannot
overlook in asserting her interests in the Red Sea.

A commando unit of the South Yemeni NLF captured Perim
island just before the British left Aden. Shortly afterwards Abdul
Fattah Isma'il, the present Secretary-General of the NLF,
announced that his country would use Perim to block the straits
of the Bab al-Mandeb to Israeli shipping.[56] Repeated on
several occasions in the coming years, this threat was quite
realistic in view of the strong ideological and other ties between
the NLF and the Marxist Palestinian guerrilla organisations.
It seems nevertheless that until June 1971 an unofficial truce
existed between the Arab countries and Israel concerning

exploitation of oil and tanker movements in the Gulf of Suez and the Red Sea. Although relatively deserted since the closure of the Canal, the Red Sea witnessed in fact a two-way traffic of Israeli tankers carrying oil from the south northwards and Egyptian tankers carrying oil from the Al-Murgan field near Suez to markets in Africa and the Far East, not to mention the movement of cargo boats belonging to the two nations. The Jordanians also enjoyed the unofficial armistice in the Red Sea and their trade via Aqaba grew between 1970 and 1972 by 300%. In 1971 even the cautious Saudis decided substantially to expand their refinery in Jedda and Saudi oil is exported by way of the Red Sea to several countries in the region. The only foreign asset which is still not nationalised in the PDRY is BP's refinery which, although not exploited to its full capacity of 9 million tons, is the source of a good part of her government's badly needed foreign currency. As for the Sudan, Yemen (YAR) and Ethiopia the Red Sea is their only outlet to the open waters of the oceans.

The attack on the Israeli tanker *Coral Sea* by Palestinian guerrillas from Perim,[57] numerous reports in the Arab press on Israel's oil installations and activities in the Red Sea and the support rendered by Arab countries to the ELF and Somalia's claim to Djibouti, demonstrate the Arab awareness of the importance of the Israeli pipe-line. The *Coral Sea* incident had far-reaching repercussions. It hardened Iran's determination to gain control of the islands in the Straits of Hormuz and made Ethiopia more aware than ever of the importance of Djibouti, its only outlet to the Indian Ocean. Israel was made to see the vulnerability of her shipping in distant waters dominated by the Arabs and, as some journalists and politicians claim, could be argued to outflank the Israeli case for keeping Sharm-al-Sheikh to safeguard freedom of navigation through Tiran. If Israeli ships could be stopped at Bab al-Mandeb or any other place beyond Israel's striking power, there was no point in Israel's retaining Sharm al-Sheikh, except for the sake of annexing Arab territory,[58] an intention Israel has continuously denied.

Although the narrow passage between the PDRY's mainland and Perim is clearly within the territorial waters of South Yemen, the distance between Perim and the African coast is over 16 miles.[59] Moreover, the African coast facing Perim belongs to the French Territory of the Afar and Issa (TFAI) and Ethiopia. At present, this international passage is used quite extensively by tankers and ships going to Red Sea ports. If the Suez Canal were to be reopened, the construction of Saudi Arabia's substantially expanded Jedda refinery terminated, or the Egyptian pipe-line built, Bab al-Mandeb would be swarming with tankers and cargo boats belonging to all nations. Incidents such as the attack on the *Coral Sea* would not be taken lightly by the major maritime nations (probably including the Soviet Union) and especially by the United States, in part because of her relations with Israel.[60]

In the last few years (especially since 1971), relying mainly on information from the ELF and the PDRY, the Arab press and radio have repeatedly alleged that in return for Israeli aid Ethiopia has permitted Israel (and the United States) to construct bases on islands in the vicinity of the Bab al-Mandeb. Strongly denied by Ethiopia, these allegations were also refuted by independent observers (including the North Yemeni authorities). No doubt Israel is interested in helping preserve the integrity of Ethiopia, her only friend in the Red Sea. It is unlikely, however, that aid projects would have induced the usually cautious Ethiopians to jeopardise their relations with the Arab world by granting bases to Israel in such a sensitive area. It is also doubtful that Israel would be interested in such bases, which might compromise her relations with Ethiopia and are worthless from a military point of view.

In the light of all this, it was significant that in early 1971, Israel's army spokesman revealed the fact that the country's aeronautical industry had converted American strato-cruisers into 'flying tankers' capable of refuelling Israeli *Phantoms*, *Skyhawks* and *Mirages* in mid-air. This meant that Israeli aircraft could strike at targets well beyond Egypt and Bab al-Mandeb. In March 1972, 'Pentagon sources' disclosed that Israel was about to launch, or was already deploying, in the Red Sea, a new version of the *Sa'ar* missile FPB's which was larger, faster, more heavily armed and with a range well beyond Bab al-Mandeb (by the beginning of 1973 the Israeli government officially admitted that some of these boats, armed with an improved version of the Gabriel SSM, were to serve in the Red Sea).[61]

The extensive press and radio campaign in the Arab countries since the end of 1971 concerning the need to close the straits of Bab al-Mandeb to Israeli shipping could indicate the beginning of a new stage in Arab strategy against Israel. It is possible that the leadership in some Arab countries would now like to reopen the 1968–70 war of attrition and expand it to the southern gates of the Red Sea. Hence, the growing interest in the possible Arabisation of the Ethiopian coast,[62] the wooing of Somalia by certain Arab leaders who support her claims to the French Territory of the Afar and the Issa and parts of Ethiopia,[63] and reports about the fortification of the island of Perim,[64] all of which would facilitate the closure of Bab al-Mandeb to Israel. The Egyptian Government has realised for some time the importance of the Red Sea arena in any future confrontation with Israel,[65] but aware of the serious repercussions which military operations near Bab al-Mandeb might have, is still reluctant to give official blessing to such a plan. Nevertheless, to some extent, the Arab–Israeli conflict could potentially become an integral part of Red Sea politics, closely interrelated to the southern complex of tensions revolving around the plan for 'Greater Somalia'[66] and the balance of power in the Horn of Africa.

Tension in the Horn of Africa

The boundaries of present-day Ethiopia are the outcome of a process of expansion renewed in the nineteenth century and accelerated as a result of European imperialism. By the turn of the century, therefore, Ethiopia's heterogeneous society was comprised of a spectrum of ethnical, cultural and linguistic groups governed by a core of Amhara–Tigrean and other semiticised agriculturalists. Although a Christian kingdom, Ethiopia had large pagan and Muslim minorities. The latter were considerably strengthened by the annexation of areas inhabited by Dankali and Somali pastoralists. Still, the majority of Muslims in Ethiopia considered themselves Ethiopians and grave Muslim secessionist-irridentist problems did not emerge until after World War II.

Because of climatic conditions, the attitude of her society to commercial activities and her tendency towards isolationism, Ethiopia cared little about its Red Sea coast which was, in most periods, in the hands of foreign powers or local Muslim rulers. This indifference to the fate of her outlet to the sea gradually changed during the nineteenth century as a result of Egyptian expansionism and the scramble for Africa. Ethiopia's efforts to regain its coast were frustrated by the establishment and growth of the Italian colony of Eritrea from 1885 and the division of the southern part of the coast of the Horn of Africa between the French, British and Italians. An outcome of the dismantling of Italy's empire in northeast Africa, Eritrea was federated to Ethiopia in 1952 according to a UN decision. Ten years later the Eritrean assembly unanimously 'decided' to unite Eritrea with Ethiopia. Hence Ethiopia regained what it terms her 'historical boundaries' and her outlet to the Red Sea. In fact, however, most Eritrean Muslims, who make up half her population (of about two million), were strongly opposed to unification with Ethiopia and wish to preserve an Eritrean identity which emerged during the colonial period.[67] Already in 1961 Muslim activists, together with some Christians opposed to Amhara domination, formed the Eritrean Liberation Front (ELF). Thus Ethiopia was faced for the first time with an active Muslim secessionist movement which found sympathy and support in nearby Arab countries.[68]

The Arab countries gradually came to realize that the secessionist movement in Eritrea, the Eritrean Liberation Front (ELF), which after 1968 became essentially Muslim and Arab-oriented, could become an important asset in the struggle against Israel. In addition to bringing the 544 miles of Eritrean coast under Arab control, the success of the ELF could spark off a chain-reaction leading to the internal disintegration of Ethiopia. Ethiopia, Israel's only friend in the Red Sea, is the source of about 70 per cent of the Nile's waters, important to the economy of Sudan and the life-blood of Egypt.[69] Ethiopia's collapse could also enable the Muslim Somali Republic to gain control of the African side of Bab al-Mandeb by annexing the French Territory of the Afar and the Issa (TFAI).

From 1968 the ELF received substantial aid from several Arab countries, especially from Syria, Sudan, Libya and the PDRY. Trained guerrillas and large quantities of Soviet, Czech and Chinese light arms smuggled from the PDRY by sea to Eritrea actually enabled the ELF during 1969–70 to intensify operations and extend them to the coast. By 1970 the ELF succeeded in gaining control of most of western and northern Eritrea and part of the coast.[70] It was co-operating by then with the FLCS having received the secret blessing of the Somali military régime, which secretly hoped that ELF's success would advance the Somali Republic's territorial ambitions.

As a result of a post-World War II settlement of the long-standing disputes between Ethiopia and Italian and British Somaliland large tracts of territory solely inhabited by Somali pastoralists were confirmed as Ethiopian or annexed to Ethiopia. The number of Somali-speakers in the kingdom (presently estimated at about one million) grew considerably, thus giving rise to the Ethio–Somali border dispute. This dispute was further complicated by the claims made by both countries to the French enclave of the TFAI.

'Acquired' by France from Dankali chiefs in 1862, Obokh on the northern side of the bay of Djibouti was meant to serve as a counterbalance to Aden, especially after the construction of the Suez Canal. Incensed by the British conquest of Egypt and spurred by competition with Italy and Britain, the French expanded their colony to the southern part of the bay of Djibouti, inhabited by Issa Somali, and named their colony 'French Somaliland'. The territory turned out to be a liability rather than an asset. The tens of thousands of pastoralists who lived there were difficult to control, the 8,500 square miles of torrid desert were worthless and Djibouti never acquired the strategic-economic importance of Aden. In fact, the Djibouti–Addis Ababa railway, completed in 1917 and serving the economy of central and southern Ethiopia, contributed the major part of French Somaliland's revenue.

An age-old animosity exists between the Afar (Dankalis), who inhabit the central and northern part of the colony, and the Issa (Somali), who live in its southern parts. In spite of the new, and to them meaningless, territorial boundaries and the laws of the Djibouti government, the Dankalis and the Issa continued to raid each other. The town of Djibouti was, however, an island of security and relative prosperity due to the presence of a few thousand French administrators and soldiers and the revenue brought by the railway and the harbour. Attracted to the town from the countryside and from British Somaliland by employment opportunities, the Issa formed the 'proletariat' of Djibouti. The town's middle class was made up of several thousands of Arab and Indian merchants and 'petits blancs', whereas the administrators, the officers of the local garrison and their dependants were considered the aristocracy.

The more sophisticated Somalis of Djibouti became involved in politics before the Dankalis. But although their leaders opposed the 'French union' in the 1958 referendum, they failed to achieve a majority (significantly, their leader Muhammad Harbi escaped to Cairo). Shortly after Somalia became independent the French enclave emerged as a bone of contention between Somalia and Ethiopia. As relations with Ethiopia continued to deteriorate in the early 1960s the future of French Somaliland became a crucial issue for Somali politicians. But in contrast to areas in Ethiopia and Kenya claimed by the Somalis, and despite her being called 'French Somaliland', the majority (although small) of the original inhabitants of the territory were Afar (Dankalis) related to tribes on the Eritrean coast, which has now been administratively absorbed into Ethiopia proper. Although nominally Muslims, the southern Afar's animosity toward the Somali tribes was always strong and they were opposed to any attempt to unify the French territory with Somalia. Incensed by Somali demonstrations on his visit to Djibouti in 1966 President de Gaulle promised Emperor Haile Selassie that France would keep the territory despite Somali pressure;[71] he no doubt also took into account Djibouti's strategic and economic value in relation to the Suez Canal, and its valuable potential as an asset in Indian Ocean politics. A referendum by the French in 1967 produced a 60% majority in favour of maintaining links with France. (Thousands of 'foreign' Somalis had previously been deported to the Somali Republic and Ethiopia.) The Arab and Indian communities in Djibouti believed that their safety depended on the continuation of a French presence in the territory, and the Dankalis preferred French rule to annexation by Somalia or Ethiopia. Significantly, the territory was immediately afterwards renamed 'the French Territory of the Afar and the Issa' (TFAI).

After independence, in 1960, Somalia's relations with Ethiopia gradually deteriorated into a limited war as a consequence of the support given by Somali politicians to the plan for a 'Greater Somalia'. The Somali Republic, with its population of 3 million, was no match however for Ethiopia, with her population of 25 million and an army then considered the strongest in Black Africa. The balance of power in the 'Horn' gradually changed in the coming years as an outcome of Russia's politics in the region and the quantities of relatively modern arms which it supplied to the Somali Republic and the Sudan.[72]

Prime Minister Ibrahim Egal, who defeated his rivals in the 1968 elections in Somalia, came to power on a platform of a détente with Ethiopia (and Kenya). Nevertheless, the Front for the Liberation of the Somali Coast (FLCS) began to operate in Djibouti and in May 1968 tried to assassinate members of the Executive Committee of the TFAI. Offices of this movement, as well as of the Front for the Liberation of Western Somalia and the ELF, continued to function in Mogadishu and were probably representative of the still strong anti-Ethiopian and pan-Somali feelings in the Republic. While the military régime which took over in Mogadishu in 1969 continued to profess its intention of maintaining the détente with Ethiopia, several high-ranking Somali-delegations visited the Sudan in 1970 'to discuss matters of common interest'. It was widely rumoured that the two countries had agreed to co-operate against Ethiopia in the event of war over Eritrea or the TFAI. Abandoned by his American allies and conscious of the gathering storm, Haile Selassie, *inter alia*, visited Paris to clarify the French attitude and plans concerning the TFAI.

Some terrorist activities attributed to the FLCS, occurred in Djibouti during 1969–70. By this time, France's policy was changing; a new situation had developed and President Pompidou, who came to office in 1969, did not consider himself bound by President de Gaulle's promises to the Ethiopian Emperor. Following the Six Day War and the closure of the Suez Canal Djibouti's immediate importance had declined whereas the political situation in, and around, Ethiopia was deteriorating and the claim to Djibouti by the Muslim Somali Democratic Republic was now supported by many Arab countries. The French Government, very aware of its good Arab connections, was anxious not to be involved in a possible conflict in the Horn of Africa. France then decided to abandon the TFAI if tension in the area should continue to grow. Haile Selassie was blandly told that if hostilities broke out France would not retain the TFAI. Enraged, the emperor reiterated previous threats that TFAI was 'an integral part of Ethiopia' and once the foreign imperialists had left it would be taken by the Ethiopian army. By the end of 1970 there was no doubt that the balance of power in the Horn of Africa had shifted. Her request for modern arms ignored by her Western allies, Ethiopia's situation seemed unenviable. At this point, the Ethiopian division in Eritrea, reinforced from Ethiopia proper, opened an all-out campaign against the ELF. It met with great success partly due to the internal, personal and ideological crisis which paralysed the ELF. In addition, Ethiopian political initiatives and developments in the region during 1971 eroded the support several Arab and non-Arab countries had given to the ELF. Above all the Sudan, preoccupied with its own problems, completely reversed her policy towards Ethiopia and moved closer.[73] Left to themselves, the Somalis, at least for a time, no longer dared challenge Ethiopia.[74]

From mid-1971 French policy shifted again. The crisis in the Horn of Africa had been defused by Haile Selassie. The Afars had in the meantime consolidated their position in TFAI's government, the FLCS was inactive and the Somali population was co-operating with the authorities. Having mended her fences with NATO and after considering her growing interest in the Gulf and the Indian Ocean, France once more gave higher priority to Djibouti.[75] As both Somalis and Ethiopians would rather have France in TFAI than fight over that area, as would certainly be the case following a French withdrawal, the French could safely declare 'that TFAI is an integral part of France'.[76] With their neighbours neutralised and ELF's power in decline, the immediate threat to Ethiopia was temporarily scotched.

But what would happen if the policy of the Sudan or of France in the TFAI were to change yet again? Ethiopia, and to a certain extent, Israel and Saudi Arabia now saw the writing on the wall. They consider that the United States is determined to disengage herself from the Red Sea area. Strategically and economically the Red Sea has lost much of its importance to the West.

Even if the Suez Canal were reopened it would be of little military value to the United States which, logically, should prefer it to remain closed. Although the West's dependence on Gulf oil will probably continue to grow despite North Sea and Alaskan oil, supertankers rounding the Cape and possibly transcontinental pipe-lines (through the Soviet Union, Syria or Turkey) could carry most of the oil consumed by Europe. Thus, attempts (mainly Soviet) to establish a position of power in the Red Sea would be unlikely to meet with serious Western opposition so long as they did not threaten the flow of oil from the Persian Gulf to world markets or endanger peace in the region. The visit to Moscow in June 1972 of the Ethiopian foreign minister and of the Emperor in 1973 marked a change of policy in recognition of this new state of affairs as does the alleged willingness of the United States to supply a limited quantity of modern arms to Ethiopia in view of the more sophisticated weaponry supplied by the Soviet Union to Somalia since 1972 and the renewed tension between Somalia and Ethiopia.[77]

Geopolitics of Oil

Besides the importance of the Red Sea as a maritime route, the Soviet Union became interested in the region as a consequence of her involvement in the Middle East and belief that aid to developing countries (especially military aid), would promote her influence. After 1964, when the *Polaris* A3, with a range of 2,500 nautical miles, became operational, Soviet naval experts realised the strategic importance of the Gulf of Aden.[78] Moreover, the region was also important, especially after 1968 and the reversal of Britain's East of Suez policy, because of its proximity to the Persian Gulf.

The Persian Gulf countries control more than half of the world's proven oil reserves. They supply about 60% of Europe's oil, 90% of Japan's and will be supplying a growing percentage of American oil consumption in the future. At the present rate of growth of oil consumption the Soviet Union too will soon become a net importer of oil. Exploitation of the substantial Siberian resources will be complicated and exeedingly costly,[79] though the Soviet Union often disregards economic considerations in order to avoid spending scarce foreign currency. As against this, Iranian natural gas flowing to

Europe through the Soviet pipe-line is paid for relatively easily by Soviet goods and factories set up in Persia. The Soviet Union is contemplating building an oil pipe-line from Persia to Europe. Notwithstanding Libya's hostile attitude the Soviet Union signed in May 1972 an agreement to purchase oil from BP's Sarir field, nationalised by the Libyans. The Soviet–Iraqi agreement of April 1972 provides for the expansion of the extraction and marketing of oil by the Soviet Union from the Rumeila field, nationalised some years ago. Although the Soviet Union was probably not consulted, it is doubtful whether Iraq would have nationalised IPC's Kirkuk field without such an assurance. It is claimed that the Soviet Union's interest in Middle Eastern oil *per se*, was one of the main factors behind Soviet policy in the region; and it is also widely accepted that the Soviet Union welcomes, if not encourages, the recent developments in the Middle Eastern oil industry. Although she would not be able to absorb all the oil produced by fields recently nationalised by Arab countries, the Soviet Union has already changed her policy regarding the supply of oil to Comecon countries.[80] Soviet activities in the Middle East have enabled the Soviet Union to acquire relatively cheap oil, paid for with Soviet investment goods and weapons, to expand her oil exports and to drive a wedge into the former Western predominance in the region. Significantly a Soviet flotilla sailed into Umm Qasir immediately after the Soviet–Iraqi agreement was signed.

There is surely some relationship between these developments and Soviet activity in the Indian Ocean and Red Sea. There was a time when every Soviet move was attributed to some carefully prepared diabolical plan. Today, the opposite is the case and it is sometimes overlooked that the Soviet Union is still competing for power and strategic advantages whenever, and wherever, the opportunity arises, and especially in areas, like the Middle East or Southern Asia, which are within reach of her influence.[81] Most military analysts belittle the role of conventional navies and the Victorian system of 'showing the flag'; and Soviet experiences in Egypt and the Sudan tend to reinforce these impressions. Nevertheless, the Soviet Union owes at least some of her influence and recognition by the West as an equal in the Mediterranean to the presence and growth of her fleet there. It looks as if the Soviet Union is trying to achieve a similar status by comparable methods in the western part of the Indian Ocean. It is true that her forces there are far smaller than those in the Mediterranean and that her posture as champion of the underdog is far more ambiguous in the Persian Gulf than the Levant and Arab North Africa, and potentially is even untenable. But the West has also less strength in the Indian Ocean and is identified with conservativism both in the Gulf and the Horn of Africa. Without the necessity of resorting to force, the Soviet navy in the north western Indian Ocean reminds the West that its former monopoly of power in the region lies broken. Whatever Western policy regarding the area may be in the future, it will have to take into account both Soviet actions and interests.

From this point of view, influence in the countries of the Red Sea and the Gulf of Aden, though it may seem marginal to the situation in the Persian Gulf, is nevertheless important to Soviet policy. Its potential would have been still plainer without the débâcle in the Sudan and Egypt and might become so again if Ethiopia were to look in future for patronage to Moscow rather than to Washington. Such influence helps to shape the milieu, in Arnold Wolfers' phrase, of regional politics. This has its parallel in naval terms. There was a pause in the growth of the Soviet naval presence in the Mediterranean between the first appearance of Soviet ships there in 1964, and the subsequent increase in the naval presence after 1968. It is possible that there is something like this in the north-west Indian Ocean and Red Sea today. The Soviet Union has an interest in preparing for the next phase and does so in certain ways in conditions harder than those in the Mediterranean in the late 1960s.[82]

The Soviet navy still does not have the independence and freedom of action which aircraft carriers have given to the American and, to a lesser extent, other Western navies. In the east (though not west) Mediterranean, it has been able to compensate for this by the use of air bases in Syria and, until recently, Egypt. (Present developments may lead to at least a partial renewal of Soviet privileges in Egypt.) This small Soviet flotilla in the Indian Ocean lacks this support. If a 30,000 ton total draught weight vessel, being built by the Soviet Union in the Black Sea, is the prototype of an aircraft carrier, we may be on the verge of a new era in Soviet naval strategy. But to build a sufficient number of carriers will take 7 to 10 years, at least. In the near future the Soviet Union in the Red Sea and Indian Ocean will lack air cover. 'Facilities' in the Red Sea and Gulf of Aden are therefore potentially useful. They could become even more so if the Suez Canal were to be reopened and the Soviet Union could rotate ships between the Mediterranean and Indian Ocean by way of the Red Sea.

The Soviet Union, as a responsible world power, with interests in the Middle East, would be the last to wish for hostilities to break out in the Red Sea, especially in a period of rapprochement with the West. Moreover, it has to take account of a number of competing influences. Hostilities in the Red Sea, especially directed against Israel, or if they seemed potentially to put Western oil supplies in disarray, could bring American attack carriers into the area. There are signs that the United States is becoming increasingly uneasy about Soviet activities and, even before the Soviet–Iraqi agreement was signed in April 1972, was inclined to reassert her interests, at least in the Gulf. The leasing of Diego Garcia from Britain, the basing agreement with Bahrain and the sale to Iran (and to some extent to Saudi Arabia) of very large quantities of arms, particularly Phantoms, followed by visits from American military and political leaders to Saudi Arabia and Iran, all point to that conclusion.[83] The renewed concern of France to remain in the TFAI and, if confirmed, to patrol with some combat vessels in the Indian Ocean, would point modestly in the same direction.[84]

While the West nevertheless remains essentially reconciled to Soviet activities in the Red Sea and the Gulf of Aden, China seems to be trying to undermine the Soviet position there. In spite of her new dialogue with the United States, she may even exploit (and in fact is already doing so) the Arab–Israeli conflict as a lever against the Soviet Union. China does not have, however, the economic and technical resources to provide an alternative to the Soviet Union. Impressive as they look, her aid programmes and loans take long to materialise and consist principally of labour, construction materials and Chinese-made goods. Some Arab (including Egyptian) politicians, are keen to expolit the Sino–Soviet rivalry. More responsible ones, aware of China's limitations, realise that this could prove to be a dangerous experiment at a time when the Arabs are heavily dependent on Soviet support and aid. They also realise that the Chinese may have ulterior motives in using Arab nationalism and not be wholly reliable. China's influence in most Arab and non-Arab countries of the Red Sea littoral should not be, therefore, overestimated. At present, it is difficult to determine whether China's policy in the Red Sea and its environs is influenced by ideology or whether, like the Soviet Union, China has become pragmatic and opportunistic. Besides, her rivalry with the Soviet Union and the quest for power and influence, China may also have an eye on Arab oil, which she might have to import in future.[85]

Soviet aspirations in the Red Sea are also meeting with mounting resistance from Arab nationalism. Libya and the Sudan accuse the Soviet Union of neo-colonialism and together with Saudi Arabia, though for different reasons, they wish to see the Soviet Union out of the Red Sea.[86] Egypt, which may have wished in the past for some sort of Soviet naval presence in the Red Sea (during the war of attrition) has gradually become uneasy about Russia's presence and aims in the area,[87] and the YAR, having become more dependent on Saudi Arabia, and fearing the Soviet Union's massive support to PDRY, would prefer to see the Russians leave the Red Sea altogether. Even 'progressive' PDRY and Iraq, dependent on Soviet aid, are uneasy about the Soviet presence in the Red Sea because it might interfere with their plans concerning Israel and the Horn of Africa. Since the beginning of 1972 'revolutionary' Arab countries, notably Libya, Iraq and the PDRY, have been trying to revive tension in the Horn of Africa probably as part of the new Arab strategy towards Israel.[88] Trying to exploit Somalia's financial difficulties and her partial disillusionment with Soviet aid before Marshal Gretchko's visit, the 'revolutionary' Arab countries incited her to take a firmer stand on her plans for a 'Greater Somalia' and thus revive the pressure on Ethiopia and France.

Ethiopia is well aware of the fact that the basic problems which led to the 1970–71 crisis are latent and have not really vanished. Some Ethiopian intellectuals and younger government officials are of the opinion that their country should disengage from her ties with the United States and Israel and develop relations with 'progressive' Arab and non-Arab countries.[89] But though she tries to improve relations with moderate Arab countries, Ethiopia's government remains suspicious of 'progressive' countries. Moreover, the majority of Ethiopia's Christians doubt that the Muslim countries will truly change their hostile attitude to a Christian kingdom in their midst which is the source of most of the Nile's water.[90] Partly as a result of the *détente* with Ethiopia, which led to the termination of the southern Sudan rebellion, Sudan has been strengthening her African orientation. If, however, General Numeiri's government which has lost much of its popular support, were to be overthrown and the new régime were to renew its support to the ELF, Ethiopia, which successfully exploited the southern Sudanese rebellion in the past, might find herself in a more difficult situation even than in 1970–71, especially due to its mounting internal instability.

The fragile peace in the Horn of Africa and the Red Sea also depends to a large extent on whether France continues to hold on to the TFAI. So long as the French remain in Djibouti, the possibility of war between Ethiopia and its neighbours greatly diminishes. Moreover, as long as the African side of Bab al-Mandeb is not controlled by the Arabs or Somalia, imposing a blockade against Israeli shipping would be complicated and even impossible. But France values her special relations with the Arabs from which she has benefited both economically and politically. There is always a possibility that she might again reverse her policy in TFAI rather than endanger relations with the Arabs.

A renewal of a war of attrition between Israel and the Arabs and its likely expansion to Bab al-Mandeb depends on whether Egypt joins the activists' camp. In spite of certain threats made by President Sadat, the uneasy peace in the Middle East continues.[91] With the plans for the construction of two oil pipelines between the Gulf of Suez and Alexandria, and with more Egyptian oil shipped through the Red Sea to East Africa and Asia, Egypt could become just as vulnerable here as Israel. However, there is always the possibility that the internal situation in Egypt might deteriorate to the point where the activists overthrow Sadat and those who support some form of peaceful settlement.

Israel went to war in 1956 and 1967 partly because her interests in the Red Sea were threatened, and partly because her credibility, considered a safeguard to her very existence, was put in question by the closing of the Suez Canal and the Straits of Tiran. Her material interests in the Red Sea have grown substantially since the Six Day War. An Arab attempt to interfere with Israeli shipping in the Red Sea would impel Israel to take military action. Obviously this was the reason why Israel demonstrated, and indirectly publicised, her ability to protect her shipping by striking beyond Upper Egypt and Bab al-Mandeb. Such a confrontation is probably fairly remote. It would require a concatenation of very diverse circumstances and a loss of control by the Soviet Union for such a conflict to break out against the interests of all the major maritime nations, the Soviet Union included. Nevertheless, it is not inconceivable. In the nature of things, a conflict which stretched through the Red Sea to the Gulf of Aden and possibly affected large areas of the Arabian Peninsula, with all its oil, could have even more dangerous implications for the world economy and world peace than any of the three Arab–Israeli wars of the past.

Notes

1. *Mois en Afrique*, January 1971, 'Ethiopie'; Bruce Oudes, View Point, in *Africa Report*, May 1971; Raouf el Gammal, *The Plain Truth*, January 1972.
2. Oudes, *op. cit.* J. F. Campbell, 'Rumblings along the Red Sea', in *Foreign Affairs*, April 1970.
3. Diego Garcia. Bruce Oudes, *op. cit. The Times*, 26 February 1971. *Ha'aretz* (Israel), 19 January 1971.
4. J. F. Campbell, 'The Red Sea', in *Survival*, August 1971, p. 274.
5. Stephen Page, *The USSR and Arabia* (London: Central Asian Research Centre, 1971), chapter 1.
6. Page, *op. cit.*, pp. 37, 48–9.
7. Page, *op. cit.*, p. 80.
8. Page, *op. cit.*, p. 75. The Russians gave priority to the Hodeida complex. 650 experts were employed in the port and other projects—see Page, *op. cit.*, p. 89.
9. See, for example, on Soviet Military Aid: *Jerusalem Post*, 14 November 1969; *Al-Hayat* (Beirut) 11 March 1972; *Al-Bilad* (Saudi Arabia) 17 December 1969; *Arab Report and Record* July 1970; *Egyptian Gazette* 14 April 1971, 29 April 1971; *Frankfurter Allgemeine Zeitung (FAZ)*, 17

April 1971, 16 April 1972, 5 May 1972; *The Observer* (London), 9 January 1972; *Sunday Telegraph*; *The Guardian* 15 March 1972; *Le Monde* 31 May 1972.

Internal Security (mainly East Germany): *Daily Telegraph* 11 December 1970, 18 May 1972; *The Times* (London) 2 January 1971; *Financial Times* (London), 13 January 1971; *FAZ* 5 May 1972; FBIS see note 16, 14 January 1972; Radio Aden, 13 January 1972.

Communications: *Commerce de Levant*, 26 June 1971, 7 July 1971; IMF/IDA/R71–13, 1 April 1971; *Le Monde Diplomatique* 26 June 1972; BBC (Economic Report), 19 January 1972; Radio Aden, 18 January 1972; BBC, 11 April 1972; ANA, 26 March 1972; *Financial Times* (London) 13 January 1971 (airfields).

Aid and Loans (East German): East Germany in 1970 $3 million (for industry) and $3 million in 1971 (for telephone system), ANA, 11 October 1971. Bulgarian loan of $5 million, ANA, 27 July 1971. It is impossible to evaluate the aid programmes of East European countries and the information concerning Soviet aid in different fields is confusing.

10. One-third as a grant and about two-thirds low interest long-term loans. *Le Monde*, 10 February 1972; *FAZ*, 2 May 1972. Eric Rouleau in *Le Monde*, 31 May 1972 mentions the figure £25 million.

11. On details of military aid; *Sunday Times* (London), 12 December 1970; *The Observer* (London), 9 January 1972; *Sunday Telegraph* (London), 5 March 1972.

12. Foreign journalists were flown over the Island of Socotra to disprove claims that there were military installations on this island.

13. *Christian Science Monitor*, 11 April 1972. Also: *Al-Hayat* (Lebanon), 14 March 1972; *Al-Bilad* (Saudi Arabia), 17 December 1969; *Sunday Times*, 12 December 1970; *Ha'aretz* (Israel), 10 May 1971, according to *New York Times*.

14. *Al-Nahar* (Lebanon), 9 April 1972 (quotation marks in original text); Geoffrey Jukes, *The Indian Ocean in Soviet Naval Policy*, Adelphi Paper No. 87 (London: IISS, 1972), p. 18 is sceptical of the naval uses of the Soviet fishing fleets in the region. See also chapter 2, 'Crisis in Southern Arabia'.

15. Cf. Soviet interest in Perim (*Arab Report and Record*, 21 March 1971, p. 178) which may be connected with the shelling of the French destroyers which approached the island in March 1972.

16. *Christian Science Monitor*, 23 January 1971: *Le Monde Diplomatique*, 4 June 1971, p. 4; *Neues Deutschland*, 19 August 1971; BBC Monitoring, Middle East and Africa, 15 October 1971, radio Mogadishu, 13 October 1971; *Daily Telegraph*, 4 November 1971; Foreign Broadcasting Information Service 15 'December 1971, radio Hargeisa, 12 December 1971, on Somali–Soviet naval manoeuvres in the area of Berbera following the completion of the project.

17. *Daily Telegraph*, 5 January 1971, 4 November 1971; *CSM*, 23 January 1971; *Ha'aretz*, 7 April 1972 according to Hanson Baldwin in *New York Times*; *The Times* (London), 19 May 1972, 2 November 1972.

18. Of a military HQ and naval base built by the Russians not far from the Kenyan border possibly to serve their activities in this part of the Indian Ocean—*The Times* (London), 19 May 1972. Of 33 oil storage tanks the Soviets are constructing 15 near Berbera, 10 near Kisimayu and 8 near Mogadishu—BBC, 4 January 1972; Radio Mogadishu, 4 December 1971.

19. *Daily Telegraph*, 4 November 1971; Peter Stewart, *The Listener* (London), 12 November 1970—2 Soviet warships appeared off Mogadishu when there was a threat of an upheaval in Somali's government in October 1970.

20. For instance: *Pravda*, 15 September 1970; BBC economic report, 18 January 1972; Radio Mogadishu, 11 January 1972; *Neues Deutschland*, 19 August 1971.

21. Russia agreed to finance part of the £50 million Juba irrigation and hydro-electric project—BBC, 14 December 1971; Radio Mogadishu, 14 December 1971.

22. FBIS, 2 December 1971, radio Mogadishu, 30 November 1971; *Al-Usbu' al-'Arabi* (Lebanon), 22 November 1971, alleges that Siyad discussed in Moscow and Cairo, 'among other things, Somalia's role in the Red Sea strategy'.

23. BBC, 21 February 1972; Radio Mogadishu, 18 February 1972. In a speech before leaving Mogadishu, Marshal Gretchko claimed that the Soviet Union and Somalia 'were now linked by strong, excellent and deep-rooted ties'—BBC, 18 February 1972; Radio Mogadishu, 16 February 1972.

24. *The Military Balance, 1972–73*, (London: IISS), p. 39. Somali ports are those most frequently visited by the Soviet navy in the region, see Adelphi Paper by G. Jukes, *op. cit.*, p. 16. On Soviet (strategic?) 'line' stretching between the Horn of Africa and Aden, see Muhammad Hasnein Haykal, weekly column, *Al-Ahram*, 27 October 1972. On new Soviet arms delivered to Somalia see *JP*, 11 April 1973, according to *NYT*.

25. *Ha'aretz* (Israel), 19 March 1970, 13 April 1970, 21 January 1971; *Ma'riv* (Israel), 29 May 1970, 26 March 1971; *Time*, 1 March 1971; W. Scherndorff, 'East European Countries in Forefront of Soviet Aid in the Third World', in *Bulletin of the Institute for the Study of USSR*, Vol. XVIII, February 1972, No. 2.

26. See for instance: *Süddeutsche Zeitung*, 22 January 1971; *New Middle East*, April 1971, p. 33, according to *Neue Züricher Zeitung*'s (*NZZ*) correspondent; *Jerusalem Post*, 2 June 1971, according to Elias Nagib (Beirut OFNS).

27. See *inter alia*, *Al-Hawadith* (weekly, Beirut), 3–4 June 1972.

28. *Al-Ayyam* (Khartoum), 11 August 1971; BBC, 16 June 1971. Radio Umdurman, 14 June 1971; *Financial Times Supplement*, 23 November 1971; General Numeiri's speech—FBIS, 20 December 1971; Radio Umdurman, 17 December 1971.

29. According to *Al-Hawadith* (Beirut), 3–4 June 1972, Soviet experts in 'Port Sudan' and elsewhere are being phased out by the Sudanese government.

30. *Egyptian Gazette*, 13 July 1971; *Nida al-Wattan* (Lebanon), 17 February 1972; *L'Orient le Jour* (Lebanon), 15–16 February 1972.
31. All these privileges were withdrawn in October 1972 as a result of political differences between Egypt and Sudan concerning Arab politics and the more African-oriented policy of Numairi.
32. *The Times* (London), 24 March 1972.
33. *The Times* (London), 17 May 1972. See also *Financial Times* (London), 19 May 1972, on new USSR–Egypt arms.
34. *Jerusalem Post*, 11 February 1972.
35. *Jerusalem Post*, 22 March 1972; Radio Cairo, 20 March 1972. Russians undertook to expand Safaga port which was attacked by the Israeli Air Force during the war of attrition—*Arab Report and Record* 1971, p. 588; *Ruz al-Yusuf* (Egypt, weekly) 3 January 1972.
36. *Daily Telegraph* (London), 6 January 1972—The Aswan base was used by the USSR for reconnaissance flights as far as the Indian Ocean. *Ha'aretz* (Israel), 27–28 January 1972, reported that Egyptian officers were complaining at not being allowed into two new airfields between Aswan and the Sudanese border. Also see Arnold Hottinger, *Swiss Review of International Affairs*, August 1971, pp. 4–5.
37. Soviet boats visiting Port Louis in Mauritius quadrupled between 1967 and 1971—see Jack P. Mener, L'Expansion Soviétique dans l'Océan indien', in *International Problems*, June 1971. By 1971 one out of four ships rounding the Cape was Russian, even though the cost of sending Soviet vessels around the Cape must be high—Neville Brown, 'Soviet Naval Expansion', in *New Middle East*, March 1971.
38. There are signs to the contrary. *Christian Science Monitor*, 25 September 1972, *Ma'riv* (Israel), 26 September 1972, according to *Aviation Week*.
39. *Ha'aretz*, 1 November 1972, according to UP, London, 31 October 1972. This trend in Soviet policy is further strengthened by the re-establishment of relations with the Sudan and renewal of some aid programmes as reported at the end of October 1972, despite continuous Sudanese persecution of local Communists—*Jerusalem Post*, 30 October 1972, according to AP, Khartoum.
40. For instance West Germany's Defence Minister Helmut Schmidt—*Daily Telegraph*, 31 November 1971.
41. The Russians are gradually becoming the main supporters of PFLOAG, see for instance: *Al-Hayat*, 11 March 1972, *Al-Nahar*, 9 April 1972.
42. *Ha'aretz* (Israel), 17 March 1972.
43. NCNA, 31 July 1971, 8 August 1971; *JP*, 20 July 1972 (according to AP); MENA (Cairo), 28 July 1972; *FT*, 8 August 1972.
44. *Daily Telegraph*, 11 October 1971; *The Guardian*, 11 October 1971; *International Herald Tribune*, 11 October 1971. The last two sources speak of $150 million.
45. According to Eric Rouleau (*Le Monde*, 31 June 1972), $60 million. Also: *Daily Telegraph*, 8 May 1972; *FAZ*, 2 May 1972. See also chapter 2 'Crisis in Southern Arabia'.
46. In view of China's new relationship with Ethiopia it is unlikely that

it would build the strategically oriented road-network between Hargeisa and the Ethiopian border.

47. *The Guardian* (London), 13 May 1971. Because of Soviet pressure, the loan was only partly used.

48. FBIS, 21 December 1971; AFP, 20 December 1971; FBIS, 23 December 1971; Radio Khartoum, 21 December 1971; *Egyptian Gazette*, 10 April 1972.

49. BBC broadcasts in Arabic, 17 April 1972 according to radio Umdurman. On Chinese military aid—*Al-Hawadith* (Beirut, weekly), 3–4 June 1972.

50. *Sunday Times*, 23 July 1972; *Ha'aretz* (according to AFP), 1 October 1972; *Ma'riv* (Irsael), 9 January 1973, 8 April 1973; *International Herald Tribune*, 13 March 1973.

51. On the growth of this trade—*Ha'aretz*, 24 April 1972; *Financial Times* (London), 2 June 1972. The volume of trade through Eilat in 1971 exceeded 600,000 tons, *Ha'aretz*, 8 June 1971, 18 February 1972.

52. The Eilat–Ashkelon pipe-line is expected to carry 45 million tons of oil a year as early as 1973; and tenders have been invited for a further expansion of the oil terminal in Ashkelon. *Ha'aretz* (Israel), 6 November 1972.

53. *Ha'aretz*, 30 June 1972, according to Dr. Z. Dinstein, Deputy Minister of Finance who claimed that Israel's investments in the oil sector in the coming decade will amount to $526 million.

54. *The Times* (London), 21 March 1972, 1 May 1972, 16 May 1972; *Financial Times* (London), 22 March 1972, 18 April 1972, 1 May 1972.

55. For example the nationalisation of IPC's Kirkuk field and pipe-line by Iraq and Syria.

56. *IHT*, 16 November 1967.

57. The attack on the *Coral Sea* was probably an isolated incident initiated by radical Palestinians. But these may have been in collusion with a certain element in the PDRY government known for its extreme position on the Palestine question. The PDRY has been threatening to stop Israeli shipping at Bab al-Mandeb ever since the British evacuated Aden—*International Herald Tribune*, 16 November 1967. When the North Yemenis occupied the islands of Kamran, a few miles off their coast, from the PDRY, they apparently found there a large guerrilla training centre and an arsenal valued at several million dollars alleged to belong to the ELF and financed by Libya—*Jerusalem Post* 18 October 1972, according to AP (Beirut), *Ha'aretz*, 11 October 1972 etc.

58. Raouf el Gammal, *The Plain Truth*, January 1972; *Al-Hadaf* (Lebanon), 8 January 1972; *Financial Times* (London), 1 April 1972. Sadat's speech—*Al-Anwar* (Lebanon), 5 April 1972. Haykal, *Al-Ahram*, 27 October 1972.

59. This is one of the Straits where the extension of territorial limits at sea to 12 miles could have the most explosive potential effects.

60. Evidence of Soviet sensitivity to American and Israeli reaction to the attack on *Coral Sea*—radio Moscow (in Russian), MAYAK, 17 June 1971. Attack on the *Coral Sea* and report that a Soviet warship signalled the Israeli vessel *Natanya* to identify itself near Bab al-Mandeb brought

CIA's director Richard Helms, to Israel—*Christian Science Monitor*, 1 July 1971.

61. On their way from France the *Sa'ar* boats are said to have been refuelled in mid-sea. In this way their range could be extended beyond 800 miles. *Jerusalem Post*, 21 March 1972; *Ha'aretz*, 21 March 1972; Radio Moscow (in Russian) MAYAK, 17 June 1971; *Financial Times*, 1 April 1972—on President Sadat's speech in which he accused the United States of deploying FPB's near Bab al-Mandeb; FBIS, 14 January 1972; Radio Baghdad, 13 January 1972.

62. *Al-Ahram*, 15.6.71; *Kul-Shai* (Lebanon), 11.9.71; *Al-Kifah* (Lebanon), 3.11.71; *Al Ba'th* (Damascus), 18.1.72; *G*, 10.3.72; FBIS, 14.1.72; Radio Baghdad, 13.1.72; *JP* (according to Reuters Beirut), 13.7.72; *T*, 17.8.72; *Daily Express* (London), 24.4.73; *Observer*, 13.5.73.

63. INA quotes Radio Baghdad, 18.10.71; MENA (Cairo), 1.12.71; BBC, 21.1.72; radio Baghdad, 27.1.72; *M*, 21.1.72; MENA (Cairo), 19.1.72; *JP*, 4.6.72.

64. *JP*, 4.6.72.

65. Muhammad Hassanain Haykal's weekly column in *Al-Ahram*, 4.7.69, 27.10.72; Sadat's speech—*FT*, 1.4.72.

66. To unite all the areas largely inhabited by Somali-speaking peoples such as south-eastern Ethiopia, NFD of Kenya and the TFAI with the Somali Republic.

67. Ironically, part of Eritrea was the seat of the ancient kingdom of Ethiopia.

68. See chapter 4, 'Conflict in the Horn of Africa'.

69. The drawing off of even 10% of Ethiopia's water to irrigate areas on the Sudan frontier could create a life-and-death crisis for Egypt; and Ethiopia has not dared carry out irrigation plans.

70. D. Laporte, *Revue de Défense Nationale*, July, 1971, p. 1131; *FT*, 20.5.69; *L'Unità*, 12.9.70; *T*, 10.5.70, 2.1.71, 26.2.71; *NZZ*, 12.5.70; *Time Magazine*, 1.3.71; BBC, 10.7.71, Damascus SNA, 8.7.71; *Atlas*, February, 1972, p. 4.

71. Ethiopia considers the TFAI part of her territory and would fight for it if France left.

72. See chapter 4, 'Conflict in the Horn of Africa'.

73. See chapter 4.

74. The discovery of natural gas and possibly oil in Ethiopia not far from the Somali border at a time when Somalia was supplied with quantities of modern Soviet arms is the cause of the renewed tension between the two countries which emerged in the first half of 1973. Evidently Libya is partly responsible for this new crisis. *JP* (according to the *NYT*), 11.4.73; *Daily Express*, 24.4.73; *Africa Confidential*, 1973, Vol. 14, No. 8; *Observer*, 13.5.73. Of a new Libyan co-ordinated campaign against Ethiopia involving the ELF, Somalia and the OAU see: *JP* (UP Beirut), 18.10.72; *Ma'riv*, 9.5.73, as well as the other sources mentioned above.

75. For instance, *DT*, 29.11.71; MENA (Cairo), 17.2.72. *The Jerusalem Post*, 7.5.72, quoting the Afrikaans newspaper *Di Oosterlig* reported the

French Military Attache in South Africa as saying that the French now had ten to twelve modern warships sailing in the Indian Ocean, more than any country including the super-powers. The build-up was being undertaken, the Attaché was alleged to have said, to oppose the Russians and meet obligations towards certain French-speaking nations in Africa. The ships do not seem in fact to have been part of a permanent squadron in the area.

76. For the latest expression of this see Mesmer's speech, *M*, 3.2.72. The culmination of this process was President Pompidou's state visit to Ethiopia in January 1973, the strengthening and modernisation of the Djibouti garrison and the French fleet in the Indian Ocean. *Africa Research Bulletin*, Vol. 19, No. 12, 15.1.73, p. 2699a; *Mois en Afrique*, No. 86, February 1973, pp. 5–7; *Africa*, No. 19, March 1973, pp. 39–41.

77. Reports in the international press around the time of the emperor's visit to the US in May 1973.

78. Jukes, *op. cit.*, p. 4.

79. *Pravda*, 15.1.71

80. 'Why Middle East oil is vital to the Soviet Union' in *The Times*, 17.7.72.

81. However, so long as the Suez Canal is closed, the Arabian/Persian Gulf is one of the areas farthest from the USSR by sea—13,000 miles from Odessa, 16,000 miles from Vladivostok, 27,000 miles from Murmansk.

82. Reports on Soviet headquarters and communications centre, probably at Bir Gavo in Somalia, tend to support this view—*T*, 2.11.72; *JP* (according to *NYT*), 11.4.73.

83. On the growth of American interests in Oman and activities in the Gulf—INA, 24.4.72; *Al-Nahar* (Lebanon), 9.4.72; *Ha'aretz* (Israel), 9.4.72, 12.4.72; *Al-Anwar* (Lebanon), 3.5.72; *T*, 31.5.72.

84. More important, if confirmed, are the claims made by President Sadat and the Arab press about United States naval patrols in the Red Sea penetrating as far as Jedda in Saudi Arabia (*FT*, 1.4.72; Haykal in *Al-Ahram*, 27.10.72).

85. Recognition of the Gulf Emirates and the intensification of China's trade with Kuwait, could be an indication of this tendency.

86. This is consonant with Libya's opposition to the Soviet naval presence in the Mediterranean and to Soviet bases in Egypt. Libya helped Numeiri break the communist coup in July 1971.

87. See Haykal, *Al-Ahram*, 27.10.72.

88. Support to the ELF and Somali Liberation Front by the PDRY and Iraq—*Atlas*, February 1972; MENA (Cairo), 21.4.72; BBC (in Arabic), 20.4.72; *Al-Kifah* (Lebanon), 6.11.71; ANA, 16.4.72; MENA (Cairo), 21.4.72; INA, 24.4.72. On Libyan support to Somalia, the ELF and the PDRY's subversive activities—MENA, 19.1.72; AFP, 27.1.72; FBIS, 21.3.72, radio Mogadishu, 31.3.72; *Al-Nahar* (Lebanon), 4.5.72; *Ha'aretz*, 22.5.72; *JP*, (according to UP Beirut), 18.10.72, on a Libyan-financed ELF training camp in the Kamran islands; *JP*, 22.3.73 (AP Addis Ababa); *Daily Express*, 24.4.73; on Libyan financial support to Somalia to acquire modern arms; *Observer*, 13.5.73, on the

Islamic conference decision (in Tripoli) to support the ELF and Libya's support of this organisation. Numerous reports in the world press in May 1973 on Libya's attempt to transfer the OAU summit meeting from Addis Ababa.

89. For instance, Taye Germaw, 'Rebellion in Eritrea', *NME*, April 1971.
90. Ethiopia has a large Muslim minority which may even be a majority. It is no accident that there has been no census.
91. Many reports of Sadat's threats to renew the war of attrition appeared in the world press in 1972 and 1973.

IV

Conflict in the Horn of Africa

Many factors make the Horn of Africa potentially an ideal area for conflicts. Its population is extremely heterogeneous, both ethnically and culturally. The Christian kingdom of Ethiopia marks the southern border of the Arab world. She is nearly surrounded by Muslim countries and has her non-Christian population in the majority. The relatively rich plateau was always the target of incursions by pastoralists who inhabit the semi-circle of desert to the east and to the south. At present, Ethiopia controls a vital part of the Red Sea coast, has grazing areas crucial to tribes living in the Somali Republic and is the source of the two rivers which provide most of the water for the limited agriculture of Somalia. She is also the source of more than 70% of the water of the Nile upon which depends the very existence of its northern neighbours and especially Egypt.

The Ethiopian plateau rises dramatically from the torrid deserts of the coast. It enjoys a high average annual rainfall and, in spite of its proximity to the Equator, an extremely pleasant and mild climate. It is not surprising therefore that the plateau, with its natural defences, has throughout the centuries attracted many peoples of different linguistic and cultural features. The original inhabitants were submerged by waves of Cushitic–Hamitic immigrants who moved into the Horn of Africa thousands of years before Christ. Migrants from Arabia with languages belonging to the semitic group, began to reach the plateau and intermarry with its population in the first millennium B.C. The main recipients of the 'semitic' cultural influences were the people today called Amhara and Tigreans,[1] who from the fourth century A.D. became Christians and more or less dominated the history of Ethiopia. Ironically, the foundations of the kingdom of Ethiopia were laid in the area which now is partly Eritrean and which local secessionists wish to tear away from Ethiopia.

In the sixth and seventh centuries the northern tip of the plateau was overrun by the Hamitic Beja pastoralists and the centres of the Christian kingdom shifted southwards.

In the Horn of Africa, although Islam was adopted by Arab merchant communities and the pastoral tribes of the coast, it made little headway on the plateau until the second millennium A.D. The constant tension between the Christian kingdom and Muslim principalities had by the end of the fifteenth century assumed the form of a religious war. In the second quarter of the sixteenth century a jihad was declared against Ethiopia, the country was conquered and many of its inhabitants temporarily converted to Islam. Although relatively short, this conquest left bitter memories which still linger in the minds of Christian Ethiopians.

The confrontation between Muslim and Christian was exploited by the Hamitic Galla pastoralists, who moved into the fertile highlands from a semi-desert area to the southeast of the plateau. From the middle of the sixteenth century and until the nineteenth century, while the Ethiopian kingdom declined and the Muslim principalities disintegrated, the Galla overran and settled large parts of the Horn of Africa.

The revival and reunification of modern Ethiopia was initiated by the northern 'semitised' elements under Emperor Tewodros (1855–68). However, the great expansion of the kingdom was spearheaded by the Amhara of Shoa, whose blood is mixed with that of the Galla, and who were led by the founder of the present dynasty, Emperor Menelik II (1889–1916). In contrast with most African countries whose boundaries were delimited by Europeans during and after the scramble for Africa, the frontiers of present-day Ethiopia are mainly the outcome of Menelik's policy of expansion, which was accelerated in order to forestall European imperialism and to establish Ethiopia's 'historical boundaries'.

Even before its great expansion in the nineteenth century Ethiopia was far from homogeneous. Differences existed between the recipients of semitic influences and other Cushitic–Hamitic elements as well as between these two groups and remnants of the ancient negroid inhabitants of the highlands. Because of mutual toleration and cultural kinship, religious differences between Christian, Muslim and pagan were of secondary importance. The conquests of Menelik brought into the fold of the empire multitudes of pagan negroid tribes, Cushitic pagan and Muslim agriculturalists, and small groups of (Muslim) Dankali and Somali pastoralists. The number of the latter was, however, greatly augmented following the World War II border settlement and later when Eritrea was federated with Ethiopia. Although the growth of the proportion of Muslims in Ethiopia further complicated the traditional problems of a heterogeneous multi-religious society, the country was now faced with the additional problem of active secessionism.

Reliable statistics are hard to come by in Ethiopia, an area of half a million square miles, with a population of nearly 25 million. It is commonly believed that nearly 45% of the country's inhabitants are Christians, about 40% are Muslims and the balance, mainly Galla, are animists. The main semitised groups in Ethiopia, the Amhara[2] and the Tigreans, do not amount to more than 35% of the whole population with the Amhara accounting for about two-thirds of this group.[3] The Amhara and Tigreans, however, cannot be considered as a cohesive group because in addition to cultural and linguistic differences, the latter have always resented the predominant position achieved by the former. The largest ethnic group in Ethiopia is the Galla, who make up about 40% of the population, and they are lately becoming more and more aware of this.[4]

In some parts of the country the Galla have assimilated to various degrees with the Amhara, and in other parts with Muslims. But the majority of the Galla have preserved their language and many aspects of their original culture. This is especially true of the Galla of the southern provinces conquered by Menelik in the last decades of the nineteenth century. These provinces were divided as fiefs among his Shoan and Galla officers. With 80% of the population living at subsistence level and the per capita income in Ethiopia about $50 per annum (among the lowest in Africa), the condition of the farmers of southern Ethiopia is unenviable. In spite of the régime's efforts to proselytise the Galla heathens they resent their exploiters and many have adopted Islam as a form of protest. Others have resorted to rebellions, the most recent of which broke out in the province of Bale in the mid 1960s and was put down only over 1971–72.

The preservation of Ethiopia's integrity will depend in the future, to some extent, on the success of the government in reforming land ownership and in assimilating the Galla.[5] The Galla have nothing directly to do with the Eritrean liberation movement as very few Galla live in Eritrea. Indirectly however the Galla problem is crucial in the long run to what happens to Eritrea and to Ethiopia as a whole.

The Eritrean identity is a by-product of the colonial period, its roots lie in the fact that since the seventh century, except for short periods, the Ethiopian coast has been under Muslim control. The Christian highlanders always abhorred the torrid coast, despised merchants and never took to the sea. Only in the first half of the nineteenth century, as a result of Egyptian expansionism and European activities in the Red Sea basin, did Ethiopian rulers begin to consider the reconquest of the lost coastal areas.

The Ottomans, who captured part of the Ethiopian coast in the sixteenth century, leased their possession in the nineteenth century to Muhammad Ali of Egypt. He and especially his grandson Isma'il gradually expanded their government along the lowlands and into the northern corner of the plateau. Their occupation accelerated the process of Islamisation which had begun at the turn of the eighteenth century with the revival of Islam in Arabia and elsewhere.

Provoked by the Mahdist rebellion in the Sudan (1881–98) and in spite of promises made by the British to the Tigrean emperor of Ethiopia, Yohannis, the Italians established in 1885 their colony of Eritrea which included all the Ethiopian coast and the northern plateau previously held by Ethiopia. Even after his victory at Adowa in 1896 Emperor Menelik allowed the Italians to retain Eritrea, for political reasons. He also encouraged the French to develop French Somaliland and to build the Djibouti–Addis Ababa railway.

Under the Italians Eritrea developed and prospered. The Italian authorities and immigrants introduced modern systems of agriculture, industry and administration. The schools built in the colony produced a class of indigenous intelligentsia years before a similar class had emerged in Ethiopia. The roads and rail network built by the Italians in Eritrea are by far superior to those of Ethiopia. However, the pro-Muslim and pro-Arab policy of Fascist Italy further widened the gap between Muslim and Christian. Thus when the British took control of Eritrea in 1941, there already existed an Eritrean 'identity' (especially among the Muslims).

It is commonly believed that about half of Eritrea's 1·6 million inhabitants are Christian and about half Muslim. Such a description is, however, too general and misleading. Most Eritrean Christians are Tigreans who belong to the Ethiopian church and live south of Asmara (an extension of the Tigre province population). Among the Muslims about 400,000 are Tigre (not Tigrinya) speaking (mainly Bani 'Amr and related groups). Western and northern Eritrea, however, are also peopled by a wide spectrum of ethnic, religious and linguistic groups. Tigreans and Agew (Cushitic) moved into the northern tip of the plateau from about the fourteenth century. Some were assimilated with the local population, but others kept to themselves. Especially during the nineteenth century many were converted to Islam. Others, under the influence of missionaries, became Catholics or Protestants, while the Barya–Kunama negroid group between the Gash and Setit rivers is still partly animist. The pastoral Dankalis and the Shiho Muslims who, it is claimed, number about 300,000 live along Eritrea's coast. However, the highly fragmented and backward Dankali society does not with some exceptions consider itself Eritrean.

Following the collapse of the Italian empire in northeast Africa Ethiopia demanded the annexation of the Italian colonies which, she claimed, were part of 'historic Ethiopia'. The British also coveted the area as did the Soviet Union and Italy once it joined the allied camp. Hence in the immediate post-war period the future of Eritrea and Italian Somaliland remained unsettled and Britain continued to administer them.

While their future was being debated by the great nations the Eritreans were themselves divided about it. Many Christians favoured some sort of association with Ethiopia, while others, fearing Amhara domination, preferred independence. The Muslim Tigre-speakers were for independence, but some supported union with the Sudan. Yet even among Muslims some (mainly Tigreans) wished to renew the traditional ties with Ethiopia, whereas most Dankalis were indifferent to the future of Eritrea.

Several parties emerged in Eritrea during the period of British administration (1941–52). The 'unionist party', founded about 1943, supported a union with Ethiopia. Most of its members were Tigrean Christians but it included Muslims, Protestants and Catholics as well, and its leader, Tedla Bairu, was a protestant. The 'Liberal Progressive Party' (LPP), established shortly after the unionist party drew its membership mainly from among Christians who opposed union and wanted either federation with Ethiopia or independence. It was led by Woldeab Wolde-Mariam, founder of 'The Syndicate of Free Workers in Eritrea'.

The Muslims were organised at first in several parties. However, by 1945–46 they had united in the 'Muslim League', which demanded complete independence for Eritrea. Towards the end of the 1940s the 'Muslim League' and the LPP created the 'Independence Bloc'. Because it feared Muslim domination, however, the LPP soon changed sides and joined the 'unionists' in supporting an Eritrean–Ethiopia federation.

After prolonged haggling in the United Nations Italy in 1951 was awarded the trusteeship of Italian Somaliland. In the case of Eritrea the United States, still sceptical in the 1950s of 'British imperialism', supported Ethiopia. Thus, in spite of British reservations, the United Nations in 1951 decided to federate Eritrea with Ethiopia in the following year; Haile Selassie was to be titular head of the federation and Ethiopia responsible for Eritrea's defence, foreign affairs, finance and communications. The Eritreans, however, were granted a seperate assembly and internal autonomy.[6]

It was the decision to federate Eritrea with Ethiopia which caused the first wave of refugees to leave Eritrea. Among them were political leaders, mainly Muslim, who opposed the federation; they included Ibrahim Sultan Ali, Idris Muhammad Adum, Osman Salih Sabbe of the Muslim League and Woldeab Wolde-Mariam of the LPP. The majority of these men were merchants, landowners and wealthy intellectuals who found refuge in Cairo. A second element was made up of collaborators with the Italians and Muslim soldiers who had served with the Italian forces during and after the conquest of Ethiopia. A third element comprised the semi-nomadic Beja tribes who lived on both sides of the Eritrean–Sudanese border and had caused endless trouble to the Italians, as they were unwilling to accept any restriction on their movements or to give up the age-old practices of raiding their neighbours and of highway robbery (*shifta*).[7] Following clashes with the Ethiopian army after 1952, some of these tribes fled to the Sudan and their raiding across the frontier gradually assumed the form of a challenge to Ethiopian authority. Such raids, notably of the Bani 'Amr, could be considered as the origin of ELF rural guerrilla activities.[8]

The economy of Eritrea began to decline shortly after the federation was established. The province lost the revenue derived from British administration and personnel. Some Italian settlers left the country while others, realising the far greater opportunities in Ethiopia, moved their business from Eritrea. An exodus of Eritrean intellectuals and capitalists had also begun, inspired by better chances of success in Addis Ababa, to Ethiopia proper. On the other hand, Amhara federal officials began to arrive in Eritrea and their presence and attitude were resented by many Eritreans. It was only to be expected that the standards of Eritrean–Ethiopian administration would be inferior to those of the British. As *shifta* activities increased the Ethiopian army was called in to preserve law and order. Whether successful or not it was always blamed, rightly or wrongly, for mistreating the rural population and for being the cause of new waves of refugees which crossed into the Sudan.

Events following 1952 thus polarised the opposition of Eritreans, especially Muslims, to the federation. Yet, except for sporadic *shifta* 'incidents', this opposition remained verbal, with exiled politicians petitioning the United Nations and embassies abroad in an attempt to gain political support and funds. Their activity, however, intensified about 1960 when it became evident that Ethiopia was preparing to incorporate Eritrea.

Once the federation was created it was inevitable that Ethiopia should try to annex Eritrea and ensure her hold over its economically and strategically crucial coast. Tedla Bairu, leader of the unionists had become chief executive in Eritrea, but it was not long before he clashed with Addis Ababa and resigned in 1955.[9] In the next several years, Ethiopia spent (it is claimed) substantial sums to strengthen the pro-unionists and to 'bribe' the opposition. Gradually the Eritrean assembly was purged of all members who opposed unity with Ethiopia. In 1962 the Eritrean assembly decided unanimously to unite Eritrea with Ethiopia.

Nothing would be more incorrect than to conclude that there was overwhelming opposition in Eritrea to union with Ethiopia. Many Christians genuinely supported such a move because they believed that Eritrea and Ethiopia had a common heritage and that in spite of the drawbacks, Eritrea would benefit.[10] Others were influenced by the very presence of the Ethiopians in Eritrea and their determination to unite 'historic Ethiopia'. The Ethiopian national church, a traditional ally of the Solomonic dynasty, was also solidly behind Haile Selassie's efforts to unify the country. However, although most Eritrean Christians belonged to this church it is difficult to gauge its influence in purely political matters. Much more important was the Christian fear of Arab–Muslim domination following the wave of panarabism which swept the Middle East in the 1950s and which impinged upon Eritrea. This fear was enhanced by the Sudan's independence in 1956 and the declaration of some Sudanese politicians that they supported Eritrean independence. In 1960, Somalia also became independent and its leaders declared their dedication to the plan of a 'greater Somalia'.[11] For different reasons therefore the majority of Eritrea's Christians and a minority of its Muslim population supported union with Ethiopia.[12]

The Eritrean Liberation Front (ELF) 1961–67

Recently the ELF captured Arab and world attention by its allegations that Ethiopia had granted bases to Israel near the Bab al-Mandeb as part of an American plot directed against the Arab countries and associated with Western interests in the Persian Gulf.[13]

Many writers have claimed that the ELF emerged as a result of the annexation of Eritrea in 1962. Even its leaders do not attribute the *shifta* activities in Eritrea prior to 1961 to the

ELF; they assert that it was established in Asmara by a handful of people in September 1961.[14] Be that as it may, it is doubtful whether after its conception the ELF was anything but a small urban underground organisation in Asmara connected with exiled Eritrean politicians in the Arab capitals. 'Political shiftas'[15] were already active in this period in western Eritrea and along the Sudanese border, but their activity was uncoordinated and unrelated to the ELF. The ELF leadership abroad was at first still preoccupied with petty jealousies, had no programme and could not agree on anything apart from opposition to the union of Eritrea with Ethiopia. This situation gradually changed from 1963 onwards. A general command of a sort emerged with Idris Muhammad Adum as president, Woldeab Wolde-Mariam director of the Cairo office and Osman Salih Sabbe secretary-general and roving ambassador of the movement.[16] Gradually the new general command succeeded in asserting some authority over the 'political shiftas' in the field.

In spite of her sympathy with the ELF the UAR was unwilling to help the movement because of Egypt's role in the OAU and the special relations which existed between President Nasser and Emperor Haile Selassie. The ELF was supported in this early period mainly by the Sudan, where most Eritrean refugees had found shelter. However, Sudanese aid was limited and inconsistent as it depended on internal political developments and was influenced by the fact that the Ethiopians could retaliate by supporting the Southern Sudan rebels. Nevertheless, the Sudan provided the ELF with essential facilities such as staging bases, supply depots for smuggled arms and shelter from the Ethiopian army. An important achievement of the general command was the link-up with the Syrian Ba'th régime, which provided the movement with military and financial aid by way of the Sudan from about 1964.[17]

The Syrian Ba'th began to compete with Egypt for the leadership of Arab nationalism after the disintegration of the UAR and the collapse of reconciliation efforts in 1962. The Ba'th ideology was a compound of socialism and panarabism. Hence Syria became the champion of the ELF which, it claimed, was an Arab liberation movement fighting a reactionary pro-Israeli régime.[18]

The military and financial support received from Syria had an immediate affect on the ELF and its activities. ELF forces grew from a few hundred men armed with antiquated weapons to about 2,000 men with relatively modern weapons. The small Ethiopian garrison in Eritrea (less than 6,000) was unable to cope with the new situation, as it was fully occupied in patrolling the Sudanese border and the main roads. Hence an Eritrean anti-guerrilla commando unit was organised, allegedly with the help of Israeli experts. But this force, said to number at first between 1,000 to 2,000 men, was inadequate to comb the vast and physically difficult terrain of western and northern Eritrea. In the meantime ELF forces continued to grow and gradually gained control of most of the rural area of western and northern Eritrea.

By 1966, following the example of the Algerian FLN, the ELF divided the 'liberated areas' into five military zones. All commanders were theoretically subordinate to the C-in-C, Idris Awate, a man who had served during World War II in the Italian colonial army. The 'liberated areas', it was claimed, were controlled by a militia a few thousand strong which also collected taxes from the population and the Italian planters and farmers. Occasionally road blocks were set up in broad daylight on the main roads and drivers and passengers were made to contribute to the ELF treasury. Even Eritrea's capital, Asmara, was not immune to ELF activities and some prominent personalities and rich merchants were made to pay such taxes.[19]

The majority of ELF guerrillas came from among the Muslim pastoralists and farmers of western Eritrea and the Sudan border. The organisation had, however, many Christian and animist members. Tension between the different groups in the ELF persisted despite the general command's efforts, and this reduced the latter's ability to assert its authority and to make the ELF more effective. In 1967 the embittered Tedla Bairu escaped to Cairo and joined the ELF command. But the propaganda value of his defection and his broadcasts from radio Damascus was offset by his contribution to the disunity within the leadership of the ELF.[20] Another element which began to assert its place in the ranks of the ELF was the Eritrean students in Ethiopia and abroad. They were, however, critical of the purely pragmatic nationalistic policy of the ELF and its general command, and (to some extent) of the growing panarabist–Muslim orientation which it was acquiring. This orientation was attributed mainly to the activity of the all-powerful secretary-general Sabbe and to the influence of the Syrian Ba'th.[21]

Until 1967 the existence of any insurrectionary activity in Eritrea was denied by the Ethiopian government. Ras Asrate Kassa, the governor of Eritrea since 1963, claimed as late as 1969 that Eritrean secessionism was mainly a socio-economic problem and therefore could be solved largely by economic development and better opportunities of advancement for Eritreans. Yet the governor did not ignore the military aspect of the problem and was intrumental in building up Eritrean commando forces.[22] Although an able governor, his approach was unrealistic: constructive solutions do not offset the hardships and reactions of an unfriendly rural population while a rebellion is being suppressed in their midst. Moreover the government was unable to provide from its 'shoe-string' budget the funds needed for development of the province. Consequently, the situation in Eritrea continued to deteriorate in 1966 and early 1967.

Eritrean secessionism served as an added incentive for Addis Ababa to develop its relations with African and non-aligned countries. This policy provided Ethiopia some assurances against outside intervention and gained for it an important position in the OAU and in the 'Third World'. Eritrean secessionism, on the other hand, reawakened and sharpened the tension between Christian Ethiopia and the Arab–Muslim world and thus drove Ethiopia to develop, although cautiously, closer relations with Israel.

Following her success in breaking the Egyptian blockade of the straits of Tiran in 1956 Israel began to develop her maritime and commercial relations (including oil) with Asian and East African countries. Some Arab countries began to take greater interest in the possibility of an independent Eritrean state (Arab–Muslim?) controlling the 544 miles of the Ethiopian coast. If Somalia were also to annex the territory of the Afar and the Issa (TFAI) the Red Sea would become an 'Arab lake' with its southern entrance controlled by a Muslim state. Israel was not unaware of what was at stake and that it was in her interest to help Ethiopia maintain its coastline. A contemporary version of the historic relationship between King Solomon and the Queen of Sheba began to emerge. Notwithstanding sizeable American aid[23] Ethiopia, although hesitant, was not in a position to reject the help offered by the only country in the region facing problems similar to hers. As ELF activities intensified and as it became apparent that certain Arab countries were supporting the rebels, relations between Ethiopia and Israel were quietly formalised. By 1967 the world press reported that Israeli officers were training the Eritrean commando unit and that Israeli experts were helping Ethiopia in non-military fields such as agriculture, education and public works.[24]

It would be outside the scope of this work to deal with the internal problems which affect the integrity and unity of Ethiopia.[25] Suffice it to say that Ethiopia as well as her enemies and other nations realise that the secession of Eritrea could start a chain reaction which might lead to the disintegration of the Ethiopian kingdom. Such an eventuality is not unattractive to the Somali Republic with its aspiration for a 'greater Somalia' including southwestern Ethiopia and the TFAI (Djibouti). The disintegration of Ethiopia would not displease the Arab countries, as it would turn the Red Sea into an Arab lake. The Arab countries of northeast Africa would rather have a Muslim–Arab nation, or a weaker Ethiopia, in control of the most important sources of the Nile, which are essential to the very existence of Egypt. In the case of the Sudan the issue has been further complicated by problems connected with her internal stability, the southern Sudan rebellion and Ethio–Sudanese border disputes. However, until 1967 the balance of power in northeast Africa was such that there was little chance of changing the *status quo* unless Ethiopia disintegrated as a result of internal developments.

The Arab supporters of the ELF were far too occupied with their own affairs following the Six Day War with Israel. With funds and arms dwindling to a trickle ELF activities were drastically reduced. Taking advantage of this Addis Ababa reinforced its army in Eritrea and by the end of 1967 had regained control over most of western Eritrea and the Kunama–Baria region. Some of the field commanders and political leaders escaped from Eritrea to Damascus. Others, however, mainly Christians disillusioned with the growing Muslim–Arab orientation of the movement, chose to surrender to the Ethiopian army.[26]

The 'Unbalancing' of the Balance of Power in Northeast Africa 1968–70

The decline in ELF activity and the relative tranquillity in Eritrea did not last for long. Arab aid, especially from Syria, had begun to flow again to Eritrea by the beginning of 1968 and Damascus radio daily broadcast ELF propaganda. The support of Syria for the Eritrean rebellion was still motivated by the fact that she considered the ELF an Arab liberation movement and Ethiopia an ally of Zionism and American imperialism. However, the possession of the Eritrean coast became even more important to the Arabs than in the past. After the Six Day War Israeli shipping used the Red Sea more extensively and a 42-inch oil pipe-line was constructed from Eilat to Ashdod. President Nasser was unwilling to act openly against Ethiopia because of his relations with Haile Selassie and Egypt's membership in the OAU. Syria, however, had no such inhibitions and did not hesitate to undermine the 'sacred' principle of territorial integrity adopted by the OAU in 1964.

Although Iraq vociferously condemned Ethiopia for its relations with Israel and the United States, her aid to the ELF was limited and aimed at undermining Syria's influence over the organisation. Far more important has been the new relationship developed since 1968 by the ELF with the government of Southern Yemen (later the PDRY). Ideologically the PDRY was close to the extremist Marxist Palestinian guerrilla organisations, and had already declared her intention of closing the straits of Bab al-Mandeb to Israeli navigation in 1967.[27] Because of her dedication to 'world revolution' and because she considered Ethiopia 'a reactionary agent of world imperialism', the PDRY considered the ELF worthy of support.

Another factor which could have influenced the PDRY's attitude to the ELF may have been China. Chinese influence in Southern Yemen was established at the end of 1967 but it grew substantially after the radicalisation of the régime in 1969. In spite of their reverses in Africa in the early 1960s the Chinese were still pledged to support liberation movements and subversive organisations in non-socialist countries of the 'Third World'. In northeast Africa and the Arabian peninsula they were active in countries which had already turned to the Soviet Union. However, whereas the Soviet Union had now outgrown her period of irresponsible activities and now followed a pragmatic policy, the Chinese still clung to an inflexible revolutionary Marxist–Leninist ideology. They could not compete with the Russians in military and economic aid, but supporting subversive and guerrilla organisations was not only cheaper but was even, it seemed, more rewarding. Hence news of Chinese aid to the ELF occasionally appeared in the world press after 1969.[28] By this time Chinese- and PDRY-trained guerrillas, as well as large quantities of arms, were being smuggled from Aden to Eritrea across the Red Sea.

In 1969 the ELF had offices in most of the Arab capitals and was receiving financial support even from conservative Arab countries such as Saudi Arabia.[29] One element in the ELF command was determined by then to bring the Eritrean struggle to the attention of the world. The ELF has been closely connected since 1967 with the Palestinian guerrillas and especially al-Fatah, but this element, under Iraqi or PDRY influence, courted the Popular Front for the Liberation of Palestine (PFLP). With the latter's help a special ELF unit was trained early in 1969 in hijacking and sabotage. Throughout 1969 and 1970 several incidents involving the hijacking or attempted hijacking of EAL planes and attacks on Ethiopian embassies were reported by the press. The ELF not only gained the publicity it sought but also the support of international radical movements and the sympathy of several Muslim countries.[30]

Military coups in countries flanking Ethiopia accelerated a change in the balance of power in the Horn of Africa. In May 1969 the Sudanese army supported by panarabist and communist elements brought General Numeiri to power. Five months later a coup by leftist officers in Somalia brought General Siyad to power. Both military régimes publicly declared their intention of maintaining the friendly relations with Ethiopia established by their predecessors. However both countries secretly stepped up their aid to the ELF.[31] Following a number of visits of Somali ministers to the Sudan and Sudanese ministers to the Somali Republic it was believed in Ethiopia that the two countries had agreed to co-ordinate their activities in case of a war with Ethiopia, either over the Eritrean problem or the TFAI.[32]

By the beginning of 1970 ELF forces were said to number about 10,000 men, of which, 2,000 to 3,000 were regulars and the rest militia. The five military commands system was abolished and a unified command set up. The 'regulars' were armed with modern automatic weapons of Russian and Chinese make and organised in small and mobile units. ELF representatives claimed that their forces now controlled and collected taxes from two-thirds of Eritrea, and this was not far from the truth. The Ethiopian second division, some 8,000 soldiers armed with American M-1 rifles, and the 3,000 anti-ELF commandos, were utterly inadequate to deal with the new situation. They abandoned a good part of the inaccessible rural area and kept the roads open only by constant patrolling and a system of escorted caravans during daylight. Even in Asmara, where the ELF had many Muslim sympathisers, the government was unable to prevent occasional 'incidents'.[33] Probably the most serious development in this period was the success of the ELF in opening a third front (in addition to the western and northern ones) by involving the Dankalis in its activities. It seems that with the help of some educated Dankalis who joined its ranks the ELF gained the co-operation of a number of Dankali chiefs against the payment of money, and these helped smuggle through their respective territories arms and the guerrillas trained in China and the PDRY. During 1970 mines were planted in the few secondary roads crossing the Dankali desert and a new 'liberated zone' was established by the ELF in the vicinity of the Bay of Zula. This area was used for operations against Ethiopian installations along the coast and the vital road linking the Assab port and refinery with Dessie and Addis Ababa. It is also alleged that the Zula area may have served as the staging base for attacks on the Christian villages to the south of Asmara.[34]

During this critical period Ethiopia's endemic economic crisis had increased further because of the decline of the price of coffee on the world market. Naturally, Ethiopia did not have the financial resources to modernise and expand her army.[35] The ELF leadership, aware of the connection between economics and success in the field, declared that it would endeavour to damage Ethiopia's economy.[36] By this time it was realised that if American aid to Ethiopia was discontinued the country would be unable to maintain her armed forces at their existing strength and might even disintegrate.

Until the end of 1969 the ELF command maintained a tolerant attitude towards the United States in spite of American aid to Ethiopia and the communications and satellite-tracking centre at Kagnew near Asmara.[37] Kagnew base had been leased from the British in the early 1940s but in 1953, after Eritrea was federated with Ethiopia, Washington and Addis Ababa signed a 25-year agreement for its use. The United States promised to assist Ethiopia in her economic development and undertook to equip, train and help maintain an Ethiopian army of about 40,000 men. Between 1953 and 1970 Ethiopia received from the United States nearly $170 million in military aid and about $230 million in economic aid, in addition to a few million dollars spent annually by American personnel in the country. The American aid and presence were therefore vital to Ethiopia.[38]

By 1970, although the general command of the ELF was still composed of self-appointed traditional politicians the rank and file consisted of a good number of ideologically oriented radicals. Under their pressure and with the aim of stopping American military aid to Ethiopia, in late 1969 the ELF opened an anti-American campaign centring on 'American neo-imperialism and Israel' and use of Kagnew as a centre of electronic spying against Arab countries. This campaign gathered momentum towards the end of 1970 and culminated with the killing of an American courier on the Massawa road in January 1971.[39]

In November 1970 a unit of the ELF ambushed and killed General Teshome Erghetu, the commander of Ethiopia's second division stationed in Eritrea. Shortly before this incident a Syrian journalist who accompanied the guerrilla forces witnessed and took photographs of several rebel operations. As his return to Damasus coincided with the death of General Erghetu, his photographs and account of ELF activities were given prominence in the international press. The situation in Eritrea seemed therefore even worse than it was in reality, and a number of American congressmen, newspapermen and political analysts clamoured for the termination of American aid to Ethiopia in order to avoid a Vietnam situation in north-east Africa.[40]

Great apprehension was aroused in Ethiopia by the attitude of alarm in the United States about the situation in Eritrea. Following the visits to the United States of the Emperor in 1969 and the Ethiopian C-in-C in 1970, Addis Ababa found to its dismay that, in spite of the changing balance of power in the area, the Americans were hedging on the question of Ethiopia's requests to modernise their army. They realised that following public reaction to developments in Vietnam, American policy was undergoing a fundamental change regarding military commitments and bases in overseas territories, especially in areas of potential local conflict. Contrary to claims that Kagnew was essential to the Americans after they gave up Wheelus base in Libya, the truth was that modern technology had made Kagnew expendable. As a result of the deteriorating situation in Eritrea Addis Ababa feared that Washington might evacuate Kagnew and terminate the military aid agreement even before 1977.[41] Ethiopia was truly alarmed because just at this time the Soviet Union was helping to modernise and expand the armies of her neighbours.

Although the Soviet Union consistently refused to support the ELF[42] it did help this organisation indirectly. Soviet weapons supplied to the Sudan, Somalia, the PDRY and Syria 'somehow' reached the ELF. But far more important was the fact that by 1970 Russian military aid to Ethiopia's neighbours had completely changed the balance of power in the area.

The idea of a 'Greater Somalia', unifying all the areas inhabited by Somali-speaking people, was a brain-child of the British Foreign Office in the early 1940s. Although later dropped by the British the idea was incorporated in the Somali constitution on the country's independence in 1960. At first only the most extreme of Somali nationalists laid claim to TFAI (Djibouti) which had a non-Somali majority[43] and which owed its economic survival to Ethiopia's trade. However, as relations with Ethiopia deteriorated the claim to TFAI became as important to the Somalis as their claims to areas in Ethiopia and Kenya inhabited by Somali tribesmen.

Skirmishes between Somalis and Ethiopians occurred even before independence. After 1960 these gradually developed into a 'mini war' which reached its peak about 1965. Somalia, a desert country with a population of less than 3 million, had a relatively small para-military force (with an assortment of British- and Italian-made weapons, armour and planes) and was no match for Ethiopia. She therefore requested her Western patrons to assist her in building an army of 20,000 soldiers. The Western powers, fearing a full-scale war in the area, only agreed to help Somalia organise an army of 5,000 men.[44] In its frustration the Somali government turned to the Soviet Union, which was more than willing to oblige.

Once Russia was firmly established in the Middle East and its fleet had made its appearance in the Mediterranean she was determined to expand her influence into the Red Sea. Populous, relatively influential and potentially rich, Ethiopia was Russia's first choice. She undertook several minor development projects in different parts of the country and in 1960 granted Ethiopia a large loan. But the conservative régime of the country remained suspicious of Soviet intentions and until recent years never drew upon this loan. Given the circumstances the Soviet Union signed in 1962 an aid agreement with the Somali Republic granting her an initial loan of $32 million (which later rose to $55 million) and undertaking to build up, equip and train a Somali army of about 14,000 men with the aim of bringing its force to 20,000 in future.[45]

During the 1960s the Soviets supplied Somalia with quantities of automatic arms and modern artillery, 150 T-34 tanks, 60 APC's and about 25 Mig-15 and Mig-17[46] and about 20 Yak reconnaisance-trainer planes. A Soviet military mission of about 300 advisers (one source claims 1,200) established itself in Somalia to train the army and new armoured brigade, while over 500 Somalis underwent, and are undergoing, training in the Soviet Union as pilots, officers and technicians.[47] Throughout this period the Soviets did their utmost to maintain friendly relations with the Ethiopians reassuring them that the agreement with Somalia stipulated that Soviet arms should be used only for defence purposes.

From around 1965 the Somalis have realised that their best chance to achieve their territorial aspirations lies in the disintegration of Ethiopia. Already in 1964 the ELF had an office in Mogadishu and many of its leaders were provided with Somali passports.[48] Radio Mogadishu started broadcasting in Gallinya, inciting the Galla of the south against their 'Amhara oppressors', and it was alleged that Somalia was helping Galla rebels in Bale. The demands of the Issa Somalis since 1965 to unite the TFAI with the Republic were encouraged, if not initiated, by the Somali government. Even after the election of Prime Minister Egal in Somalia and the détente in relations between Ethiopia and Somalia in 1968, the offices of the two fronts for the liberation of western Somalia and the Somali coast remained active in Mogadishu as did that of the ELF. Although the military régime which came to power in Somalia in 1969 professed its intention of continuing peaceful relations with its neighbours it has never given up Somali territorial claims.[49] In the next several years the Chinese gradually established their influence in the Republic. It is claimed that unlike the Soviet Union, they actively helped subversive activities against Ethiopia.[50]

The 'progressive' government which emerged in 1968 in the Sudan fully supported the UAR in her struggle against Israel for restoration of the 'occupied territories'. A symptom of the new Sudanese policy was a £50 million arms deal signed about the middle of 1968 by Prime Minister Mahgub with the Soviet Union. The agreement provided for the purchase of Mig-21 fighters, T-34 and T-54 tanks, an assortment of modern artillery and large quantities of automatic light arms. It also provided for the training of pilots, officers and technicians in the Soviet Union and for Soviet experts to train the Sudanese army.[51]

The powerful panarabist and communist elements in the army, the intelligentsia and trade unions who brought General Numeiri to power opened a new era in the Sudan's relations with the Arab world and the Soviet Union. The panarabists, though more numerous, were disunited and lacked an organisational framework. The communists, though fewer in number were dedicated and well organised. The inconsistent and sometimes contradictory policy of the Sudan in the next two years was an outcome of the tension between these two rival factions in power.

With the exception of the new Marxist approach to economic affairs, the policy of the new government seemed to be similar to that of Mahgub's period. It did however lay greater stress on panarabism and on involvement in the Arab–Israeli struggle, on relations with Russia and the strengthening of the army. It was also determined to find a solution to the endemic problem of the south and to accelerate economic (mainly agricultural) development. Hence the Sudan became more interested in the cause of the ELF than before. ELF success could lead to the arabisation of the Red Sea and the Bab al-Mandeb and to the disintegration of Ethiopia, Sudan's only neighbour willing and able to support her régime's internal enemies. Such a new policy could also solve the Sudan's growing anxiety over Ethiopia's agricultural development programme in the Humera–Setit and Gash regions and a number of irrigation and hydro-electric projects affecting branches of the Blue Nile.[52] Although enraged by Ethiopian encroachments on what they considered their territory, the Sudanese (and the Egyptians) were even more worried about Ethiopia tapping water sources (originating on the plateau) which were important to Sudanese agricultural projects undertaken with Soviet aid.

In spite of the growing tension between panarabists and communists in Numeiri's government, the Sudan strengthened her relations with the Soviet Union. Sudanese ministerial delegations frequently visited Russia and its satellites during 1969 and 1970. Soviet loans were granted to the Sudan and several aid agreements signed between the two countries. The most impressive agreements, however, were military. In addition to selling large quantities of modern arms, the Soviets undertook to help expand the Sudanese army from about 30,000 to about 50,000.[53] Even before the first shipments of arms were delivered (beginning of 1970) around 100 Sudanese were sent to Russia to be trained as pilots and a very large training mission and a host of Soviet experts arrived in the Sudan. By the last months of 1970 the Sudanese army had received large quantities of automatic arms and different types of modern artillery. It had the equivalent of two armoured-motorised brigades with 150 T-54s and T-55s, an unknown number of

T-34 tanks and about 200 APC's. The Sudanese air force received about 30 Mig-21 fighter-interceptors, organised in several squadrons, a squadron of 6 Antonov bombers, two squadrons (of 6) Tupolov 16s and ten to twelve MI-8 helicopters. This was of course in addition to the assortment of Western weapons and planes which the Sudanese already had.[54]

Compared to the Sudanese army the Ethiopian imperial army by the end of 1970 still looked quite formidable. Ethiopia's regular army of about 40,000 soldiers is organised in four divisions, an armoured brigade, several other armoured elements and artillery and engineers units. Her navy is insignificant but so are the navies of her neighbours. Her air force however was considered in the 1960s to be the best and strongest in black Africa. In 1970 it consisted of a squadron of six Canberra B-2 bombers (purchased from Britain), a squadron of eight Saab-17 ground support planes (purchased from Sweden), a squadron of eight supersonic F-5A fighter-interceptors (American aid), a squadron of 12 sub-sonic F-86 fighter bombers (American aid), a reconnaissance squadron of six T-28 and three T-33 trainers, a transport squadron of DC-3s and several small helicopters. In addition to the regular army Ethiopia had a 3,000-strong commando unit (said to have been greatly strengthened in 1971), and a territorial army said to number between 10,000 and 20,000 troops.[55] It also had a police and border guard para-military force of about 25,000 men. Impressive as it looked on paper, by 1970 Ethiopia's army was by far inferior to the armies of her neighbours. The territorial army is in fact a loosely organised, badly disciplined and poorly armed militia. The infantry division, though relatively well trained and organised, are armed with World War II American weapons (standard rifle M-1). The air force, while it has excellent pilots, has only one squadron of (six) supersonic fighters, inferior to Mig-21's. As for Ethiopia's armoured units they had about the same number of tanks as the Somali army, but Russian T-34s are relatively superior to American World War II M-41s and M-24s. Moreover, the antiquated American tanks are no match for the modern T-54s and T-55s acquired by the Sudanese.[56]

Addis Ababa was not unaware of the dangerous external threat developing from the end of 1969. Ominous signs of the hostile attitude of its neighbours could be detected in news about talks between Sudanese and Somali defence experts, comments in the Arab press about accusations of Ethiopia's involvement in Hadi al-Mahdi's rebellion in the Sudan and Arab pressure to transfer, in the first month of 1970, the conference of the non-aligned countries from Addis Ababa to Dar-es-Salam.[57]

When it became evident that America was unwilling to extend her commitments in Ethiopia and as Ethiopia could not afford to modernise her army, Emperor Haile Selassie resorted to politics. During his visit to Moscow in the first half of 1970 he discussed the utilisation of the Russian loan and assured his hosts of Ethiopia's friendship. But the main purpose of his visit was to convince the Soviets to use their influence with Ethiopia's neighbours in order to reduce the tension. On his way back to Addis Ababa the Emperor stopped at Cairo for talks with President Nasser and Babakr Awadallah, the Sudanese deputy prime minister. It seems that these meetings only convinced Haile Selassie that the Arab countries (and possibly the Soviet Union) had no intention of stopping their aid to the ELF and that they would support Somalia over the question of Djibouti. The joint defence agreement which he signed shortly afterwards with President Kenyatta in Nairobi was of limited importance in view of the weakness of the Kenyan army. Yet Ethiopia refrained at this stage from turning to Israel, its natural ally, in order not to antagonise the Arabs. But the death of General Erghetu at the end of 1970 and reports of the American reaction to the situation in Ethiopia forced the emperor to adopt more aggressive political and military policy.

The Disintegration of the Anti-Ethiopian Front and the Erosion of ELF Power

Ethiopian efforts to isolate the ELF and to erode its power began shortly after the death of General Erghetu. These efforts combined political activity with wide-scale military operations in Eritrea. An immediate and impressive achievement was the winning over of China (PRC). By now the Cultural Revolution was fading away and a new phase had opened in China's foreign policy, especially regarding relations with countries of the 'Third World'. This was the phase of 'respectability', designed to establish China as a world power partly by gaining the recognition and respect of governments rather than by association with subversive organisations whose future was doubtful. Ethiopia's position in Africa and the 'Third World' and her position as the centre of the OAU, made relations with Addis Ababa most desirable. Following Ethiopian recognition of the PRC in December 1970 and her willingness to have China open an embassy in Addis Ababa the Chinese undertook to stop their aid to the ELF and promised, it is alleged, to use their influence in the PDRY to the same effect. In January 1971 Ethiopia's foreign minister Ketama Yifru visited Aden and told the Southern Yemenis, among other things, that unless they stopped supporting the ELF the large South Yemeni community in Ethiopia would be deported or (at least) its remittances blocked. In the light of the PDRY's financial situation this threat could not be ignored. It seems, however, that the decline in the PDRY's support to the ELF was mainly the outcome of an internal struggle which nearly paralysed this organisation during 1971.[58]

Relations between the communist and panarabist supporters of Numeiri progressively deteriorated throughout 1970. The Soviets were unable, or unwilling, to persuade the Sudanese communists to bow to the wishes of the panarabists in the government. Hence by the first months of 1971 tension in the Sudan was approaching a climax. In the meantime the Anyanya rebels in the south were becoming more effective, better organised and armed with the help of Ethiopia and, it is alleged, Israel.[59] Thus when Ketama Yifru visited Khartoum in March 1971 the Sudanese were willing to curtail their aid to the ELF if Ethiopia would do the same with the southern rebels. Khartoum also agreed to work towards a better understanding between the two countries and to set up joint committees to deal with outstanding border problems.[60]

In June the Ethiopian foreign minister visited Saudi Arabia. By now King Faisal was incensed by the radicalisation of the ELF, agreed not to support the movement and requested facilities for elements hostile to the PDRY. Shortly afterwards an Ethiopian delegation visited Egypt and Syria to discuss Ethiopia's relations with these governments. Although Egypt was sympathetic the Syrians were unco-operative.[61]

The coup and countercoup in the Sudan in 1971 and purges in

the army which followed strengthened the position of traditional elements in the country. The unstable internal situation forced Numeiri to seek better relations with Ethiopia, the country most likely and able to help his enemies. ELF offices in Khartoum and Kassala were closed and in November General Numeiri arrived in Addis Ababa, officially for a state visit but in fact to reach a settlement. As Ethiopia negotiated from a position of power, Numeiri's visit resulted in important concessions, namely the settlement of border disputes and Sudan's agreement to move Eritrean refugee camps further inland from the border and to stop ELF activities. On their part Ethiopia promised not to support disaffected elements in the northern Sudan and to help settle the problem of the southern Sudan.[62] Emperor Haile Selassie's visit to Khartoum at the end of 1971 and the beginning of 1972 signalled, in fact, the complete success of his policy regarding the Sudan. He was treated with the greatest respect and gained further concessions. Among other things the Sudanese agreed to the opening of an Ethiopian consulate in Port Sudan, the main function of which would, it is expected, be to prevent the smuggling of arms to the ELF and to keep Eritrean refugees in the eastern Sudan under surveillance.[63] Ethiopia was thus able by the end of 1971 to isolate the ELF from most of its supporters.

With the communist coup and the successful countercoup in July relations between the Sudan and the Soviet Union became extremely strained, a fact which inevitably affected the Sudanese armed forces. The Somalis left to themselves could not openly challenge their strong neighbours. Thus a military confrontation between Ethiopia and her neighbours was at least temporarily avoided.

A state of emergency was declared in most parts of Eritrea as early as the end of November 1970. The governor of the province, Ras Asrate Kassa, opposed this measure and was dismissed; General Debebe Haile Mariam, commander of the bodyguard division, was appointed in his place. General Debebe arrived in Eritrea with some units of the bodyguard division and armoured elements. At the same time several squadrons of the Ethiopian air force were moved from their main base in Debra Zeit (near Addis Ababa) to Eritrea. An amnesty was declared for ELF members who surrendered within a given time. The scores of guerrillas who laid down their arms, how-however, were mainly Christian; in fact the majority of Christian members of the ELF had already defected from the movement after 1967 when the ELF leadership adopted a pan-arab and to some extent pan-Islamic orientation.[64]

At the beginning of December 1970, the Ethiopian army opened a large-scale military operation against areas held by the rebels. ELF spokesmen, and in their steps the Arab and international press, claimed that the Ethiopian air force was systematically bombing villages and towns along the coast and in northern and western Eritrea. Following the air activity, it was alleged, the Ethiopian army moved in the beginning of 1971 into areas previously held by the rebels, burned villages and executed or detained men suspected of collaborating with the ELF. These allegations were strengthened by a wave of refugees from Eritrea which reached the Sudan at the end of 1970.[65] The reports were greatly exaggerated; in fact, the ELF did not hold any town and there are hardly any villages worth bombing on the coast or in the northern part of the Eritrean plateau. Moreover, some villages claimed to have been destroyed south and northeast of Asmara were Christian and, according to eye witnesses, had been destroyed by the ELF.[66]

ELF control over large parts of Eritrea had resulted, it seems, from the inability or unwillingness of Ethiopian regular forces to penetrate the rugged and nearly inaccessible terrain of different parts of the region. Many of the inhabitants of those areas belonged to ethnic, cultural or religious groups. They accepted ELF authority because the ELF represented the only power in the area rather than because they were fired by revolutionary zeal. Some ELF units, especially those trained in China or the PDRY, following Chinese–Russian guerrilla techniques tried to indoctrinate, educate and integrate them-selves with the people among whom they lived. These tactics were in some instances a cause of friction with backward and introverted communities. In other areas predominantly Mus-lim Tigre-speaking ELF units oppressed and mistreated the population which did not belong to the Muslim majority group.[67]

From the beginning of 1971 Ethiopian army engineers and sappers began to open new roads into the relatively fertile and more densely populated western Eritrea, the lowland along the Sudanese border and the coast areas which had previously been inaccessible to motorised transport. Once the roads were finished the Ethiopian army moved in and gained control there. Although the population sometimes fought fiercely alongside the ELF, in other areas, peopled by ethnic or religious minorities, the residents actually welcomed the soldiers as deliverers.[68]

Once they had established some control over most of rural Eritrea, the Ethiopians exploited the heterogeneous character of the population and resorted to tactics similar to those used by the Americans in Vietnam. They moved the inhabitants of hamlets belonging to 'friendly' groups to large and fortified villages, supplied them with arms and formed local militia units so that they could resist ELF pressures. Harsher methods, it seems, were used against groups known to be friendly to the ELF in order to dissuade them from co-operating with the rebels. In the lowlands, and particularly in the Tesene–Gash area and the enclave inhabited by the Baria–Kunama negroid groups, the Ethiopians succeeded in establishing a line of fortified villages along the border. The war-like character of the population and their age-old feuds with their Beja neighbours caused many to volunteer for anti-guerrilla auxiliary units.[69]

The coastal strip of Eritrea with its Dankali population was detached from Eritrea and divided among adjacent provinces of the plateau. Thereafter the governor of each province was responsible for administering, developing and policing the part of the coast attached to his domain. Police and army centres were established next to strategically important routes and water sources. Some minor agricultural projects and plans connected with mineral exploitation are being carried out and the Dankalis have been told that they will be held responsible if guerrillas and arms pass through their respective areas. Hence an area neglected, and only nominally governed by Ethiopia until 1971, is being gradually brought under the control of the central government.[70]

During 1971 Ethiopia became less timid in its relations with the Arab world because Syria, Iraq, the PDRY and Libya openly supported the ELF. Although careful not to antagonise its friends in the Arab camp, Addis Ababa strongly criticised the role of some Arab countries in what was happening in

Eritrea.[71] Moreover, it seems that during 1971 Ethiopia cautiously developed its relations with Israel. In September 1971 Israel's C-in-C visited the country, and the Arab press then alleged that Israel had undertaken to supply Ethiopia with electronic equipment, a radar network, coast guards and missile boats. It was also claimed that Israeli officers were stationed in Ethiopian ports and that Israeli experts would train Ethiopians in the use of electronic equipment. These claims were strongly denied by Addis Ababa and it is unlikely the emperor would have gone that far or that Israel could supply weapons which she herself finds difficulty in obtaining. The ELF, however, used the opportunity to reiterate its allegations that 'bases' were given to Israel on two islands in the bay of Assab, not far from the Bab al-Mandeb. These allegations were refuted by the Ethiopians as well as by Swedish observers who flew over the islands and found them uninhabited.[72] Western and other sources claim, however, that Israel, interested in preserving the integrity of Ethiopia, in 1971 stepped up her economic co-operation and trade with her[73] and that the Israeli-trained Eritrean commando force was substantially strengthened.[74]

The appeals of ELF leaders to world public opinion to stop 'the massacres in Eritrea', demonstrations of radicals in front of Ethiopian embassies and some ELF broadcasts from Damascus in the second half of 1971 suggest that the Ethiopian military operations were successful.[75] Deprived of shelter, food and revenue, ELF units were gradually forced to abandon areas previously considered their strongholds. Many members of the ELF found it prudent to escape to nearby Arab countries. Others, surrendered to the government and some even joined the Ethiopian auxiliary forces.[76]

In spite of the decline in ELF power it would be utterly wrong to assume that the rebellion has been broken. 'Incidents' still occurred throughout 1971 in different parts of Eritrea, trains and bridges are blown up and even the main roads are still not completely safe. However, especially since about the middle of 1971 the number of 'incidents' has fallen sharply and most of these could be classified as 'hit and run'. Moreover, if ELF communiqués are closely examined it is evident that the activities reported usually occurred in the semi-deserted area in northern Eritrea, its coast and along the Sudanese border.[77] It is clear that the 'liberated areas' of the ELF have shrunk in size and, if they still exist, it is mainly because the Ethiopian army is unwilling to pay the price for opening and holding them. Hence, what seemed to be a strong and cohesive popular organisation was proved to be lacking the popular and general support with which it was credited and to be far weaker than claimed by its leaders.

The present decline of the ELF should not be attributed solely to the political and military successes of the Ethiopians. It is also the outcome of the serious internal crisis which the ELF underwent throughout 1971 and which resulted from a clash of personalities and ideologies within the ELF and from the conflicting policies of its supporters.

The ELF between Pragmatism and Ideology

When founded in the early 1960s the ELF served as an organisational framework for all Eritreans who opposed the annexation of their country by Ethiopia. It consisted of an element (mainly Christian) which wanted to return to the federal arrangement, or a form of loose relationship, with Ethiopia. A small minority supported a union of Eritrea with the Sudan. The majority of ELF members, however, opted for complete independence. The policy of the ELF leadership could be described as nationalistic and pragmatic, lacking any socio-economic ideology. This is not surprising as the exiled leadership of the ELF came from middle-class merchants and the well-to-do intelligentsia of Asmara and other towns in Eritrea.

Although its Muslim members by far outnumbered its Christian, the ELF claimed until 1971, and even later, that it was a non-religious, non-sectarian movement. Nonetheless, the panarab–Muslim character of the organisation had become evident as early as the mid-1960s. By 1968 it depended heavily on the military, financial and political support of Arab countries (and on Arab nationalism), and did little to hide its panarab–Muslim orientation. Hence most ELF Christian members defected; and some of them abroad began to try to create a common front with the 'progressive' opposition to the Ethiopian régime. This opposition was composed of Ethiopian students, intellectuals and political refugees in European capitals and in the United States. The Christian members of the ELF also made common cause with those Eritrean students in Ethiopia and abroad who joined the ELF and were truly above religious and sectarian prejudices. These students had been critical of the non-ideological policy of the ELF general command, but they lacked the power to influence the leadership.[78]

The Six Day War of 1967 was a turning point in the history of the ELF. The support of Syria and other Arab countries had been important in the past, but after 1968 they gradually stepped up their aid. The ELF also received help and facilities from the Palestinian guerrilla organisations and especially from al-Fatah. Hence, and because of circumstances arising from the Arab–Israeli conflict, the ELF leadership found it prudent by 1969 openly to declare this revolution to be an Arab–Muslim revolutionary movement and to identify themselves with the Palestinian struggle.[79]

To attract world public opinion to their struggle a faction of the ELF general command decided in the beginning of 1969 to hijack Ethiopian Airlines planes and to attack Ethiopian government offices in Europe. This necessitated manpower of the highest calibre. Most suitable for this purpose were Eritrean students in the Arab countries, in Europe and in America.

Until 1969 the burden of the armed struggle against Ethiopia rested on the shoulders of rural guerrillas who were mainly semi-literate Muslim tribesmen and villagers. Although there were indications that field commanders were dissatisfied with the political leadership this hardly ever came into the open. Once the students became more important to the ELF they allied themselves with some of the dissatisfied commanders and 'retired' political leaders. The students, courted by the Marxist 'Popular Front for the Liberation of Palestine' (PFLP) and Iraq,[80] had called upon the ELF command to adopt a socialist ideology. They had also opened a dialogue with 'progressive' elements in Ethiopia who opposed the 'autocratic and traditional' régime in their country. About the middle of 1969, supported by the Iraqi Ba'th, they demanded the convening of a national Eritrean congress to discuss the reorganisation, structure and aims of the movement. For a time some of the commanders in the field also refused to co-operate with the general command. Iraqi support however was more verbal than practical and under the pressure of Syria and other Arab countries the split in the ELF was temporarily patched up. The all-powerful secretary-general of the ELF, Osman Salih Sabbe, continued to lead the organisation, at least abroad.[81]

A far more serious threat to the unity of the ELF emanated from Southern Yemen's (presently the PDRY's) aid to Eritrean secessionism. Whereas the Syrian Ba'th and other Arab governments supported the ELF because it served a purpose in the struggle against Israel and was considered an Arab liberation movement, the PDRY did so as well because of her Marxist revolutionary ideology. From about the beginning of 1969 guerrillas trained in China and Southern Yemen and large quantities of automatic arms were smuggled from Aden across the Red Sea to the Eritrean coast.[82] Gradually, the Marxist-trained guerrillas consolidated their position and by 1970 had established a separate command calling themselves 'The Popular Forces'. They, as well as other ELF guerrillas, by this time refused to recognise the authority of the general command led by Osman Salih Sabbe.[83]

The double-pronged campaign launched by Ethiopia at the end of 1970 found the ELF stronger in numbers and arms but disunited and in a state of confusion. In view of developments in Eritrea in 1971 the opposition to the traditional leadership intensified its efforts to depose Sabbe and his supporters, to reorganise the ELF and to give it an ideological programme. Exploiting the rivalry between Baghdad and Damascus, the Eritrean students and their allies elected in the first half of 1971 a committee to prepare the 'Eritrean General National Congress', whose office was in Baghdad. In August they convened a congress of 'The Federation of Eritrean Students', which elected an aggressive executive committee which strongly supported the demand to convene a national congress in the 'liberated areas'.[84] Soon after their meeting the student leaders prudently approached the Syrian régime and the Palestinian guerrillas to explain their actions and demands. Shortly afterwards the Syrians abandoned the isolated traditional leadership and thereafter became the main patron of those elements pressing for democratisation and radicalisation of the ELF. By now it was realised in Damascus, and possibly in Cairo, that unless a more dynamic and socially conscious leadership took command of the ELF the movement would either disintegrate or abandon the mainstream of 'progressive' Arab nationalism and became a client of the PDRY and also of Iraq which was by this time co-operating with the former regarding the Persian Gulf and Eritrea.[85]

The ELF national congress was held, it is claimed, in the 'liberated areas'[86] in October and November of 1971 despite the opposition of the traditional leadership and its supporters in Eritrea. The congress elected a new military command and a new 'General Command', whose president was the veteran Muslim League politician, Idris Muhammad Adum. and whose other members were students (including Tedla Bairu's son, Herui Bairu) and some field commanders. The 'internal and external programmes' adopted by the congress were clearly the result of a compromise between the more radical and non-sectarian students and the panarabists. The congress adopted a relatively radical socialist ideology, denouncing what it termed 'Eritrean Bourgeois nationalism'. Yet it was also decided that the ELF should be closely associated with Arab nationalism and co-operate with the Syrian Ba'th party. The previous leadership was strongly denounced for its attempt to prevent the convening of the congress and for a mistaken policy which had caused the division within the ranks of the ELF and its present weakness. The congress and its resolutions, however, were it seems rather an attempt to eliminate the 'Popular Forces' and to undermine the influence of the PDRY in the area. The new military command was instructed to establish its authority, if necessary by force, over all ELF forces, with specific mention of the 'Popular Forces'. Finally a policy was formulated for regaining, either by indoctrination or coercion of the population, the territories lost by the movement.[87]

It was only to be expected that the PDRY would not send a delegation to the congress; neither did it send a cable of congratulations to its organisers. However, the fact that Iraq was not mentioned among the countries thanked for their help to the organisers of the congress was an indication of its co-operation with the PDRY and a reflection of her displeasure at being used to win over the Syrian Ba'th.[88] The new General Command, needing all the support it could obtain and in order to deny such support to its rivals, prudently despatched to Baghdad in the beginning of 1972 a delegation led by Idris Muhammad Adum to patch up relations with the Iraqi Ba'th. This occasion was exploited to reiterate allegations about Israeli bases being built on islands near the Bab al-Mandeb. Because of Iraqi concern at developments in the Gulf the ELF denounced 'imperialist plots' in the whole area between the Horn of Africa and the Persian Gulf.[89]

In spite of the impressive resolutions of the congress and lengthy communiqués issued in the months that followed by the new ELF General Command the Eritrean rebels are still weak and divided. The traditional leadership led by Osman Salih Sabbe disregards the new leadership and claims that the congress, organised by a handful of students and disgruntled old politicians, took place outside Eritrea. Sabbe and his faction are seemingly supported by Libya because of their traditional Islamic–Arab nationalism.[90] On the other hand there is some evidence to indicate that the PDRY has quietly reactivated the ELF office in Aden and renewed her help to the 'Popular Forces'.[91] Be that as it may, the fact is that up to the present ELF activities in Eritrea are limited and the areas it still controls, are relatively small, sparsely inhabited and inaccessible.

In the case of the ELF, as in the case of other liberation and secessionist movements, foreign aid and the support of a country bordering on the area of its activity are essential. The dependence of ELF success on continuous Arab aid has twice been demonstrated: following the Six Day War when the ELF, left to itself, lost the initiative and shrunk in size and importance, and—a more striking example—what happened to the ELF, then at the peak of its power, as a result of the success of Ethiopian political and military initiatives in 1970–71 in isolating the movement. Hence as long as Ethio–Sudanese relations remain as they are, the route from Somalia, long and hazardous, and with supply by sea complicated by extensive patrolling, radar and other detecting devices, there is little chance of a sudden dramatic upsurge in ELF rural activities.

For a decade Eritrean secessionism frustrated Ethiopia's

efforts to achieve homogeneity and national unity. It held back the economic development of the country because a substantial part of Ethiopia's budget was absorbed by military expenditures. The ELF therefore enhanced the dissatisfaction of the Ethiopian intelligentsia with the economic stagnation of their land and with its régime. It even gained the sympathy of some 'progressive' Ethiopians who consider the ELF the only active opposition to their government. A serious upheaval in Ethiopia, remote as it may seem today, is nonetheless possible and could lead to a period of instability. Such a development might provide the ELF with an opportunity to achieve its goal even without massive aid from neighbouring countries. But such an eventuality is remote in present circumstances despite Libyan aid.

The fortunes of the ELF have fluctuated since its conception in September 1961. The problems which gave rise to the movement—an Eritrean (Muslim?) identity which emerged from the colonial period, a large Muslim population with a growing panarab orientation, economic stagnation and dislike of Amhara domination—still remain unresolved. Hence ELF activity may be limited but not altogether stopped. Internal developments in Ethiopia, a change in the present détente between Ethiopia and its Muslim neighbours or the intervention of one of the Great Powers, may bring the Eritrean conflict to boiling-point again.

Notes

1. Speakers of Tigrinya, most of whom belong to the Ethiopian church and live in the province of Tigre and the southern parts of Eritrea; not to be confused with speakers of Tigre, mainly Muslim Beja and related elements.
2. In the widest sense of the term, including many of mixed blood.
3. The figures given by J. Spencer Trimingham (*Islam in Ethiopia*, 1965, p. 15), based on sources from the 1930s, can serve as an indicator to the present situation. Also: American Geographical Society, *Focus Ethiopia*, No. 8, April 1965; *Le Monde*, 9–10.4.1971.
4. *Focus Ethiopia*, No. 8, April 1965; Ethiopia: Ministry of Information, Addis Ababa, 1969, p. 76 and evidence collected by the author.
5. *Time Magazine*, 1.3.71; *M*, 9.4.71, 5.11.71; D. Laporte, 'Problèmes Ethiopiens', *Revue de Défense Nationale*, July 1971, p. 1125; *NYT*, 11.7.71.
6. In recognition of United States' help Ethiopia supported United States' action in Korea.
7. When referring to ELF, the Ethiopians always called them *shifta*.

8. Laporte, *RDN*, p. 1132; J. F. Campbell, 'The Red Sea', *Survival*, August 1971, p. 269.

9. He was appointed ambassador to Sweden, but was recalled in 1958 and appointed a senator, which meant political retirement.

10. Many Eritreans who benefited from Eritrea's superior educational system were to be found by 1962 in the highest positions in the government of Ethiopia.

11. See below, page 177.

12. The main sources for the period of British administration and the federation are: J. K. H. Trevaskis: *Eritrea. A Colony in Transition*, London, 1960; R. Hess: *Ethiopia. The Modernization of Autocracy.* Cornell University, 1970; R. Greenfield: *Ethiopia. A New Political History.* London 1965 and pamphlets issued by ELF Damascus office.

13. *Al-Dustur* (Lebanon), 26.10.71; *Kul Shai'* (Lebanon), 11.9.71; FBIS, 18.1.72, radio Baghdad, 14.1.72. On this subject see below, page 199.

14. Osman Idris, ELF director of Aden office. *Dawn* (Pakistan), 10.8.69; *Mois en Afrique*, No. 61, January 1971, Ethiopia.

15. A term which was widely used in Ethiopia to describe the ELF in the early 1960s.

16. Tedla Bairu, who joined the ELF in 1967, became vice president of and member of the general command. See below page 170.

17. *AR*, News in brief, February 1966, p. 25; J. F. Campbell, 'Background to the Eritrean Conflict', *AR*, May 1971; Hess, pp. 185–6; Laporte, *RDN*, p. 1128.

18. In 1964 Syrian newspapers published a map with Eritrea included in the Arab world. Syrian support of the ELF became common knowledge in 1965 when a Syrian plane with arms for the ELF was detained by mistake (?) in Khartoum airport.

19. Hess, pp. 186–8; *AR*, February 1966, 'News in Brief', p. 28; Laporte, *RDN*, p. 1128; J. F. Campbell, 'Rumblings Along the Red Sea: The Eritrean Question', *Foreign Affairs*, p. 544; *JP*, 5.11.69 and oral evidence collected by the author.

20. Campbell, 'Rumblings'; and 'Background'; Hess, p. 188. The command was split into two with the old enmity between Woldeab and Bairu coming up once again.

21. Information gathered by the author when Associate Dean at H.S.I.U. 1966–67; Laporte, *RDN*, pp. 1126–7; Hess, pp. 188, 203.

22. *NYT*, 1.9.69; *AR*, April 1971.

23. See below, p. 176.

24. *JP*, 5.11.69; Campbell, 'Rumblings', p. 544; ISC report beginning 1970.

25. M. Abir, 'Education and National Unity in Ethiopia', *African Affairs*, 1970, pp. 44–59.

26. Taye Germaw, *NME*, p. 277; Hess, p. 188; Laporte, *RDN*, p. 1128; *AR*, February 1966, p. 28; *JP*, 5.11.69; Campbell, 'Rumblings', p. 544.

27. *Economist*, 25.11.67, p. 838.

28. *NYT*, 3.3.69, 18.8.70; *CSM*, 5.4.69; *M*, 9.1.71; *Mois en Afrique*, No. 61, January 1971, Ethiopia; *Time Magazine*, 1.3.71; Taye Germaw, *NME*, April 1971, p. 277.

29. *Observer*, 22.6.69; *Mois en Afrique*, No. 61, January 1971, p. 23; Campbell, 'Background', *AR*, May 1971.

30. *T*, 13.3.69; *M*, 5.4.69; *G*, 19.6.69, 21.6.69, 13.8.69; *IHT*, 20.6.69; Many news items in *Dawn* (Pakistan), June–September 1969; *Dawn*, 17.12.69; *NYT*, 14.9.69, 9.8.70; *FAZ*, 4.3.70; *S. Times*, 8.3.70; *Mois en Afrique*, No. 61, January 1971, Ethiopia.

31. *ARCE*, 2.1.70, 11.3.70; *FBIS*, 1970, No. 47, Vol. 42, radio Mogadishu, 8.3.70; *ARB*, June 1970, October 1970; Laporte, *RDN*, p. 1132; *East African Journal*, Vol. 8, No. 2, February 1971; *Daily Star* (Beirut), 3.11.71.

32. ISC report mid-1970.

33. *CSM*, 5.4.69, 21.1.70; *NYT*, 1.6.69, 18.8.80; *Dawn*, 10.7.69, 10.8.69, 9.11.69; *JP*, 5.11.69; *IHT*, 30.12.70; ISC report end 1970; *Mois en Afrique*, No. 61, January 1971; *Al-Kifah* (Lebanon), 3.11.71.

34. *FT*, 20.5.69; *S. Times*, 10.5.70; *NZZ*, 12.5.70; *L'Unita*, 12.9.70; Laporte, *RDN*, p. 1131; *ARB*, Vol. 6, No. 8, p. 1503B; *T*, 2.1.71, 26.2.71; ICS report end of 1970; *Time Magazine*, 1.3.71; BBC, 10.7.71, Damascus SNA, 8.7.71.

35. One-third of Ethiopia's $208 million budget of 1970–71 was earmarked for defence and security. *Time Magazine*, 1.3.71. On the deficit of balances of payment 1970—*ARB*, 31.7.71, VIII/6, p. 2085. Trade deficit 1969–70—*EH*, 4.7.71.

36. *CSM*, 21.1.70; ISC report, 31.10.70; *NYT*, 29.1.71; *M*, 10.4.71; E. Schwarzenbach, 'Trouble in Ethiopia', *Swiss Review of World Affairs*, May 1971, p. 18; *ARB*, 31.7.71, Vol. 8, p. 2086; *G.*, 4.1.71.

37. *CSM*, 5.4.69; *Observer*, 22.6.69; Campbell, 'Rumblings', p. 537.

38. United States' source of 30% of Ethiopia's budget—*S. Times*, 30.5.71. Also: Hess, p. 199; *Mois en Afrique*, No. 61, January 1971; *M*, 6.4.71, 9.4.71; Bruce Oudes, 'The Lion of Judah and the Lambs of Washington', *AR*, May 1971; *L'Unità*, 3.7.71; *The Plain Truth* (South Africa), January 1972.

39. *DT*, 10.4.69, 18.1.71; *NYT*, 18.7.70, 22.1.71; *IHT*, 30.12.70; *Ha'aretz* (Israel), 19.1.71; *Mois en Afrique*, No. 61, January 1971, Ethiopie; *T*, 26.2.71; *Time Magazine*, 1.3.71; Germaw, pp. 277–8; FBIS, 21.12.71, radio Damascus, 20.12.71.

40. *Ma'riv* (Israel), 18.12.70; *DT*, 18.1.71; *NYT*, 22.1.71; *T*, 26.2.71; Germaw, p. 278; Oudes, *AR*, May 1971; Campbell, *Survival*, p. 274.

41. Hess, p. 203; *Ma'riv* (IL), 25.2.70, according to *Washington Post* Service; Oudes, *AR*, May 1971; ISC reports from 1970.

42. *CSM*, 5.4.69; *M*, 6.4.71.

43. TFAI's population is presently estimated at more than 100,000 of which Issa Somali make up nearly 40%.

44. Laporte, *RDN*, p. 1133; Hess, p. 186; E. A. Bayne, American University Field Staff, October 1969; A. A. Castagno, *AR*, February 1970, pp. 26–8; *DT*, 4.11.71.

45. Not including police and other para-military units.

46. Richard Booth, 'The Armed Forces of African States', Adelphi Paper No. 67, *IISS*, pp. 20–1; Castagno, *AR*, February 1970, p. 26; *MD*, June 1971, p. 4; *DT*, 4.11.71. Two destroyers were promised (?) and it is claimed that in last years some T-54 tanks and a number of Mig-19s were delivered—ISC report end of 1970; *DT*, 4.11.71.

47. Castagno, *AR*, February 1970, p. 26; *DT*, 4.11.71. Hundreds of Soviet technicians are employed in development projects, including the ones who built Berbera naval base.

48. Hess, p. 186; *DT*, 10.4.69; *CSM*, 4.5.69; *Dawn* (Pakistan), 10.7.69; 25.8.69.

49. Somali speakers in Ethiopia are estimated between three-quarters and one million.

50. ISC report mid-1970; *Mois en Afrique*, No. 61, January 1971, Ethiopia; *FT*, 20.5.69; *Dawn* (Pakistan), 20.7.69; *ST*, 20.12.70.

51. *Ha'aretz* (Israel), 23.4.69, 19.3.70.

52. *M*, 5.11.71; *NYT*, 29.1.71; *EG*, 3.8.71; *FT*, 23.11.71, Sudan Supplement, Karl Lavrencic; BBC, radio Umdurman, 22.11.71.

53. In brigade groups, ISC report end of 1970; *Ma'riv* (Israel), 17.3.71; A. Sylvester, *NME*, July 1971.

54. *Ha'aretz* (Israel), 19.3.70, 13.4.70; ISC report end of 1970; Booth, pp. 7–8. Booth's excellent paper is badly in need of updating in view of large deliveries in 1970–71. It is claimed that 25 Sudanese Mig-21s took part in rocketing rebels on Aba Island in March 1970—*Ha'aretz* (Israel), 5.4.70.

55. Richard Booth, *ISS* 1970, p. 18; *JP*, 5.11.69; *Ma'riv* (IL), 25.2.70; Ethiopia. Ministry of Information (Addis Ababa 1969), p. 108; ISC report end of 1970; *G*, 10.3.72.

56. The Sudanese defence budget, £37 million in 1968, soared to £65 million in 1970. The 1971–2 military budget was 7% higher than that of 1970–1—*Observer*, 11.7.71; ISC report from end of 1970.

57. *ARB*, March 1970, May 1970; Laporte, *RDN*, p. 1132; *East Africa Journal*. February 1971, Vol. 8, No. 2; *Ha'aretz*, 26.6.70; ISC reports from middle and end of 1970.

58. *T*, 18.1.71; *ARR*, p. 73, January 1971; NCNA, 13.2.71; *M*, 6.4.71; FBIS, 8.11.71; *Daily Star* (Beirut), 3.11.71. Regarding the split in the ELF, see above, page 192.

59. Cecil Eprille, 'The Southern Sudan', *Conflict Studies*, 1972.

60. *Ha'aretz* (IL), 28.3.71; Laporte, RDN, p. 1132; *M*, 6.4.71; *Al-Usbu' al-'Arabi* (Lebanon, 27.9.71) claims that Ethiopia agreed not to grant Israel military or other facilities.

61. *JP*, 4.6.71; RWA 52/2, July 1971; MENA, Cairo, 29.7.71; FBIS, 4.11.71, Aden ANA, 4.11.71.

63. This led to the settlement lately reached between the Sudanese government and the Anyanya rebels in Addis Ababa.

64. *T*, 5.11.71; FBIS, 8.11.71, Cairo MENA, 7.11.71; FBIS, 21.12.71, radio Umdurman, 20.12.71; FBIS, 3.1.72, radio Umdurman, 31.12.71; FBIS, 4.1.71, radio Umdurman, 31.12.71; FBIS, 5.1.72, radio Umdurman, 4.1.72.

65. *Dawn*, 10.7.69, 19.7.69, 25.12.69; *M*, 18.12.69; *CSM*, 21.1.70; Campbell, *Rumblings*; *T*, 17.12.70; *IHT*, 30.12.70; *G*, 31.12.70; *Mois en Afrique*, No. 61, January 1971; Germaw, pp. 277–8.

66. *NYT*, 18.12.70; *M*, 29.12.70, 31.12.70; *T*, 30.12.70; *EFR*, 31.12.70.

67. *Time Magazine*, 1.3.71; ISC report beginning of 1971.

68. Resolution of ELF congress—FBIS, 15.12.71, radio Damascus, 13.12.71; Germaw, p. 278.

69. ISC report middle of 1971; *G*, 10.3.72.

70. *Time Magazine*, 1.3.71; FBIS, 15.12.71, radio Damascus, resolution of ELF congress, 13.12.71; ISC report end of 1971; *G.*, 10.3.72.

71. ISC report middle of 1971.

72. *Ethiopian Herald*, 21–22.4.71; *NZZ*, 24.12.70; Radio Baghdad (Reuters), 24.4.71; MENA, Cairo, 29.7.71; *G*, 10.3.72. The Iraqi support is limited. There are allegations of some Egyptian aid and although the PDRY stopped its support for a time, lately the ELF office in Aden was reactivated and arms were smuggled across the Red Sea.

73. *Kul Shai'* (Lebanon), 11.9.71; *Al-Aharam*, 15.9.71; *Al-Ba'th* (Damascus), 18.1.72; FBIS, 18.1.72, radio Baghdad, 14.1.72; FBIS, 25.1.72, radio Damascus, 24.1.72; ISC report mid-1971.

74. *Time Magazine*, 1.3.71; *Ma'riv* (IL), 17.5.71; *Ha'aretz* (IL), 25.1.71; 8.8.71, 6.2.72; *FT*, 16.2.72.

75. *Time Magazine*, 1.3.71; *EG*, 3.8.71; *G*, 10.3.72.

76. *IHT*, 30.12.71; *T*, 30.12.70, 26.2.71; *EFR*, 31.12.70; *L'Unità*, 21.1.71; FBIS, 21.9.71, radio Damascus, 20.9.71; FBIS, 7.12.71, radio Damascus, 6.12.71.

77. FBIS, 15.12.71, radio Damascus, 13.12.71; ISC report mid-1971.

78. *S. Times*, 30.5.71; BBC, 10.7.71; Damascus SNA, 8.7.71; BBC, 29.7.71, SNA, 27.7.71; BBC, 4.8.71, SNA 2.8.71; FBIS, 5.8.71, radio Damascus, 2.8.71; FBIS, 5.11.71, radio Baghdad, 2.11.71; FBIS, 15.11.71, radio Damascus, 14.11.71; BBC, 27.1.72, SNA, 24.1.72; *T*, 15.2.72.

79. Hess, pp. 188, 203; Laporte, *RDN*, pp. 1126–7; Taye Germaw, *NME*, April 1971; Campbell, 'Background', AR, May 1971; FBIS, 21.9.71; radio Damascus, 20.9.71; *Daily Star* (Beirut), 31.11.71 and evidence collected by the author.

80. *DT*, 10.4.69; *Dawn*, mid-1969 to beginning of 1970, numerous reports on Arab–Islamic character of the movement; Campbell, 'Rumblings', April 1970; Taye Germaw, *NME*, April 1971; Campbell, 'Background', AR, May 1971.

81. *M*, 8.4.71; *L'Unità*, 13.7.71.

82. *CSM* (London edition), 6.12.69; *CSM*, 21.1.70; *ST*, 10.5.70; *NYT*, 18.8.70; Taye Germaw, *NME*, April 1971, p. 277; FBIS, radio Damascus, 20.9.71; *Al-Kifah* (Lebanon), 3.11.71; *Daily Star* (Beirut), 3.11.71; *Al-Yaum* (Lebanon), 27.11.71.

83. *CSM*, 5.4.69; *Observer*, 22.6.69; *NYT*, 18.8.70; *L'Unità*, 12.9.70; *G*, 3.12.70, 31.12.70; *T*, 2.1.71; *Time Magazine*, 1.3.71.

84. *T*, 26.2.71; *Time Magazine*, 1.3.71; FBIS, 7.12.71, radio Damascus, 6.12.71; FBIS, 15.12.71, radio Damascus, 13.12.71.

85. BBC, 30.6.71, radio Baghdad, 27.6.71; INA, 4.8.71, 6.8.71; FBIS, 13.8.71, radio Baghdad, 12.8.71; FBIS, 21.9.71, radio Damascus, 20.9.71; FBIS, 21.12.71, radio Damascus, 20.12.71.

86. BBC, 19.8.71, SNA, 17.8.71; SANA, 9.9.71; FBIS, 21.9.71, radio Damascus, 20.9.71; *JP*, 20.10.71; *Al-Hurriyah* (Lebanon), 25.10.71; *Daily Star* (Beirut), 3.11.71; FBIS, 21.12.71, radio Damascus, 20.12.71, resolutions of ELF congress. ANA, 24.12.71.

87. Some doubts were expressed regarding whether the congress was actually held within Eritrea as well as regarding the participation in the congress.

88. FBIS, 7.12.71, radio Damascus, 6.12.71; FBIS, 15.12.71, radio Damascus, 13.12.71, resolutions of the congress; FBIS, 18.1.71, radio Baghdad, 14.1.72. The resolutions reveal the mass desertion from the ranks of the ELF and the effectiveness of the anti-guerrilla commando.

89. *Al-Yaum* (Lebanon), 27.11.71; FBIS, 7.12.71, radio Damascus, 6.12.71; FBIS, 21.12.71, radio Damascus, 20.12.71.

90. *Al-Kifah* (Lebanon), 3.11.71; FBIS, 12.1.72, radio Baghdad, 11.1.72; FBIS, 18.1.72, radio Baghdad, 14.1.72; *Al-Ba'th* (Damascus), 18.1.72; FBIS, 25.1.72, radio Damascus, 24.1.72.

91. *Al-Thawra* (Tripoli), 15.11.71; *NYT*, 15.12.71; FBIS, 29.12.71, Libyan News Agency, 28.12.71; FBIS, 1.2.72, AFP (Cairo), 28.1.72; *T*, 15.2.71. Strangely enough they were accused by their rivals of aiding and abetting the growth of the 'Popular Forces'.

92. *Al-Yaum* (Lebanon), 27.11.71; ISC report end of 1971; *G*, 10.3.72. The 'resolutions of the congress' hint at the existence of other factions among the ELF guerrillas.

V

Conclusion

Although at times seemingly dormant the situation in the Red Sea and the Gulf could be compared to a volcano which erupts occasionally with varied degrees of violence. In the past, the tensions and conflicts of the region were considered of local importance and easily contained by the Great Powers. Nowadays, however, the ability of the Great Powers to control these conflicts has greatly diminished: they cannot only get out of hand, but have far reaching international repercussions as is shown by the new round of Arab–Israeli conflict in the last months of 1973.

The temporary defusion of the explosive situation in the Horn of Africa in 1971 was short-lived. Despite Ethiopia's friendly relations with Sudan, encouragement and support of 'progressive' Arab countries (notably Libya, the PDRY and Syria) was partly responsible for the revival of large-scale guerrilla warfare in Eritrea and the reactivation of the Ethio–Somali border dispute. In addition to its economic and other internal difficulties and the alleged discovery of fuel resources by Ethiopia near its borders, Somalia received in the meantime substantial quantities of modern Soviet arms. The new crisis which caused both countries to despatch reinforcements to their common border at the begining of 1973 became a major issue in May 1973 at the Addis Ababa OAU summit conference. Moreover, in addition to ELF operations, other subversive organisations in Ethiopia said to enjoy a varied amount of Arab support expanded their activities.

Already from the OAU summit conference it was quite apparent that the growing Arab pressure on Ethiopia was connected to the latter's relations with Israel and the Arab 'Red Sea strategy'. But evidently Islamic affiliations and pan-arabism are factors which cannot be overlooked when analysing Ethio–Arab relationships as a whole. The American disengagement policy and the tensions with the Arabs and Somalia nevertheless increased the dissatisfaction of Ethiopians critical of their government's foreign policy and the power of those who had advocated the improvement of relations with the Soviet Union and the Arabs. This development, Israel's mounting internal troubles and the gradual erosion of her position in Africa, began to affect Ethiopia's relations with the country from the end of 1972 and, after heavy Arab pressure, led to the breaking of relations between the two countries in October 1973. There are, nevertheless, elements in Addis Ababa which doubt that this decision will diminish the pressures on Ethiopia but think rather that it will leave the 'Christian kingdom' even more exposed to Arab–Muslim aggression. Be that as it may, the Arab countries undoubtedly gained a political, and to some extent strategic, victory over Israel. This victory (even before the relations with Israel were finally broken) may, among other things, have paved the way for the Egyptian blockade against Israeli shipping at Bab al-Mandeb during the 1973 war.

The Arab blockade on Bab al-Mandeb clearly indicates that Israel's deterrent tactics against the 'new Arab strategy' in the Red Sea have failed. In addition to other factors, this was due to the fact that by October 1973 Israel's tiny Red Sea navy had not received the long-range missile boats which according to 'Pentagon sources' were being built for service in that area. Two such boats excelled in their performance during the October war, together with their smaller sisters the S'ar type, helped to paralyse the Egyptian and Syrian navies in the Mediterranean. As expected, the Egyptian blockade enabled the Arabs (and indeed caused some of Israel's friends) to challenge the viability of the Israeli arguments for the strategic necessity of maintaining control of Sharm al-Sheikh. If ships going to, or coming from, Eilat could be stopped at a point beyond Israel's striking power, there was no justification, it seemed, for the occupation of Sharm al-Sheikh by Israel except for the sake of annexing Arab territory. Logical as it may sound, this argument is, nevertheless, groundless because it is based on the ability of the Arabs to establish naval superiority at a point temporarily beyond the reach of Israel's armed forces. Moreover, whereas the Straits of Tiran (near Sharm al-Sheikh) are less than a mile wide and were never recognised by Egypt as an international waterway, Bab al-Mandeb is sixteen and a half miles wide, its African side is 'neutral' and its international character was never questioned. Indeed, it is to be expected that the Great Powers should view with apprehension the possible outbreak of hostilities in the vicinity of the Gulf of Aden, not far from the main maritime lanes from the Persian Gulf. The presence of an American task force in the region and the Soviet silence (with the exception of a mild article in Pravda long after it happened) concerning this matter could be an indication of such an attitude. Finally, if the Suez Canal were to reopen as a result of the 1973 war thousands of tankers and ships would be sailing the Red Sea. In such an eventuality a blockade against Israel is unlikely while Sharm al-Sheikh remains in its hands, whereas it is possible if Egypt would regain control of the Straits of Tiran, as was the case in the past. Despite the fact that it has only an insignificant navy and air-force much will depend on the policy of the PDRY, which controls Perim, and the Soviet ability to restrain this impulsive ally-client, which, in addition to its ideology, is motivated by its inter-Arab relations.

It is doubtful whether tensions in southern Arabia and the Gulf will diminish as long as the present dogmatic Marxist revolutionary régime rules the PDRY. Despite the ludicrous agreement signed in Tripoli at the beginning of 1973 to unite the two Yemens (partly in order to facilitate the struggle against Israel) the situation in southern Arabia during 1973 continued to deteriorate. Unification has already been postponed and border clashes between the two countries are commonplace. The southerners have, moreover, stepped up their subversive activities in the north and are quietly supporting a limited guerrilla warfare and sabotage campaign around the capital and in the southern parts of the YAR. In San'a, however, the conservative elements, strengthened by Riyadh's generous financial aid and its growing political influence in the Arab world seemed by the end of 1973 to have gained the upper hand over the progressives, although the struggle for power is still far from over.

Together with Saudi Arabia, Jordan, Iran and allegedly the United States, Britain supports Sultan Qabus's government in Oman. With such formidable opposition, the attempts of Iraq, the PDRY, PFLOAG and other local progressive elements to revive guerrilla activities in Oman-proper were unsuccessful, whereas in Dhofar the situation could be termed a stalemate. Nevertheless, all the ingredients for a possible overthrow of the conservative pro-Western régime in this strategically important corner of the Peninsula are still very much in existence. In fact they are aggravated by Sultan Qabus' connections with the west and its conservative allies in the region, and his inability to use Oman's oil revenues to solve the country's economic and social problems.

With part of its army and national guard deployed along the PDRY border and another in Jordan, Saudi Arabia stretched its armed forces to its limits when a whole division was moved to the Kuwaiti border during the crisis with Iraq in March 1973. Had this crisis escalated into a full-scale war, the Saudi government, with a huge country to control, would have found itself in an awkward position. For this reason Saudi Arabia was probably unable, even if it had wished, to play a more significant role in the 1973 war against Israel. Little is known of the internal situation in Saudi Arabia because of the strict censorship existing in the country, and information emanating from sources inimical to the régime is, in many cases, unreliable. On the surface all is well in Riyadh, and Faisal's outstanding position among the leaders of the Arab world, especially the more moderate ones, is unquestionable. Because of his manipulation of the 'oil weapon' against Europe, Japan and even the United States, and his uncompromising stand concerning the Palestinian problem in general and Jerusalem in particular, Faisal has won widespread admiration among the Arab masses. There are, however, those who say that not enough is being done, that Faisal is only risking an insignificant part of his currency reserves, and that in spite of American support for Israel he is still very much an American 'pawn'.

With the country's economy flourishing and its education system expanding, but with Faisal unwilling to bring about meaningful reforms while tenaciously clinging to his anachronistic Islamic policy, dissatisfaction with his régime must be spreading among the growing ranks of the intelligentsia and the semi-educated younger generation. This process is accelerated by the influence of the many 'foreign' Arabs employed in the country. The substantial acquisition of sophisticated weapons since 1972 will obviously lead to the expansion of the more specialised units of the Saudi armed forces and consequently to a growth in the power of the new elites. Faisal is old and sick. Although a sudden upheaval in the country's government resulting from his death or a coup d'état is unlikely to bring a 'socialist revolution', it certainly could bring about at least a 'white revolution' similar to that in Iran.

Disillusioned with Faisal's internal policy and apprehensive of Soviet–Iraqi ambitions in the Gulf, Iran has been investing several billion dollars in building up its military power so that, if the need should arise, it would be able to act independently. Its formidable military, and to some extent economic, power has already aroused fear among its Gulf neighbours as well as other Arab countries. The Arab world as a whole is concerned with the future of the Gulf and its vast oil resources—to a great extent the source of its financial and political power. It is true that in order to safeguard its rear, Iraq has temporarily mended its fences with Iran in the last months of 1973, and the latter has even rendered limited support to the Arabs in the recent war against Israel. Nonetheless most Arab countries still regard Iran with suspicion and they are not overlooking the possibility that under certain circumstances it may try to occupy part, or all, of eastern Arabia. Although Iran is an active member of OPEC and usually co-operates with its other members, some Arab countries claim that it is exploiting the situation resulting from the Arab 'oil strategy' to further its own interests to the detriment of the Arabs. Moreover, as a staunch ally of the west, they claim, Iran may try, if the necessity arose, to undermine the Arab 'oil strategy' against the west. Hence, the ambivalent attitude to Iran of east Arabia's sheikhdoms and other Arab countries including Saudi Arabia, despite persistent attempts to improve relations. For its part, Iran is worried about the instability in the region and increasing Soviet influence in the Arab countries. With its economic revolution moving into high gear, but its political and social problems only partly solved, Iran is trying to maintain an independent oil policy, to strengthen its armed forces further, and to retain its special relations with the west.

Any doubts remaining before 1972 concerning Soviet intentions in the Gulf have since been completely dispelled. It is evident that the Soviet Union is determined to expand its influence in the Gulf and to acquire a far greater share of its oil production and distribution, while further eroding the western economy and strategic-military potential. Allegations of secret clauses in Russia's 1972 treaty with Iraq seem to have been substantiated by events. So too is the fact that Iraq, both for its own ends and as a result of Russian manipulations, has been subverting the conservative Gulf régimes and Iran. The Soviet Union, although openly supporting the PDRY and even PFLOAG, is nonetheless careful not to antagonise the Gulf's governments and indeed is constantly trying to improve relations with them; it may even have been instrumental in bringing about the détente between Iraq and Iran in the second half of 1973. Despite its ambivalent policy, it is clear that the Soviet Union would welcome any upheaval which would replace the Gulf's conservative pro-Western régimes with more progressive ones, friendly to the socialist block.

In view of the new developments in the Gulf and the increasing internal, social and other pressures, the governments of the Gulf principalities seem to have reached a cross-road. They have to decide whether to encourage rapid progress and allow their citizens a greater share in the government, as Bahrain and Kuwait are already doing, or to follow Saudi Arabia and preserve a conservative authoritarian régime by ruthlessly crushing any opposition to it. At least in the case of Kuwait, the former policy seemed to have justified itself during the crisis with Iraq in March–April 1973. This incident and its aftermath, however, eroded the hopes of the rulers of east Arabia that they could buy security and non-interference just by donations, loans and grants to the poorer Arab countries, especially those confronting Israel.

Having refused to join a Gulf defence pact, fearing that it would compromise their relations with Arab countries, the Gulf States found themselves completely exposed to aggression from their more powerful neighbours. Riyadh rather than Teheran was their obvious resort. But, because of historic animosities and because Saudi Arabia itself is not sufficiently strong and stable, east Arabia's sheikhdoms vie with one another in militancy over the Palestine problem and in providing funds for the struggle against Israel. They also follow each other in a mad scramble to acquire large arsenals of sophisticated weapons. Years will pass before these relatively backward countries will receive and will be able to deploy the new weapons. Even then they are unlikely to add significantly to the military potential of these small countries. On the other hand, the arsenals of modern weapons in the Gulf may further contribute to the tension in the region, which is already inflamed by the distrust existing between some Gulf Arab countries and between these countries and Iran, and by fear of Iraqi and Saudi Arabian policies. In the meantime these countries are continuing to 'buy time' and goodwill by generous donations to inter-Arab development plans, by co-operating in the use of the 'oil weapon' against the west and by supporting a 'hard line' in relation to Israel and its friends.

Agreements for the sale of sophisticated western weapons, aircraft and warships to the conservative régimes of the Arabian Peninsula during 1973 were expected to effect the Arab–Israeli conflict and aroused Israel's apprehension and criticism. The funds and political influence of these countries were, and are, increasingly exploited for the Arab struggle against Israel. Thus the sale of such weapons could to a certain extent be taken as showing that even the policy of the United States, not to mention that of several European countries, could be influenced by the increasing importance of Arab (mainly Saudi) oil reserves. This is probably why several senior Israeli cabinet members declared in May 1973 that developments in the Gulf could force Israel to reconsider its strategy and its limits. In view of the massive support of the Arab–Gulf countries for Egypt, Syria and even Jordan in the recent war, Israeli fears seem to have been fully justified. The Gulf interests of Europe and Japan, and to an extent the United States, are, it would seem, far too important for these countries to permit them to antagonise their oil suppliers.

The United States was not unaware of the delicate situation emerging in the Gulf and the Red Sea in the last two years. Wishing to gain essential time and maintain the *status quo* in the region, America is determined to strengthen the position and power of the Arabian Peninsula's conservative régimes, which have been, and may be again, subject to considerable pressure. The Soviet Union, being in a far better position to exploit the

Arab–Israeli conflict, wishes to erode this *status quo* and capitalise on Western losses arising from wars and political upheavals in the area. The October 1973 war enabled Russia to strengthen its influence in several Arab countries and, to some extent, solved the problem of foreign currency or suitable merchandise with which to pay Arab oil producers. Since the war, the latter have paid Russia several billion dollars for the vast quantities of sophisticated arms supplied to the 'confrontation' countries. Moreover, the use of the oil weapon by the Arab producers and the dramatic rise in oil prices since 1973 greatly accelerated international interest in the development of Russia's Siberian fuel resources. When the Suez Canal re-opens the Soviet Union will undoubtedly gain a most significant military-strategic advantage over the West. Nevertheless, the Soviet Union as a responsible world power is as determined as the United States, especially during the present détente, not to allow tensions for which ironically both powers are partly responsible to escalate beyond their control. Unfortunately, the energy crisis, the power of the oil weapon, the currency reserves and the vast quantities of arms in the hands of some Arab countries undermine the ability of the Powers to control the situation.

Since its emergence, panarabism has aimed at, *inter alia*, the revival of the Arabs' past glory and the regaining of their 'rightful place' in the family of nations. The different panarab ideologies have stressed as a precondition the unification of the Arab 'homeland' stretching from Maghreb to the Gulf (not specifying which side of the Gulf), thus giving the Arab people, in addition to oil wealth and control of strategic straits, the territory and numbers which are a pre-requisite to becoming a world power (and making a land bridge between the Asian and African Arab countries even more essential). But even an outstanding panarab leader such as Nasser could not foresee the importance which oil would assume and the magnitude of the wealth and power which it could bestow upon the Arab countries in the 1970s. The Red Sea and the Gulf littorals are not just a part of the envisaged Arab 'homeland', but a most essential part of it. Although this area includes some of the poorest and most backward Arab countries it is the focus of Arab oil wealth and consequently of Arab power.

Roughly classified, the conflicts in the region discussed in this book may be divided into inter-Arab struggles motivated respectively by ideological, economic and personal factors. Another set of conflicts comprises those between Arab countries and non-Arab elements and countries in the region. Such for instance is the suppression of attempts to achieve Kurdish self-determination in Iraq (on the fringe of the region), the tensions with Christian Ethiopia, the suspicion and fear of Iran and the claims concerning Khuzistan based on its large Arab elements; but above all, the Arab–Israeli conflict which overshadows all the other conflicts and over which all Arabs seem to be able to unite despite their great differences. The most important motivation for this set of conflicts is the wish to preserve the 'Arab character' of the region and Arab predominance in it (an extreme example is the insistence on calling the Gulf the 'Arab Gulf', despite historic and general use of the term 'Persian Gulf'). It is, however, not just a political problem, but rather a religio-cultural one.

Fascinated by their tremendous newly-gained economic and political power, Arab politicians and press constantly discuss and are pre-occupied with the possibilities opened by the use of the 'oil weapon' (*silāh al-betrol*) to achieve Arab political aims. Theoretically, however, oil wealth should not only gain glory and power but benefit all the Arabs, some of whom have the highest per capita income in the world, whereas others are at the bottom of the scale. No doubt this is one of the major reasons for various conflicts which exist between Arab countries and will persist in the future although temporarily over-shadowed by events arising from the 1973 war. Having reconciled themselves for the time being to the existence of such internal strifes, the Arabs are determined at least to maintain their solidarity over the Arab–Israeli conflict and several other international issues. Inter-Arab struggles are, therefore, in most cases patched up temporarily by the Arab countries themselves. Alas, the preservation of the *status quo* in inter-Arab relations and especially the present delicate relationship between conservative and 'progressive' nationalist and socialist régimes cannot depend for ever on solidarity resulting from conflicts against Israel and other non-Arab countries. They could easily be unsettled by the interference of the Big Powers, a change in leadership, or other circumstances in the Arab countries.

Because deep emotional and psychological factors are involved, the conflicts between Arab countries and non-Arab countries seem at present to be potentially far more dangerous than inter-Arab issues. A marginal case, that of Ethiopia (although connected to the Arab–Israeli conflict), succeeded in rallying a number of Arab countries to support the ELF and Somalia. If the question of defending 'holy Arab land' were to arise, even the most conservative Arab régimes would be bound to join their 'progressive' brethren and would no doubt disregard the interests of their Western allies. Unquestionably, if convinced that their control of the Gulf and its resources were threatened by Iran or another non-Arab country, the Arabs would unite to defend it. In the case of the Arab–Israeli conflict, where many factors have combined to add to the bitterness of the struggle, such an Arab front, exploiting the 'oil weapon' against the West has already emerged and seems to have gone far beyond its initial aim. Apprehensive that this conflict may affect 'stability' in the Gulf, Iran, considering its own delicate relations with the Arabs, has not only sided with them, but is said to be putting pressure on the United States to coerce Israel to withdraw from the occupied territories; but, despite growing pressures within the country, Iran is acting cautiously because it would be against its interest to undermine Israel's security and western power.

The Arab masses and especially their leaders, are still overwhelmed by the power achieved through the use of the 'oil weapon' and the success of co-operation between the different Arab countries. The contention of the panarabists, and especially of President Nasser in the 1950s and 1960s, that unity would bring a revival of past Arab glory, seem now to have been fully justified. (Nasser, however, also advocated an upheaval of all the régimes of the Arab countries). Most Arabs are convinced that the industrial countries are completely at their mercy and will become even more so in the future. The moderate leaders, however, are beginning to carefully examine the possible outcome of their policy and the reaction which it may arouse. They also realise that they should not over-exploit the 'oil weapon' and that the game can only be played as long as the rivalry between the Great Powers protects them from retaliatory measures and even conquest. The more conservative leaders, although the most vociferous and extreme in their attitude, already fear that in the long-run they may be undermining their own positions and régimes. But the 'progressives' of the different camps, especially those with little to lose, perhaps encouraged by the Soviet Union for its own reasons, clamour in the name of 'anti-imperialism' and the revival of Arab greatness, for the continued use of the oil weapon for various political and economic aims in addition to the struggle against Israel. Such a policy, no doubt, may give birth to new conflicts in the region both with non-Arab elements and between the Arabs themselves.

The vast quantities of modern arms accumulating in the countries around the Red Sea and the Gulf breed new dangers rather than containing local conflicts and outside threats, as the West, especially America, hope. For as long as the newly acquired financial-political power bedevils some Arab countries, the Arab–Israeli and other conflicts with non-Arab countries in the region remains unresolved and the 'progressive' Arab régimes continue to undermine the conservative Gulf governments, a most dangerous crisis could easily break out. If unchecked, it could escalate to the extent that it might threaten the international economy, if not world peace. Aware of these facts, of the dangers of being dependent on such a volatile and unstable area for the fuel essential to their economies and of the effect of the fuel crisis on their balance of payments, nearly all the major industrial countries have substantially stepped up oil prospecting outside the Middle East, and even more so the development of and research into alternative sources of energy. Obviously, it is only a question of time before technologically-developed countries such as the United States, Germany or Japan can find economic substitutes for oil. Such a development may not only bring sanity to the Middle East, but could also prove disastrous for most oil-producing countries, especially those in the Arabian Peninsula. The coming decade, therefore, will be crucial not only for the world economy as a whole but also for the Red Sea and the Gulf regions.

Bibliographical Note

A great number of books and other works were consulted for background material, but only the ones actually cited appear in the short list below. The major source for the different essays was, however, the Arabic, Hebrew, European and American press as well as the British Broadcasting Corporation and the (United States) Foreign Broadcasting Information Service monitoring services.

Books

Assah, Ahmed, *Miracle of the Desert Kingdom*, London, 1969.
Becker, Abraham S., *Oil and the Persian Gulf in Soviet Policy in the 1970's*, The Rand Corp, 1973.
Burrell, R. M. and Cottrell, A. J. (eds.), *The Indian Ocean: its Political, Economic and Military Importance*, Praeger, 1972.
Ethiopia, Ministry of Information, *Ethiopia*, Addis Ababa, 1969.
Europa Publications Ltd., *The Middle East and North Africa*, London.
Greenfield, R., *Ethiopia. A New Political History*, London, 1965.
Hawley, D., *The Trucial States*, London, 1970.
Hess, R., *Ethiopia. The Modernization of Autocracy*, Cornell University, 1970.
Hopwood, D. (ed.), *The Arabian Peninsula*, London, 1972.
International Institute for Strategic Studies, *Military Balance 1972–1973*, London, 1973.
Kelly, J. B., *East Arabian Frontiers*, Faber, 1964.
Page, Stephen, *The USSR and Arabia*, London, 1971.
Phillips, W., *Oman—A History*, London, 1967.
Thesiger, W., *Arabian Sands*, London, 1959.
Thomas, B., *Arabia Felix*, London, 1932.
Trevaskis, G. K. N., *Eritrea, A Colony in Transition 1941–1952*, London, 1960.
Trimingham, J. S., *Islam in Ethiopia*, London, 1965.
United States. *Area Handbook for Saudi Arabia*, Washington, 1966.

Articles

Abir, M., 'Education and National Unity in Ethiopia', *African Affairs*, 1970.
Adie, W. A. C., 'Peking's Revised Line', *Problems of Communism*, September–October 1972.
Alkassas, Aziz and Decken, Klaus von der, 'Die Politik Chinas im Nahen und Mittelen Osten', *Orient* (Hamburg), March 1972.
Bayne, E. A., 'Somalia', *American University Field Staff*, October 1969.
Bell, J. B., 'South Yemen: Two Years of Independence', *World Today*, 1970.
Booth, Richard, 'The Armed Forces of African States', *Adelphi Papers* No. 67, IISS.
Brown, Neville, 'Soviet Naval Expansion', *New Middle East*, March 1971.
Burrell, R. M., 'The Gulf', to be published in *Washington Papers Series* (ed. W. Laqueur).
Burrell, R. M., 'Problems and Prospects in the Gulf', *The Round Table*, April 1972.
Burrell, R. M., 'The Gulf . . .', *New Middle East*, December 1972.
Burrell, R. M., 'The Gulf Pot Begins to Boil', *New Middle East*, May 1973.
Campbell, J. F., 'Rumblings Along the Red Sea: The Eritrean Question', *Foreign Affairs*, April 1970.
Campbell, F. F., 'The Red Sea', *Survival*, IISS, August 1971.
Campbell, J. F., 'Background to the Eritrean Conflict', *Africa Report*, May 1971.

Castagno, A. A., 'Somalia Goes Military', *Africa Report*, February 1970.

Cottrell, A. J., 'Shah of Iran Concerned . . .', *New Middle East*, July 1970.

Cottrell, A. J., 'A New Persian Hegemony', *Interplay*, September 1970.

Eprille, Cecil, 'The Southern Sudan', *Conflict Studies*, Institute for the Study of Conflict, London 1972.

Frauke Heard-Bey, 'The Gulf States etc.', *Asian Affairs*, February 1972.

Halliday, F., 'Counter Revolution in Aden', *New Left Review*, No. 63, September–October 1970.

Heath, M. L., 'Arabian Extremities', *Royal Central Asian Journal*, 1960.

Hottinger, Arnold, 'Ferment on the Persian Gulf', *Swiss Review of International Affairs*, February 1971.

Housego, D., 'Iran in the Ascendant', *The Round Table*, No. 248, October 1972.

Jukes, Geoffery, 'The Indian Ocean In Soviet Naval Policy', *Adelphi Papers*, No. 87, IISS, May 1972.

Laporte, D., 'Problèmes Ethiopiens', *Revue de Défense Nationale*, July 1971.

Ledger, David, 'Gulf Union', *Middle East International*, December 1971.

Lewis, B.; 'Conflicts in the Middle East', *Survival*, June 1971.

Malone, J. J., 'Yemen Arab Republic's "Game of Nations"', *World Today*, December 1971.

Mener, Jack P., 'L'expansion Soviétique dans l'Océan Indien', *International Problems*, June 1971.

Nasmyth, Jan, 'The British Leave the Gulf', *Interplay*, September 1970.

Oudes, Bruce, 'The Lion of Judah and the Lambs of Washington', *Africa Report*, May 1971.

Peck, M. 'Saudi Arabia's Wealth', *New Middle East*, January 1972.

Raouf El Gammal, 'The Eritrean Conflict', *The Plain Truth*, January 1972.

Scherndorff, W., 'East European Countries in Forefront of Soviet Aid in the Third World', *Bulletin of the Institute for the Study of the USSR*, Vol. XVIII, No. 2, February 1972.

Schwarzenbach, E., 'Trouble in Ethiopia', *Swiss Review of World Affairs*, May 1971.

Taye, Germaw, 'Rebellion in Eritrea', *New Middle East*, April 1971.

Viennot, J. P., 'Aden de la lutte pour la libération', *Orient* 1967 (Published 1968).

Viennot, J. P., 'Zanzibar Programme' (French translation), *Orient* 1967 (Published 1968).

Watt, D.C., 'The Arabs, the Heath Government and the Future of the Gulf', *New Middle East*, March 1971.

Watt, D.C., 'The Persian Gulf Cradle of Conflict', *Problems of Communism*, May–June 1972.

Yodfat, A., 'The People's Republic of South Yemen', *New Outlook*, March 1971.

Other Material

Dirasat 'Arabiya (Beirut monthly), Watha'iq (Documents):

    Vol. 7, No. 2, December 1970 (Proposed constitution of the PDRY).

    Vol. 7, No. 4, February 1971 (A press conference with 'Abd al-Fattah Isma'il).

    Vol. 7, No. 5, March 1971 (The agricultural problem in the PDRY).

    Vol. 7, No. 7, May 1971 (The proclamation of the central committee of the General Workers Union of the PDRY).

    Vol. 8, No. 2, December 1971 (The political programme of the people's forces of Oman).

    Vol. 8, No. 5, March 1972 (Documents of the founding committee of the

Popular Front for the Liberation of Oman and the Arab Gulf, held in Ahlish—in the liberated area, December 1971).

Dhofar, Britain's Colonial War in the Gulf, A collection of documents and articles, The Gulf Committee, London, January 1972.

Focus Ethiopia, American Geographical Society, No. 8, April 1965.

Government of Saudi Arabia, Ministry of Agriculture, 'Saudi Arabia offers a rich potential of water development', issued by the Embassy of Saudi Arabia, Washington 1967.

Muhammad J. Nadir, (Minister Plenipotentiary, Embassy of Saudi Arabia), 'The Modernisation of Saudi Arabia', Embassy of Saudi Arabia, Washington 1971.

United States, Department of Commerce, Overseas Business Report, Saudi Arabia, Washington, December 1967.

United States, State Department, Background Notes, Saudi Arabia, Washington, March 1971.

Index